Fast & Festive Meals
for the Jewish Holidays

ALSO BY MARLENE SOROSKY

Entertaining on the Run
Cooking for Entertaining
Marlene Sorosky's Cooking for Holidays and Celebrations
The Dessert Lover's Cookbook
Season's Greetings
Easy Entertaining

Fast & Festive Meals
for the
Jewish Holidays

Complete Menus, Rituals, and Party-Planning Ideas for

Every Holiday of the Year

Marlene Sorosky
in collaboration with
Joanne Neuman and Debbie Shahvar

William Morrow and Company, Inc.
New York

Several of the Passover dessert recipes contained in this book previously appeared in
Gourmet magazine, April 1995.

The English text for the blessings is reprinted with permission from *On the Doorposts of Your House*,
Central Conference of American Rabbis Press, New York, 1995.

Library of Congress Cataloging-in-Publication Data

Sorosky, Marlene.
    Fast & festive meals for the Jewish holidays : complete menus, rituals, and party-planning ideas
for every holiday of the year   /   Marlene Sorosky, in collaboration with Joanne Neuman and
Debbie Shahvar.
        p.   cm.
    Includes index.
    ISBN 0-688-14570-1
    1. Cookery, Jewish.   2. Holiday cookery.   3. Fasts and feasts—Judaism.
    4. Entertaining.   5. Menus.   I. Neuman, Joanne.   II. Shahvar, Debbie.   III. Title.
    IV. Title: Fast and festive meals.
    TX724.S644   1997
    641.5'676—dc21   97-11188
                                                                                CIP

Printed in the United States of America

First Edition

1 2 3 4 5 6 7 8 9 10

BOOK DESIGN BY BEVERLY WILSON

To my children, Cheryl, Caryn, Margi, and Kenny
To their children
And their children's children

Acknowledgments

Without the assistance, talent, inspiration, and friendship of Debbie Shahvar and Joanne Neuman this book might never have been written. They worked with me tirelessly and devotedly for over a year, researching, developing, testing, eating, and laughing. Debbie and her husband, David, own the Buttercup Kitchens in Vallejo and Oakland, California, and the Buttercup Grill in Walnut Creek, California, where Debbie does all the recipe development for their menus. If you are in the northern California area, drop in and say hello. They will welcome you with open arms. Joanne's artistic talents shine through in her centerpieces and party decorations. She owns a large and well-stocked party shop in Walnut Creek called Party City. If you don't find what you're looking for, she'll do everything in her power to get it or find you something better.

A big thank-you to Brent Lindstrom and J. Michael Tucker for the beautiful photographs and many long days, short nights, and lots of hard work. For her excellent food styling, my deepest appreciation to Ann Olstad, whose optimism and humor are surpassed only by her creativity and dedication. Ann has a special talent for turning work into fun. I also thank Joanna Kong for her assistance in the kitchen; Buffy Tucker for props; L'Chaim Gifts for Jewish Life, in Danville, California, and bob and bob in Palo Alto, California, for donating their beautiful china, silver, and giftware for the photographs.

I also thank Beverly Wilson for her creative illustrations. This is my second book with Beverly and I am continually impressed with her talent, flexibility, and generosity. Thanks also to my editor, Gail Kinn, for her patience, endurance, and her many efforts to make this book special.

I am indebted to Rabbi Roberto D. Graetz of Temple Isaiah in Lafayette, California, for proofreading the text and advising me on the prayers and rituals. And to Rabbi Harold Shulweis of Temple Valley Beth Shalom in Encino, California, for his words of wisdom.

I also want to thank several people, some for helping with the book and others for touching my heart:

To Marion Cunningham, who encouraged me to write the book when I was wavering, for being such a dear, honest, and wise friend. To my sister and brother-in-law, Beverly and Herb Liberman, for their never-ending support and for so generously giving my books to so many friends and colleagues. To Leal Roberts, my neighbor, for all her recipe testing, and to her bridge club for sampling the recipes and giving me feedback.

To my dear friends, Aileen and Bill Souveroff, for never being too busy to answer questions, offer advise, test recipes, and provide support. To Susan Jacob, for the many gifts she's given me through her insight, spirituality, and encouragement. And last, but not least, to my children, their spouses, and my grandchildren, the greatest blessings in my life.

Contents

Introduction

✧

I believe that life has a plan, nothing happens by accident or coincidence, and this book is part of mine. This may sound philosophical for a cookbook, so let me explain.

I remember with vivid clarity when my editor called and asked me to write a book on the Jewish holidays. The moment is etched in my mind because my heart began pounding and I could barely catch my breath. Of all the subjects I didn't feel emotionally ready to tackle, it was Judaism. Not because I didn't know about it, or because I didn't feel qualified, but because it was such a traumatic part of my childhood. I had included Hanukkah and Passover menus in past books, but they were done by rote. If I were to write a book on Jewish holidays, it would have to come from my heart. And I wasn't sure I wanted to revisit the pain.

I was brought up in Beverly Hills by a tyrannical, Orthodox father and a mother who bent to his every religious desire. She herself was not religious and often grumbled about the hardships the observances placed on her. My parents met in the 1930s in Germany before World War II, where my father, who was American, was stationed as an undersecretary to the American ambassador. I was told he was the highest Jewish official in the diplomatic corps at that time. They met in Berlin, she was eighteen and he thirty-six, and they married shortly thereafter. After the destruction of the synagogues on Kristalnacht, he was told to leave Germany, and to take with him my mother's family. Only recently did I learn that he had been able to get two of my mother's cousins out of Buchenwald, where they had been for six weeks. My parents and relatives were never willing to discuss the Holocaust, or shed any light on their lives in Germany during that fateful time. Whenever I asked, I got a look that said, "This is not a subject we talk about." Eventually I stopped asking.

While my two sisters and I were growing up, we were told that my father hadn't been Orthodox before the war. He became religious when he returned from Germany to the U.S., after seeing the atrocities. We know there is more to the story—but it remains buried with those who chose not to share it.

In my home, holidays were not for celebrating. There was no warmth or happiness in their observance. They were about control, dominance, and penitence. Everything was done in excess. On Passover the Haggadah was read in Hebrew and English, and after every few pages my father would stop to sermonize, extending the Seder to many hours.

At the age of five, I began reading Genesis with my father. Not in English—I read it in Hebrew and translated it into English. The consequences for mistakes were stringent. Besides those dreaded at-home "lessons," I went to Hebrew school three times a week, plus Sunday school, until I graduated Hebrew high school at sixteen.

Although over 80 percent of my classmates at Beverly Hills High School were Jewish, they did not lead the life I led. They went to dances and football games on Friday nights, while I stayed home enduring agonizingly long and austere Shabbat dinners. Saturdays, while my friends went to the movies, I sat in synagogue daydreaming about the places I'd rather be.

When my four children were growing up, we joined a temple and a Havurah, a group of ten families who celebrated the holidays together. These were fun times and so different from my childhood. But I was only playing the part, I wasn't living it. I was giving Judaism lip service, taking it at face value because I felt it was the right thing to do.

I was about to decline writing this book, when fate stepped in and handed me two gifts—Joanne Neuman and Debbie Shahvar, whom I met at a book signing. They had come because they enjoyed my previous books and wanted to meet me. Joanne was making centerpieces for parties at the time, and Debbie was developing recipes for her restaurants. They both love every aspect of Judaism and embrace every holiday with enthusiasm and fervor. We met and discussed how we might work together and, I can happily admit, this book is the loving collaboration of the three of us. A part of each of our hearts and souls is in every thought, every idea, and every recipe.

Since writing this book, I have discovered the beauty of Judaism and the warmth and love that come from celebrating our rich heritage. I have found joy and meaning in the holidays. When I tried these menus on my family, my children, grandchildren, sisters, nieces, and nephews, they were enamored with the creativity of the recipes, the inventiveness of the centerpieces and invitations. For me, it was like celebrating each holiday for the first time. A part of me that was buried had finally come alive.

But healing is a lifelong process, and for the remainder of my days I shall seek to shine the light and spirituality of Judaism brighter and stronger. The greatest serenity and peace come from opening one's eyes and seeing beauty where before there was darkness.

It is my hope that this book adds a new dimension to your holidays by guiding you through the rituals and making them more meaningful and enjoyable. I hope you share my exhilaration in bringing out a cake decorated like a dreidel for Hanukkah, breadsticks assembled into a hut for Sukkot, and a giant shofar cookie for Rosh Hashanah. What a thrill it's been to take my grandmother's and mother's recipes, which I stopped making years ago because they were so time-consuming and full of fat, and update them for my children and posterity.

Life is the passage of chapters, and this book is merely one of mine. In writing it, I have fulfilled one of my life's quests. And now, with love and affection, I pass it on to you. I hope that it enriches your holidays and devotion to Judaism, and fills you and your loved ones with cherished memories to pass from generation to generation.

Marlene Sorosky
Danville, California

About the Book

One of my goals in writing *Fast & Festive Meals for the Jewish Holidays* was to make it more than a cookbook, more than a compilation of delicious recipes to embellish your holiday table, and more than a list of suggested decorations to adorn it. I've attempted to assemble a complete Jewish holiday compendium by including with each festivity a brief description of why we celebrate it, its rituals and customs, and the items and blessings needed to fulfill them. However, because this is basically a cookbook and not a book on Jewish history and traditions, the explanations and descriptions are brief. The blessings, too, are only the most basic ones. Included here are the fundamentals for celebrating each holiday: a complete menu with an advance preparation chart, or Game Plan, for making it; decorations, centerpieces, and invitations when appropriate; a listing of the essential religious items and foods, and the blessings to recite over them—in other words, the whole megillah. I hope that having all this information in one place inspires you to give thanks for the blessings of our beautiful heritage more often throughout the year.

DIETARY RESTRICTIONS

The word *kosher* in Hebrew means ritually fit. The laws of *kashrut* (keeping kosher) are based on complex biblical injunctions that govern every aspect of food preparation and specifically state which animals may be eaten. To be kosher, meat has to be meticulously handled and independently certified by a rabbinic authority. Cattle and sheep are permitted, but pigs, rabbits, and horses are not. Anything in the water with fins and scales may be eaten. This includes most vertebrate fish, but not shellfish. The eating of meat together with milk products is prohibited. Many foods, such as fish, vegetables, fruits, rice, and grains, which are not meat or dairy are considered neutral, or *pareve*, and can be eaten with any meal. All of my menus and recipes adhere to the laws of kashrut, but in some I offer alternatives. For example, in a dessert served after a meat meal, I suggest nondairy or regular margarine or butter. By doing this, I have tried to make it easier for anyone who does not keep kosher to use this book. Each recipe that offers alternatives has been tested with each of the variations.

RITUALS

Through the many years I've been teaching cooking for the Jewish holidays, I've been asked the same basic questions, such as what goes on the Shabbat or Passover table, on which holidays are the candles lit, and what is the blessing for the wine. Every year at Passover I get inquiries on how to roast the egg for the Seder plate and where to buy a shank bone. In this book I've attempted to answer these questions and more. For Shabbat and the major holidays, I've included the blessings over the candles, the wine, and the challah, plus the prayers pertinent for each occasion, and the special items needed on the table. It is my hope that having this information encourages you to recite one blessing that you've never said or celebrate one holiday you've overlooked. The blessings included here are only the most important ones. For more detailed blessings, refer to any prayerbook, available at synagogue or Jewish gift or specialty shops.

THE GAME PLAN

Even the simplest meal is easier to prepare when it's done in stages. Each menu in the book includes a Game Plan, indicating how far in advance the recipes can be made and what needs to be done before serving. You should supplement this with a working time frame of your own: 1. List each recipe and the date you plan to prepare it. 2. Make a grocery list. When you cook in stages, you won't need all the ingredients at the same time. You may prefer to purchase all the staples at one time and the perishables as needed. Making lists early helps determine what items you have to order ahead or purchase from a specialty store. 3. Select serving pieces and utensils; if they need cleaning or polishing, do it early. 4. Make a Day of Holiday Time Plan: Write down each recipe, along with its garnish, and what needs to be done before serving. If you find you're jotting down minutes and seconds, and running on a stopwatch, your menu is too ambitious.

PREP TIMES

Time in cooking is a relative factor. A recipe that is long and involved to a novice can be a quickie to an expert. I've observed students slowly and painstakingly chop onions into T-square–precision cubes, while others pulsed them in a fraction of the time in a food processor. The Prep Times were calculated on an average and are not meant to be precise. They are only a guide to help you select the recipes that fit your needs.

EXTRA POINTS

These are exactly what their name implies, the extras—centerpieces, decorations, invitations, and projects for the children—that lift the celebration above the ordinary. For me, setting the table with a creative centerpiece and unique place cards is as rewarding as cooking the food. Many of the holiday chapters offer invitation ideas as well. For example, at Hanukkah, I like to stuff a little note in a plastic dreidel and mail it to my guests rather than telephone them. If the mere thought of cooking one or two dishes causes tremors, then you'll probably want to skip right past the Extra Points.

Fast & Festive Meals
for the Jewish Holidays

Shabbat

(Sabbath)

Shabbat, which in Hebrew means rest, is the oldest of all the Jewish holidays. According to the Bible, God worked for six days to create the world, and on the seventh day He rested. In the Hebrew calendar, Saturday is the last day of the week. It is a day set aside to be different from the others, to be a haven from the tensions and troubles of the ordinary work week, a day of peace and relaxation, calmness, and harmony. Because Shabbat is welcomed with such great joy and gladness, it is often referred to as a "bride" or "queen."

According to ancient Jewish law, a fire may not be kindled on Shabbat, and all work must cease. In Orthodox homes, all the cooking must be completed by sundown Friday with enough food to last until sundown Saturday. In olden times, people would begin cooking over a heavy fire, and when the sun went down, the embers would keep the pot warm. As a result, many of the dishes associated with Shabbat are slow-cooked ones.

In order to set Shabbat apart from the other days of the week, dinner is more elaborate and should be enjoyed in a leisurely fashion. Often it consists of several courses, frequently beginning with chicken soup. Here are three different menus, each festive and easy to prepare.

THE RITUALS

The Shabbat meal begins by lighting two candles with the following blessing:

We praise You, Eternal God, Sovereign of the universe: You hallow us with Your Mitzvot, and command us to kindle the lights of Sabbath.

Ba-ruch a-ta Adonai, Eh-lo-hei-nu meh-lech ha-o-lam, a-sher ki-d'sha-nu b'mitz-vo-tav v'tzi-va-nu l'had-lik ner shel Shabbat.

O God, You are the light by which we see the ones we love. As we kindle these lights, we begin a holy time. May we and all Israel find in it refreshment of body and spirit, and the sense that You are near to us at all times.

The leader lifts a glass of wine, and all present recite the following blessing:

We praise You, Eternal God, Sovereign of the universe, Creator of the fruit of the vine.

Ba-ruch a-ta Adonai, Eh-lo-hei-nu meh-lech ha-o-lam, bo-rei p'ri ha-ga-fen.

One or two loaves of challah are on a plate covered with a decorated cloth. Everyone breaks off a piece of bread and says the following blessing:

We praise You, Eternal God, Sovereign of the universe, for You cause bread to come forth from the earth.

Ba-ruch a-ta Adonai, Eh-lo-hei-nu meh-lech ha-o-lam, ha-mo-tzi leh-chem min ha-aretz.

Extra Points

THE TABLE

Because Shabbat is referred to as the "bride" or "queen," make a centerpiece using a crown or white netting. Decorate the table with fresh flowers.

To make mini challah napkin rings, braid small loaves of bread out of thawed frozen bread dough. Bake and varnish them. Using a glue gun, attach to plain napkin rings or painted cardboard rings cut from paper-towel, toilet-paper, or gift-wrapping tubes.

FOR THE KIDS

To make a challah cover, decorate a handkerchief, napkin, or piece of fabric with felt markers, puffy paints, glitter, beads, ribbons, etc.

To make candlesticks, shape them out of self-hardening clay. When they've hardened, paint and decorate them.

To make a kiddush cup, decorate a plastic wineglass using pieces of different-colored tissue paper coated with Elmer's glue. Press the various shapes around the outside of the glass to look like stained glass.

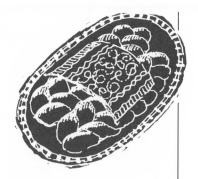

Menu

✧

Traditional Challah

*Bread Machine
Challah*

Raisin Challah

*Manna from Heaven
Challah*

Orange-Date Challah

Challah (Egg Bread) and Its Variations

The Bible says God sent manna from heaven to feed the Israelites when they wandered through the desert. On Friday, He sent enough manna to last for two days, so they wouldn't have to gather it on Shabbat, the day of rest. For that reason there are often two loaves of challah on the Shabbat table. It is braided into a long oval for Shabbat and all the major holidays except Rosh Hashanah and Yom Kippur, when it is coiled into a round. Whether you make challah in a bread machine or by hand, you will find the instructions easy to follow and the results superb.

Although home-baked bread is best freshly made because it has no preservatives, it is not always possible or practical to do this. The bread can be stored in a plastic bag and kept at room temperature overnight, but for longer storage it is best to freeze it. Don't refrigerate bread, because it dries out. If you follow the following directions for reheating, it will be almost as good as freshly baked.

To Rise Bread: Choose a warm, draft-free spot, such as inside a gas oven with the pilot light on or in an electric oven warmed to 200°F for 5 minutes and turn off before the dough is put inside.

To Freeze: Place unwrapped loaf in freezer until frozen solid. Place loaf in a heavy plastic bag, squeeze out the air, seal, and return to freezer. Defrost in the wrapping at room temperature.

To Reheat: For a crisp crust, preheat oven to 400°F. Using your fingers or a spray bottle, sprinkle the crust with water. Place the loaf on a baking sheet and bake for 10 minutes, or until crisp and warm. For a soft crust, wrap the loaf in foil and bake at 350°F for about 15 minutes.

Traditional Challah

Photograph, page 1

1 package active dry yeast
1 teaspoon plus 1 tablespoon sugar, divided
¼ cup warm water (105° to 115°F)
3½ cups all-purpose flour
2 teaspoons salt
2 large eggs
½ cup boiling water
¼ cup cold water
¼ cup vegetable oil
Poppy or sesame seeds, for topping

To Make Dough: In a small bowl, combine yeast, 1 teaspoon sugar, and warm water. Set aside for 5 minutes, or until foamy.

In mixing bowl with beaters or dough hook, mix flour, salt, and 1 tablespoon sugar on low speed until combined. In a small bowl, whisk eggs until frothy. Set aside 1 tablespoon to brush over top, and add rest to flour mixture. Add yeast mixture, boiling and cold water, and oil, and mix for 5 minutes on medium-low speed. Scrape down sides of bowl.

To Knead in Mixer: With the dough hook, knead for 8 to 10 minutes, or until dough is smooth, shiny, and almost cleans sides of bowl. Remove dough and shape into a rough ball.

To Knead by Hand: Turn dough onto a floured surface and knead until it is smooth and elastic, about 12 minutes. If dough is sticky, flour your hands.

For First Rise: Oil or spray a large bowl, place dough inside, and turn to coat with oil. Cover with a lightly dampened towel and place in a warm, draft-free place until double in bulk, 60 to 90 minutes (see page 000). When you poke the dough with your finger, an imprint should remain. Punch dough down, remove to a lightly floured board, and knead until smooth and shiny, about 2 minutes.

To Shape into a Long Braid: Divide dough into 3 pieces. With your hands, roll each into a long, smooth rope, about 20 inches long by ¾ inch wide. Place on a greased or sprayed baking sheet. To braid, bring left rope under center rope and lay it down. Bring right rope under new center rope and lay it down. Repeat to end. (See illustrations.) Pinch ends and tuck under to seal. (If desired, the loaf may be refrigerated overnight. If chilled, the second rising will take at least twice as long.)

It may be hard to believe that this magnificent, golden brown braided loaf with its soft, cakelike interior is so easy to prepare. Granted, bread making takes some practice, but the batter can be mixed and kneaded in a mixer with a dough hook, and braiding it is easier than braiding hair. When my friend Leal Roberts, a novice at making bread from scratch, attempted this recipe for the first time, she was so ecstatic with her newly discovered talent that she asked me to take her picture holding her triumph. This is the classic loaf that is on every major holiday table except Passover.

Prep Time: 25 minutes

Rise Time: 1 to 1½ hours for first rising; 45 minutes for second rising

Shape Time: 5 to 10 minutes

Bake Time: 35 to 45 minutes

Advance Prep: Challah may be stored at room temperature overnight or frozen.

To Shape into a Round Loaf for Rosh Hashanah and Yom Kippur:
With your hands, roll dough into a smooth rope, about 32 inches long.
Starting with one end, wind into a 5-inch circle, spiraling it up in a coil.
Tuck the remaining end underneath. (See illustrations.) Transfer to a
greased or sprayed baking sheet, and cover loosely with a sheet of greased
or sprayed wax paper. (If desired, the loaf may be refrigerated overnight at
this point. The second rising time will be doubled at least.)

For Second Rising: Let loaf rise at room temperature in a draft-free place
until double in bulk: about 45 minutes if at room temperature, at least 1½
hours if chilled.

To Bake: Preheat oven to 375°F. Brush loaf with beaten egg (it's easiest to
do this with your fingers) and sprinkle with seeds. Bake for 35 to 45 minutes, or until golden brown and bread sounds hollow when tapped. If crust
gets too brown, cover loosely with foil. With a spatula, remove from baking sheet and cool on wire rack. (Cooled bread may be stored at room temperature, sealed in a plastic bag overnight, or frozen. To freeze and reheat,
see page 4.)

Makes: 1 loaf

Change of Pace: To make Raisin Challah, mix ½ cup raisins into
kneaded dough before the first rising.

To make Manna from Heaven Challah, mix ¼ cup colored sprinkles or
nonpareils into kneaded dough before the first rising. Sprinkle top of loaf
with colored sprinkles instead of seeds.

To make Orange-Date Challah, substitute ¼ cup orange juice for ¼ cup
cold water. Mix ½ cup chopped dates and 2 teaspoons grated orange zest
into kneaded dough before the first rising.

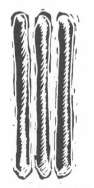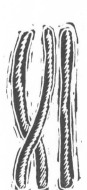

Bread Machine Challah

1-pound recipe
½ cup water
1 large egg
2 tablespoons margarine, cut up
1 teaspoon salt
2 cups bread flour
4 teaspoons sugar
1½ teaspoons active dry yeast
1 large egg yolk
1 tablespoon water
Poppy or sesame seeds, for topping

1½-pound recipe
(for 2 small loaves)
¾ cup water
1 large egg
3 tablespoons margarine, cut up
1¼ teaspoons salt
3 cups bread flour
2 tablespoons sugar
2 teaspoons active dry yeast
1 large egg yolk
1 tablespoon water
Poppy or sesame seeds, for topping

To Make Dough: To bread machine, add the water, egg, margarine, salt, flour, sugar, and yeast in the order suggested by the manufacturer. Select dough/manual cycle. When cycle is complete, remove dough from machine to a lightly floured surface. If necessary, knead in enough flour to make dough easy to handle. (For 1½-pound recipe, divide into 2 loaves.)

To Shape a Long Braid: For each loaf, divide dough into 3 pieces and shape each into a 12-inch rope. Place on greased or sprayed baking sheet. To braid, bring left rope under center rope and lay it down. Bring right rope under new center rope and lay it down. Repeat to end. Pinch ends to seal. (See illustrations for Traditional Challah, page 6.)

To Shape a Round Loaf for Rosh Hashanah and Yom Kippur: With your hands, roll dough into 1 or 2 smooth 18-inch long rope(s). Starting with one end, wind into a coil like a snail. Tuck the remaining end under the bottom. (See illustrations, page 6.) Transfer to a greased or sprayed cushioned or heavy-duty baking sheet and cover loosely with a sheet of greased or sprayed wax paper.

To Rise: Place in a warm, draft-free place (see page 4) until almost doubled in size, about 1 hour.

To Bake: Preheat oven to 375°F. Lightly beat egg yolk with water. Brush over loaf (it is easiest to do this with your fingers). Sprinkle with poppy or sesame seeds. Bake for 25 to 30 minutes, or until bread is a deep golden brown and sounds hollow when tapped. Cover with foil after 15 minutes to prevent excess browning. Remove from oven to rack to cool. (Bread may be stored at room temperature, sealed in a plastic bag overnight, or frozen. To freeze and reheat, see page 4.)

After experimenting with dozens of bread machine challot (plural of challah), I like this one, developed by Fleischmann's yeast, the best. It has a wonderful cakelike consistency, a soft texture, and a tender crumb. Do not try to form 1½ pounds of dough into 1 large loaf. It won't bake properly and the result will be doughy.

Prep Time: *5 minutes*

Rise Time: *About 2 hours in bread machine; about 1 hour for second rising*

Shape Time: *5 to 10 minutes*

Bake Time: *25 to 30 minutes*

Advance Prep: *Challah can be stored at room temperature overnight or frozen.*

Makes: 1 (1-pound) loaf or 2 (¾-pound) loaves

Change of Pace: To make Raisin Challah: Add ⅓ cup raisins to 1-pound loaf, ½ cup raisins to 1½-pound loaves according to manufacturer's directions.

To make Manna from Heaven Challah: Add 1 tablespoon colored sprinkles or nonpareils to 1-pound recipe, 2 tablespoons to 1½-pound recipe when making dough. Sprinkle top(s) with 1 to 2 teaspoons colored sprinkles instead of seeds. If desired, raisins may also be added to dough.

Orange-Date Challah (Bread Machine Version)

1-pound recipe	**1½-pound recipe (for 2 loaves)**
2 tablespoons orange juice	¼ cup orange juice
½ cup water less 2 tablespoons	½ cup water
1 large egg	1 large egg
2 tablespoons margarine, cut up	3 tablespoons margarine, cut up
1 teaspoon salt	1¼ teaspoons salt
2 cups bread flour	3 cups bread flour
4 teaspoons sugar	2 tablespoons sugar
1½ teaspoons active dry yeast	2 teaspoons active dry yeast
1 teaspoon grated orange peel	1½ teaspoons grated orange peel
⅓ cup chopped dates	½ cup chopped dates
1 large egg yolk	1 large egg yolk
1 tablespoon water	1 tablespoon water

To Make Bread: To bread machine, add the orange juice, water, egg, margarine, salt, flour, sugar, yeast, orange zest, and dates in the order suggested by the manufacturer. Select dough/manual cycle. When cycle is complete, remove dough from machine to a lightly floured surface. If necessary, knead in enough flour to make dough easy to handle. (For 1½-pound recipe, divide into 2 loaves.) Shape into a long braided loaf (see page 5) or round loaf (see page 6), and let rise as directed for Bread Machine Challah (see page 7).

To Bake: Preheat oven to 375°F. Lightly beat egg yolk with water. Brush over loaf. Bake for 25 to 30 minutes, or until bread is a deep golden brown and sounds hollow when tapped. Cover with foil after 15 minutes to prevent excess browning. Remove from oven and loosen bottom with a spatula. After 10 minutes, remove to rack to cool. (Bread may be stored at room temperature overnight, wrapped, or frozen. To freeze, see page 4.)

Makes: 1 (1-pound) loaf or 2 (¾-pound) loaves

I am especially partial to this orange-flavored loaf, perhaps because it is almost like a coffee cake.

Prep Time: 5 minutes

Rise Time: About 2 hours in bread machine; about 1 hour for second rising

Shape Time: 5 to 10 minutes

Bake Time: 25 to 30 minutes

Advance Prep: Challah can be stored at room temperature overnight or frozen.

A Dinner in Provence

Because Shabbat cuisine is often equated with long, slow cooking, Lamb Shanks with Portobello Mushrooms and Dried Cranberries fit the bill beautifully. The shanks simmer slowly in the oven, virtually unattended, leaving you free for other chores. They should be cooked the day before serving, so the sauce can be refrigerated separately and the fat scraped off the top. The sauce can then be combined with the lamb 2 to 3 hours before serving to give the meat a chance to marinate. If you wish to double the recipe, you will need to bake the shanks in two roasting pans. Round out the lamb's lusty earthiness with crunchy and sweet Peas with Leeks.

Begin this robust repast with a cool and crisp Pear Salad with Mixed Greens and Sesame-Pear Vinaigrette, or substitute Butter Lettuce Salad with Balsamic Vinaigrette (see page 207). Top it off with a comforting Warm Brownie Pudding that takes mere minutes to prepare. Once your family and friends taste it, they will beg you to make it more often. I'm sure it will become a staple in your culinary repertoire.

GAME PLAN

As Far Ahead As Desired	Make challah and freeze
	Make brownie pudding and freeze or refrigerate up to 4 days
2 Days Ahead	Make and refrigerate lamb
	Make vinaigrette
1 Day Ahead	Defrost pudding, if frozen
	Prepare peas and leeks

DAY OF DINNER	
6 Hours Ahead	Marinate onions for salad
	Bring brownie pudding to room temperature
4 Hours Ahead	Complete sauce and pour over lamb
	Bring challah to room temperature
1 Hour Before Serving	Reheat lamb
30 Minutes Before Serving	Bring water to a boil for noodles
20 Minutes Before Serving	Cook peas and leeks, if baking
	Reheat challah
Shortly Before Serving	Assemble salad
	Cook noodles
	Cook peas and leeks, if microwaving
	Reheat pudding

Menu

Challah
(see page 4)

◆

Pear Salad with
Mixed Greens and
Sesame-Pear
Vinaigrette

◆

Lamb Shanks with
Portobello Mushrooms
and Dried Cranberries

Peas with Leeks

◆

Warm Brownie
Pudding

I call this my "fallback" salad, for whenever I'm in doubt about what to serve, it comes to the rescue. The dressing is refreshingly sweetened with pureed fresh pear and orange juice, and sparked with a splash of sesame oil. It is used to marinate red onion slices as well as to coat baby greens and pear and avocado slices.

Prep Time:
Vinaigrette, 5 minutes; salad, 10 minutes

Onion Marinade Time: 30 minutes to 6 hours

Advance Prep: Vinaigrette may be refrigerated up to 2 days.

Pear Salad with Mixed Greens and Sesame-Pear Vinaigrette
Photograph, page 2

Sesame-Pear Vinaigrette
½ fresh ripe pear, peeled, seeded, and cut into chunks (about ½ cup)
¼ cup rice vinegar
1 scant teaspoon oriental sesame oil
2 tablespoons orange juice
3 tablespoons olive oil
Salt and freshly ground black pepper to taste

Salad
½ red onion, thinly sliced
2 ripe pears
10 to 12 ounces mixed baby or field greens (sometimes called mesclun)
2 avocados, peeled, pitted, and thinly sliced
1 tablespoon sesame seeds, toasted

To Make Vinaigrette: In a food processor with the metal blade, process pear and vinegar until pureed. Add sesame oil and orange juice, and process to blend. With machine running, add olive oil through feed tube. Mix in salt and pepper. Makes ⅔ cup. (Vinaigrette may be refrigerated up to 2 days.)

To Marinate Onion: Place onion slices in a plastic bag and pour over 2 tablespoons vinaigrette. Toss to coat. Marinate at room temperature for 30 minutes or refrigerate up to 6 hours.

To Make Salad: Cut each unpeeled pear in half, remove seeds (a melon baller works well), and slice thin. Place greens in a salad bowl, add onion and vinaigrette, and toss well. Divide among 6 plates. Arrange pear and avocado slices spoke-style around lettuce. Sprinkle salad with sesame seeds.

To Toast Sesame Seeds: Place in a pan in a 350°F oven for 8 to 10 minutes until golden.

Makes: 6 servings

Change of Pace: Substitute butter or Boston lettuce for mixed baby greens. For dairy meals, sprinkle salad with crumbled blue cheese.

Lamb Shanks with Portobello Mushrooms and Dried Cranberries

Photograph, page 3

Lamb Shanks
½ cup flour
1 teaspoon salt
½ teaspoon freshly ground black pepper
6 lamb shanks, about 1 pound each, trimmed of fat
2 to 3 tablespoons vegetable oil
1½ cups dry red wine
1½ cups beef broth
1½ cups cranberry juice cocktail
6 cloves garlic, minced
2 tablespoons chopped fresh rosemary

Sauce for Reheating Lamb
3 tablespoons flour mixed with 5 tablespoons red wine
2 tablespoons chopped fresh rosemary
1 bag (12 ounces) frozen pearl onions, not defrosted
12 to 16 ounces portobello mushrooms, cut into 1½- × ¾-inch strips
¾ cup dried cranberries

For Serving
1 package (12 ounces) extra-wide egg noodles, cooked according to
  package directions
Sprigs of fresh rosemary, for garnish (optional)

Preheat oven to 350°F.

To Prepare Lamb: In a large plastic bag, mix flour, salt, and pepper. Add lamb, 1 or 2 pieces at a time, shake to coat, and pat off excess. In a large, wide, nonaluminum saucepan or Dutch oven, heat 2 tablespoons oil over high heat. Brown lamb in batches, turning to brown all sides. If drippings begin to burn, reduce heat. If necessary, add more oil. Remove lamb to plate and pour off fat. Stir wine, broth, and juice into pan. Bring to a boil, scraping up any brown bits. Stir in garlic and rosemary. Return lamb to pan and bring to a boil.

To Cook: Cover and bake for 1 hour. Rearrange shanks, putting the top ones on the bottom, and bake for an additional 1¼ to 1½ hours, or until very tender when pierced with a fork. Remove lamb and immediately cover with wax paper and foil. Refrigerate sauce separately until fat rises to the top and solidifies. (Lamb and sauce may be refrigerated up to 2 days.)

To Reheat: Preheat oven to 350°F. Scrape fat from top of sauce and dis-

Shanks, the front legs of the lamb, are one of the most flavorful cuts. They are cooked like a stew in a sauce of wine, broth, and cranberry juice until the meat literally falls off the bone. With the addition of tangy cranberries, meaty mushrooms, and pearl onions, served over noodles to sop up every delectable drop of the sauce, this dish makes a down-home meal with an upscale taste.

Prep Time: 20 minutes

Bake Time: 2¼ to 2½ hours plus 1 hour before serving

Advance Prep: Shanks should be cooked 1 to 2 days ahead.

card. Simmer sauce for 10 minutes. Remove from heat and, stirring briskly, whisk in flour dissolved in wine. Add rosemary and bring to a boil, stirring constantly. Place shanks in a roasting pan and pour sauce over. Sprinkle with pearl onions, mushrooms, and cranberries, pushing them into sauce. (Lamb may be held, covered, at room temperature up to 4 hours.) Bake, covered, for 1 hour, or until bubbling and heated through. Serve over cooked noodles. Garnish with sprigs of rosemary, if desired.

Makes: 6 servings

Peas with Leeks
Photograph, page 3

2 tablespoons nondairy or regular margarine or butter
3 cloves garlic, minced
3 medium leeks, white part and 1 inch of green, washed, quartered, and sliced
16 ounces frozen peas (about 2¾ cups)
1 teaspoon sugar
¾ teaspoon salt
¼ teaspoon freshly ground black pepper
½ cup water

To Prepare Vegetables: In a medium skillet, melt margarine. Add garlic and leeks, and sauté 2 minutes. Stir in peas, sugar, salt, pepper, and water. Transfer to a heatproof casserole, microwave-safe if desired. (Casserole may be refrigerated overnight. Bring to room temperature before cooking.)

To Cook: Microwave, covered, on high (100%) for 4 to 6 minutes, stirring once. Or preheat oven to 350°F and bake, covered, for 20 to 30 minutes, stirring once, until crisp-tender.

Makes: 6 servings

G*uests seldom rave about peas, but they do when they taste these. Frozen peas are mixed with sautéed leeks and garlic, then microwaved or baked so they retain their natural crunch and sweetness.*

Prep Time: 10 minutes

Cook Time: Microwave, 4 to 6 minutes; oven, 20 to 30 minutes

Advance Prep: Peas and leeks may be refrigerated overnight and cooked before serving.

Warm Brownie Pudding

4 large eggs
2 cups sugar
½ cup all-purpose flour
¾ cup unsweetened cocoa
½ pound (2 sticks) nondairy or regular margarine or butter, melted and
   cooled slightly
¾ cup chopped pecans
2 teaspoons vanilla extract
Nondairy whipped topping, whipped cream, or ice cream, for serving

Preheat oven to 325°F. Butter or spray a 7 × 11-inch glass baking dish or 2-quart shallow gratin dish. Bring a pot of water to a boil for baking the pudding.

To Make Pudding: In a large mixing bowl with electric mixer, beat eggs and sugar until very light colored and tripled in volume, about 5 minutes. Add flour and cocoa, and mix on low speed until incorporated. Mix in margarine, pecans, and vanilla on medium speed until incorporated.

To Bake: Pour batter into prepared pan and place it in a shallow roasting pan. Pour in enough boiling water to come halfway up sides of pan. Bake for 50 to 60 minutes, or until the top is crusty and a knife inserted ½ inch from the edge comes out almost clean. The center will not test clean. Remove pan from hot water to wire rack to cool slightly. (The pudding may be refrigerated, covered, up to 4 days or frozen. To reheat, bring to room temperature and bake at 325°F for 10 minutes, or microwave on medium until warm.)

To Serve: Serve warm, chilled, or at room temperature with whipped cream or ice cream.

Makes: 8 to 10 servings

I *f you've been looking for a dessert that goes together in minutes, can be baked and served in the same dish, needs no decorating, and is incredibly rich and fudgy, you've just found it.*

Prep Time: *10 minutes*

Bake Time: *50 to 60 minutes*

Advance Prep: *Pudding may be refrigerated up to 4 days or frozen.*

Menu

Challah
(see page 4)

Easy Chicken Soup
with *Kreplach*

◆

Kid's Crusty Baked
Chicken (optional)

Chicken Kashmir

Cinnamon-Spiced
Couscous

Plum Tomatoes with
Cumin–Cornbread
Crumbs

◆

Raspberry-Glazed
Poached Pears

A Taste of the Near East

This menu touches on the exotic, but it's not so far out that finicky eaters, or most children, will take issue with the flavors. Easy Chicken Soup with Kreplach, laced with shreds of fresh spinach, is more Ashkenazic in origin than Near Eastern. Sprigs of fresh dill simmer in the broth, imparting just a mild hint of their sublime flavor. Kreplach, triangular noodle dumplings, are traditionally served in chicken soup. Once you discover how easy they are to make, consider keeping a batch in the freezer to elevate even the simplest broth to lofty heights.

For Chicken Kashmir, shred the chicken that cooks in the soup and stir it into a velvety mushroom-curry sauce. The flavors in the sauce are on the mild side, but feel free to spark them up with additional curry and/or cayenne. This saucy dish pairs well with Cinnamon-Spiced Couscous or any simple pasta or rice, such as Rice Pilaf with Fideo Nests (see page 37). Plum Tomatoes with Cumin-Cornbread Crumbs perk up the plate with their vibrant color, but the chicken has such an abundance of mushrooms, you may wish to omit a separate vegetable. This menu also includes an optional Kid's Crusty Baked Chicken, to be served with any meal when you want a separate entrée for the youngsters.

The intermingling of so many sprightly flavors calls for a light and fruity finale, like Raspberry-Glazed Poached Pears. Consider doubling or tripling the raspberry sauce (it will keep for weeks in the refrigerator) for topping ice cream or frozen yogurt or for spooning over pound cake or pancakes.

GAME PLAN

As Far Ahead As Desired
Make challah and freeze
Make soup and freeze (freeze chicken
   separately) or refrigerate up to 2 days
Make kreplach and freeze or refrigerate
   up to 8 hours

2 Weeks Ahead
Make raspberry sauce

2 Days Ahead
Make topping for tomatoes

1 Day Ahead
Make sauce for chicken
Make couscous
Poach pears

DAY OF DINNER

4 Hours Ahead
Bring challah to room temperature
Prepare kid's chicken, if serving
Assemble tomatoes
Bring pears and sauce to room
   temperature

30 Minutes Before Serving
Bake kid's chicken, if serving

20 Minutes Before Serving
Reheat challah

Shortly Before Serving
Reheat soup and cook kreplach and
   spinach
Reheat sauce and add chicken
Bake tomatoes
Microwave couscous
Dip pears in sauce and serve

Simmering chicken breasts, vegetables, and dill in canned broth enhances the flavor so much that everyone will think you made this soup from scratch. Be sure to buy breasts on the bone, because the bones enhance the flavor. It's easy to pull the meat off after it's cooked. Use the meat for Chicken Kashmir (see page 19), chicken salad, or in a casserole.

Prep Time: 10 minutes

Cook Time: About 30 minutes

Advance Prep: Soup may be refrigerated up to 2 days or frozen.

Easy Chicken Soup

10 cups chicken broth
5 cups water
2 carrots, peeled and sliced ¼ inch thick (about ¾ cup)
1 onion, peeled and quartered
12 sprigs fresh dill, tied into a bundle with string
3 to 4 pounds chicken breasts with bones, skinned (about 6 half breasts)
Salt and freshly ground black pepper to taste
Kreplach (see page 17)
2 cups spinach, thinly sliced into 2 × ¼-inch strips

To Make Soup: In a large soup pot, bring broth, water, carrots, onion, and dill to a boil. Add chicken and bring back to a boil. Using a slotted spoon or skimmer, remove foam from top as it collects. Reduce heat to medium low and simmer (small bubbles breaking above the surface), uncovered, for 20 minutes. Using slotted spoon or skimmer, remove chicken to a bowl. Reserve for another use. Remove onion and dill, and discard. (Soup may be refrigerated up to 2 days or frozen.)

To Cook Kreplach: Bring soup to a simmer and season to taste. Add kreplach (freshly made or frozen) and boil gently for 2 to 4 minutes. Add spinach and simmer 1 minute. Serve in soup bowls with 2 to 3 kreplach in each.

Makes: 8 to 10 servings

Kreplach (Meat-Stuffed Dumplings)

8 ounces beef stew meat (chuck or shoulder), cut into chunks and
   trimmed of fat
1 chicken liver, washed and patted dry (optional—but not once you've
   tasted it)
½ onion, peeled and quartered
1 large egg
½ teaspoon salt
About 36 wonton skins

To Make Filling: In a food processor with the metal blade, process meat,
liver, onion, egg, and salt until coarsely ground.

To Assemble: Place several wontons on a work surface. (Keep remainder
covered with plastic wrap.) Spoon a heaping teaspoon of filling near center of wonton. With your finger, moisten 2 joining sides of wonton with
water. Fold over to form a triangle, pressing edges to secure. (Kreplach
may be refrigerated up to 8 hours on a baking sheet that has been greased
with oil or coated with nonstick spray. Cover tightly with plastic wrap.
They may also be frozen on a baking sheet in a single layer. When solid,
transfer to a freezer bag. Do not defrost before cooking.) Cook as directed
in Easy Chicken Soup (see page 16).

Makes: about 36 kreplach.

*My grandmother
would have been
greatly impressed with
the ease of making
pasta dough in a food
processor. But it still
needs to be rolled and
cut by hand or in a
pasta machine. My on-
the-run version merges
cultures by substituting
frozen wonton skins.
Although they are softer
than traditional
kreplach dough, the
results are still
outstanding. If you
freeze a chicken liver
from a whole chicken
before roasting it, you
can add it to the filling.*

Prep Time: 30 minutes

*Cook Time: 2 to 3
minutes*

*Advance Prep:
Uncooked kreplach may
be refrigerated up to
8 hours or frozen. Cook
before serving.*

Kid's Crusty Baked Chicken

Often when you have children at your dinner table, you'll want to make an entrée you know they'll eat. This one rated high marks with my young tasters, ranging in age from 3 to 11. The adults liked it, too.

Prep Time: *10 minutes*

Bake Time: *25 to 30 minutes*

Advance Prep: *Chicken may be breaded and refrigerated up to 4 hours before baking.*

1 egg
⅓ cup Italian salad dressing
⅔ cup cornbread stuffing mix
⅔ cup plain dried bread crumbs
2 tablespoons flour
2 teaspoons dried basil
4 pounds chicken pieces, skin removed
Paprika, for sprinkling on top

Line a rimmed baking sheet with heavy foil and grease or spray it with non-stick spray.

To Prepare Coating: In a shallow dish, mix egg with salad dressing until blended. In a food processor with the metal blade or in a plastic bag with a rolling pin, pulse or roll cornbread stuffing until coarse crumbs form. Add bread crumbs, flour, and basil, and pulse or mix until combined. Remove to a shallow dish.

To Prepare Chicken: Dip chicken in egg-dressing mix and then into crumbs. Place on prepared baking sheet. Sprinkle with paprika. (Chicken may be refrigerated up to 4 hours.)

To Bake: Preheat oven to 425°F. Bake chicken for 25 to 30 minutes, or until crumbs are golden and chicken is cooked through.

Makes: 8 servings

Chicken Kashmir

3 tablespoons nondairy margarine or vegetable oil
2 onions, peeled and chopped
12 ounces mushrooms, sliced (about 4½ cups)
3 tablespoons all-purpose flour
2 cups chicken broth
¾ cup apple cider
½ cup dry white wine, such as imported dry vermouth
1¼ teaspoons curry powder (hot preferred, or add a dash of cayenne)
1½ teaspoons Dijon mustard
4 cups cooked chicken, torn into shreds or cut into chunks
½ cup sliced green onions, green parts only
Cinnamon-Spiced Couscous (see page 20) or cooked rice for serving

To Make Sauce: In a large skillet, melt margarine. Add onions and sauté 1 minute. Cover and cook on low heat, stirring occasionally, until very soft, 8 to 10 minutes. Stir in mushrooms, increase heat to medium high, and sauté, uncovered, until lightly browned, about 3 minutes. Stir in flour and cook for 1 minute, or until completely absorbed. Stir in broth, cider, wine, curry powder, and mustard. Bring to a boil, stirring. Reduce heat and simmer, uncovered, stirring often, for 5 minutes, or until thickened. (Sauce may be refrigerated overnight. Bring to a simmer before serving.)

Before Serving: Stir chicken and green onions into hot sauce and cook until heated through, 5 to 10 minutes. Serve with Cinnamon-Spiced Couscous or rice.

Makes: 8 servings

Apples and curry have long been paired in Indian cuisine because the sweetness of fruit and heat of curry are so compatible. This dish will remind you of curry with mushrooms, but the sauce is mellower and not at all spicy. It was designed to use the poached breasts and broth from Easy Chicken Soup (see page 16). If you don't make the soup, use canned broth and cooked chicken—the meat from a whole roasted bird is fine.

Prep Time: 10 minutes

Cook Time: 20 minutes

Advance Prep: Sauce may be refrigerated overnight. Add chicken before serving.

Cinnamon, allspice,
and currants add a
hint of sweetness to
granular semolina,
making it an ideal
counterpart for any
spicy, saucy dish. You
use precooked couscous,
so all you need to do is
steep it in boiling
liquid—that's why the
prep and cook times
are so short.

Prep Time: *5 minutes*

Cook Time: *10 minutes*

Advance Prep:
*Couscous may be
refrigerated overnight.*

Cinnamon-Spiced Couscous

2¼ cups chicken broth or water or a combination of both
¼ teaspoon ground cinnamon
¼ teaspoon ground allspice
1 tablespoon margarine or olive oil
¼ cup currants
1½ cups couscous

In a medium saucepan on top of the stove, or in a microwave-safe bowl, covered, in the microwave, bring broth, cinnamon, allspice, margarine, and currants to a full boil. Remove from heat and stir in couscous. Cover and let sit 5 minutes. Fluff with a fork. (Couscous may be kept at room temperature for several hours or refrigerated overnight. Reheat, covered, in microwave.)

Makes: 8 servings

Plum Tomatoes with Cumin–Cornbread Crumbs

Topping
¾ cup cornbread stuffing mix (such as Pepperidge Farm),
  crumbled with fingers
¼ cup finely chopped pecans
1½ teaspoons dried basil
2 tablespoons chopped fresh parsley or 2 teaspoons dried parsley
¾ teaspoon ground cumin
3 tablespoons olive oil

8 medium plum tomatoes
Salt and freshly ground black pepper

To Make Topping: In a medium bowl, stir together stuffing mix, pecans, basil, parsley, and cumin. Add olive oil and toss to coat. (Topping may be refrigerated up to 2 days.)

To Bake: Preheat oven to 425°F. Cut tomatoes in half lengthwise and cut out cores. Cut a small slice from the bottom so they stand straight. Place on baking sheet. Sprinkle with salt and pepper. Spoon 1 generous table-spoon topping over each half. (Tomatoes may be assembled and held at room temperature up to 4 hours before baking.) Bake for 4 to 5 minutes, or until crumbs are golden.

Makes: 8 servings

Here's a tasty side dish that adds color to the plate. Embellish cornbread stuffing mix with pecans, basil, and cumin, pile onto tomato halves, and bake. These tomatoes are simple to prepare and partner well with any meat or fish.

Prep Time: 5 minutes

Cook Time: 4 to 5 minutes

Advance Prep: Topping may be refrigerated up to 2 days. Bake tomatoes just before serving.

I prefer to poach pears in the microwave rather than on the stove. The trick is to begin with ripe but firm pears, and to microwave only 4 at a time. They look so glamorous all dressed up in a ruby-red glaze and garnished with a mint leaf.

Prep Time: Pears, 15 minutes; sauce, 10 minutes

Cook Time: 6 to 12 minutes for 4 pears

Advance Prep: Sauce may be refrigerated up to 2 weeks. Pears may be refrigerated overnight.

Raspberry-Glazed Poached Pears

Pears
8 ripe but firm pears with stems (Bosc or Bartlett preferred)
Juice of 1 lemon

Raspberry Sauce
3 packages (10 ounces each) frozen raspberries in syrup, thawed
2 tablespoons cornstarch
2 tablespoons lemon juice
1 teaspoon sugar or to taste
8 sprigs fresh mint, for garnish

To Poach Pears: Peel 4 of the pears, leaving stems intact. Using a melon baller and working from the blossom end, remove seeds, leaving top with the stem intact. Cut a thin slice off the bottom so they stand straight. Brush with lemon juice.

Stand pears in a circle around the outer edge of a round casserole or soufflé dish. Cover with a sheet of wax paper. Microwave on high (100%) for 6 to 12 minutes, rotating dish after 5 minutes. Pears are done when they feel tender when pierced with the tip of a sharp knife. Timing varies with type and ripeness of pears. Transfer pears to a plate. Meanwhile, peel and core remaining 4 pears. Microwave in same manner. (Pears may be refrigerated, covered, overnight. They will darken slightly.)

To Make Sauce: Place a medium-mesh strainer over a medium saucepan. Add raspberries with their liquid and stir until all pulp is extracted, scraping bottom of strainer frequently. Discard seeds. Stir in cornstarch, lemon juice, and sugar. Bring to a boil over medium-high heat, stirring constantly until thickened. Remove to a bowl and cool. (Sauce may be refrigerated up to 2 weeks.)

To Serve: Bring pears and sauce to room temperature. Dip pears in sauce to coat and place on serving plate. If sauce is too thick, thin with a little water. Spoon remaining sauce around and over pears. Garnish stems with a sprig of mint. Serve immediately.

Makes: 8 servings

For Passover: Substitute 2 tablespoons potato starch for the cornstarch.

Dinner on the Mediterranean

This is the most sophisticated of the three Shabbat menus. Mediterranean Fish Chowder with Red Pepper Rouille is one of my favorite company standbys because you can prepare it quickly, it's easy to serve, and universally popular. The delicate broth, brimming with chunks of fish, tomatoes, and olives, makes an excellent entrée for a crowd, since it doubles and triples effortlessly. Ladled over pasta or rice, this dish makes a complete meal in a bowl. Caesar Salad with Parmesan Wafers and Challah or another type of crusty bread round out the meal. Lemon Yogurt Cake with its delightfully zesty tang is as welcome after this hearty soup as a cool breeze on a warm day. But Raspberry-Glazed Poached Pears (see page 22), Cranberry-Apple Crisp (see page 80), or Cheesecake Pear Tart (see page 178) make fine stand-ins. The recipes in this menu can all be multiplied to serve a crowd.

Other Shabbat entrées you might consider are Chicken in the Pot with Feather Dumplings (see page 56), Herb-Encrusted Roast Chicken (see page 35), Brisket with Burgundy-Orange Sauce (see page 89), Cornish Hens with Apricots and Prunes (see page 137), Salmon Stuffed with Mushrooms, Potatoes, and Dill (see page 43), and Stuffed Cabbage Casserole (see page 208).

Menu

*Challah
(see page 4)*

◆

*Caesar Salad with
Parmesan Wafers*

◆

*Mediterranean
Fish Chowder with
Red Pepper Rouille*

◆

Lemon Yogurt Cake

GAME PLAN

As Far Ahead As Desired   Make challah and freeze
                                Make cake and freeze or refrigerate
                                   up to 2 days

2 Days Ahead   Make dressing for salad

1 Day Ahead   Make rouille for chowder
                                Prepare greens for salad
                                Make Parmesan Wafers
                                Make base for chowder
                                Defrost cake, if frozen

DAY OF DINNER

4 Hours Before Serving   Bring rouille to room temperature
                                Bring challah to room temperature

30 Minutes Before Serving   Bring water to a boil for fettuccine,
                                   if serving
                                Cook rice, if serving

15 Minutes Before Serving   Cook fettuccine, if serving
                                Reheat challah

Shortly Before Serving   Toss salad
                                Reheat chowder base and cook fish

Caesar Salad with Parmesan Wafers

Dressing
3 tablespoons fresh lemon juice
2 to 3 tablespoons olive oil
1 teaspoon Worcestershire sauce
1½ tablespoons orange juice
1 clove garlic, minced
1 teaspoon dry mustard
2 anchovies, minced, or 1 teaspoon anchovy paste
Freshly ground black pepper to taste

Parmesan Wafers
4 tablespoons good-quality shredded Parmesan cheese (do not use the
  grated kind)

Salad
2 to 3 small heads romaine lettuce or inner hearts of romaine
¾ cup croutons
¼ cup shredded Parmesan cheese

To Make Dressing: In a small bowl or wide-mouth jar, mix lemon juice, 2 tablespoons olive oil, Worcestershire sauce, orange juice, garlic, mustard, anchovies, and pepper. Taste and, if desired, add remaining oil. (Dressing may be refrigerated up to 2 days. Remove from refrigerator at least 1 hour before using and mix well.)

To Make Parmesan Wafers: Heat a medium nonstick skillet over moderately high heat until hot. Spoon 1 tablespoon cheese into center of pan. As it begins to melt, spread out with the back of a spoon into a lacy circle (it should have holes). When cheese is melted and edges are lightly golden, remove with spatula and place over a thin rolling pin or wide-handled spatula. Let set until firm, about 2 minutes. Repeat with remaining cheese. (Wafers may be stored at room temperature, covered, overnight.)

To Prepare Salad: Wash lettuce, tear into bite-size pieces, and spin dry. Wrap in paper towels and refrigerate in a plastic bag. (Lettuce may be refrigerated overnight.)

To Assemble: In a large bowl, toss lettuce with croutons, Parmesan cheese, and as much dressing as desired. Divide among 4 plates and top each serving with a Parmesan Wafer. Serve immediately.

Makes: 4 servings

Heat Parmesan cheese in a skillet until it melts into lacy wafers. Place over a thin rolling pin and they will cool into curved crisps. In addition to being a conversation piece on salads, they make wonderful hors d'oeuvres. The dressing here has all the ingredients of a classic Caesar, but it's much lighter.

Prep Time: Salad and dressing, 10 minutes; wafers, 3 minutes

Cook Time: Wafers, about 10 minutes

Advance Prep: Dressing may be refrigerated up to 2 days. Lettuce may be refrigerated overnight. Wafers may be stored at room temperature overnight.

This chowder goes together so quickly that it's a good idea to assemble all the ingredients before you begin. In French, "rouille" means rust, and that aptly describes the hue of this pungent paste. The chowder is served over a bed of pasta or rice.

Prep Time: Chowder, 15 minutes; rouille, 5 minutes

Cook Time: 15 minutes

Advance Prep: Chowder may be refrigerated overnight. Add fish before serving. Rouille may be refrigerated up to 2 days.

Mediterranean Fish Chowder with Red Pepper Rouille

Chowder
3 tablespoons olive oil
2 large onions, peeled and chopped
6 cloves garlic, minced
1½ cups dry white wine or imported dry vermouth
½ cup water
¼ cup fresh lemon juice
½ teaspoon sugar
2 medium plum tomatoes, seeded and chopped
⅓ cup sliced pimiento-stuffed green olives
⅓ cup sliced black olives

1½ pounds firm white-fleshed fish, such as orange roughy, red snapper, or rock fish, cut into 1-inch chunks
¼ cup fresh basil leaves, chopped
Cooked fettuccine, broken in thirds, or rice, for serving

Red Pepper Rouille
1 slice white, wheat, or egg bread, crusts removed
3 tablespoons broth from chowder
3 large cloves garlic, peeled
½ jar (7 ounces) roasted red peppers, drained
2 tablespoons parsley sprigs
½ teaspoon dried basil
½ teaspoon salt
8 to 10 drops Tabasco sauce
3 to 4 tablespoons olive oil

To Make Chowder: In a medium saucepan, heat olive oil until hot. Sauté onions over moderate heat until soft, about 10 minutes. Add garlic and sauté 1 minute. Add white wine, water, lemon juice, and sugar. Simmer 1 minute. Add tomatoes and olives and simmer 1 minute.

To Make Rouille: Soak bread in 3 tablespoons soup until liquid is absorbed. Mince garlic in food processor with metal blade. Add bread, red peppers, parsley, basil, salt, and Tabasco sauce and process until pureed. With machine running, add just enough olive oil to make a paste. (Rouille may be refrigerated up to 2 days.)

To Cook Fish: Before serving, bring chowder to a simmer. Add fish and basil and simmer, stirring, until cooked through, about 3 minutes.

To Serve: Spoon pasta or rice into soup bowls. Add chowder. Spoon a dollop of rouille into the center. Pass remaining rouille.

Makes: 4 servings

Lemon Yogurt Cake

Cake
½ pound (2 sticks) unsalted butter, at room temperature
  (do not substitute margarine)
1½ cups granulated sugar
4 large eggs, separated
⅓ cup fresh lemon juice
8 ounces lemon yogurt
2 cups all-purpose flour
2 teaspoons baking powder
¾ teaspoon baking soda
½ teaspoon salt
2 teaspoons grated lemon peel

Lemon Yogurt Glaze
1 cup powdered sugar, sifted if lumpy
¼ cup lemon yogurt
3 teaspoons lemon juice

Grease and flour a 12-cup Bundt pan. Preheat oven to 350°F.

To Make Cake: In a large mixing bowl with electric mixer on high speed, cream butter and sugar until light and fluffy. Add egg yolks, one at a time, beating well after each addition. Mix in lemon juice and yogurt. In a bowl, stir together flour, baking powder, baking soda, and salt. Add to lemon mixture. Mix on low speed until blended.

In a separate bowl, beat egg whites until they hold firm but moist peaks. Fold whites and lemon peel into batter. Spoon into prepared pan. Bake in center of oven for 50 to 60 minutes, or until cake tester inserted into cake comes out clean. Cool for 10 minutes and invert onto rack to cool completely.

To Make Glaze: In a medium bowl, stir together powdered sugar, yogurt, and lemon juice. Place cake on rack over baking sheet. Spoon glaze over the top, allowing it to drip over the sides. Let sit at room temperature until firm. (Cake may be stored at room temperature overnight, refrigerated up to 2 days, or frozen. Defrost, wrapped, at room temperature overnight. Serve at room temperature.)

Makes: 12 servings

For years I tried to create a lemon cake with an intense lemon flavor. The more lemon juice I added to the batter, the coarser the crumb, resulting in a cake with the texture of bread. Then one day I had a brainstorm—lemon yogurt. When my friend Marion Cunningham was doing consulting for a restaurant and looking for a lemon cake, I asked her to try this one. She was so impressed she put it on the menu.

Prep Time: 20 minutes

Bake Time: 50 to 60 minutes

Advance Prep: Cake may be stored at room temperature overnight, refrigerated up to 2 days, or frozen.

Rosh Hashanah

✦

Rosh Hashanah heads the year of Jewish festivities, foods, and traditions. It occurs on the first two days of Tishrei, the seventh month of the Jewish calendar, which normally falls in mid-to-late September or early October. Because Jewish holidays are determined by the lunar calendar and not the common solar one, they fall on different days each year. The words Rosh Hashanah come from the Hebrew words *rosh*, meaning head or beginning, and *hashanah*, meaning year. The ten-day period beginning with Rosh Hashanah and ending with Yom Kippur is known as the Days of Awe or Days of Penitence or, more commonly, the High Holy Days. According to traditional Judaism, it is during this period that divine judgment on each person's life is made and rendered. It is, therefore, a time for soul-searching, evaluating one's actions, and contemplating the meaning and precariousness of life. This period is also a time of joy and hope for the year to come.

Rosh Hashanah and Yom Kippur are celebrated in much the same way throughout the world. The *shofar*, or ram's horn, is sounded during synagogue services as a reminder of spiritual awakening, to rouse us from complacency and self-satisfaction, and awaken us to reflection and action. This tradition stems from the time when God permitted Abraham to substitute a ram for Isaac as a sacrifice. "*L'shanah tovah tikatevu*, May you be inscribed for a good year," is the greeting among worshipers around the globe.

In many ways, this ancient holiday reflects our modern life. It is celebrated at the time of year when school begins anew, committees reconvene, and families return to busy schedules after summer vacation. It is traditional to buy a new outfit and to send New Year greeting cards. Rosh Hashanah also coincides with the beginning of the agricultural year for trees, when the new moon is closest to the autumn harvest. Blessings are made over seasonal foods that are plentiful and grow in abundance, such as apples, pomegranates, avocados, and grapes. Apples are dipped in honey in the hopes of a sweet year.

THE RITUALS

Two candles are lit at sundown with the following blessing:

We praise You, Eternal God, Sovereign of the universe: You hallow us with Your Mitzvot, and command us to kindle (the Sabbath and) Festival lights.

Ba-ruch a-ta Adonai, Eh-lo-hei-nu meh-lech ha-o-lam, a-sher ki-d'sha-nu b'mitz-vo-tav v'tzi-va-nu l'had-lik ner shel (Shabbat v'shel) yom tov.

We thank you, O God, for the joy of Yom Tov and for the opportunity to celebrate it in the company of those we love.

This is followed by one of the most important Jewish blessings, the She-heh-cheh'yanu, which is recited on every new occasion or event in the cycle of the year, including the first night of holidays:

We praise You, Eternal God, Sovereign of the universe, for giving us life, for sustaining us, and for enabling us to reach this season.

Ba-ruch a-ta Adonai, Eh-lo-hei-nu meh-lech ha-o-lam, sheh-heh-cheh-ya-nu, v'ki-y'manu, v'higi-anu la-z'man ha-zeh.

The leader lifts a wineglass, and everyone recites the following blessing:

We praise You, Eternal God, Sovereign of the universe, Creator of the fruit of the vine.

Ba-ruch a-ta Adonai, Eh-lo-hei-nu meh-lech ha-o-lam, bo-rei p'ri ha-ga-fen.

Extra Points

THE INVITATIONS

Cover the lid of a small jar of honey with apple-printed fabric and tie with cord. Write a note, "Join us for dinner and apple dipping," on brown card stock and attach to cord. Drop off at your neighbor's house or mail in a small box.

THE TABLE

For the centerpiece, fill a shallow bowl with floral foam or Styrofoam. Place Date-Walnut Shofar Cookie toward the front. Prop it up against skewers or sticks so it stands upright. Place red and green crab apples on sticks and insert them into the foam. Accordion-pleat sheets of Mylar and arrange in between. Fill with flowers, ivy, and moss. Weave flowers and ivy down center of table and around candlesticks.

For napkin rings, glue dried apple slices with a glue gun around small grapevine wreaths.

A round challah is covered with a decorated cloth. Everyone breaks off a piece of bread and says the following blessing:

We praise You, Eternal God,
Sovereign of the universe,
for You cause bread to
come forth from the earth.

*Ba-ruch a-ta Adonai, Eh-lo-hei-nu
meh-lech ha-o-lam, ha-mo-tzi
leh-chem min ha-aretz.*

One or more dishes of sliced apples and honey are placed around the table. Apples and pieces of challah are dipped in honey to signify hope for a sweet year ahead. They are eaten with the following blessing:

We praise You, Eternal God,
Sovereign of the universe,
Creator of the fruit of the tree.
Our God and God of our people,
may this new year be good for us,
and sweet.

*Ba-ruch a-ta Adonai, Eh-lo-hei-nu
meh-lech ha-o-lam, bo-rei p'ri
ha-eitz.*

Erev (Evening of) Rosh Hashanah Dinner

T he shape of the challah is varied slightly for Rosh Hashanah and Yom Kippur. Instead of being formed into a long braid, as is traditional for Sabbath and other holidays, it is coiled into a round to symbolize a universal wish for a well-rounded, full, and wholesome year, and to recall the crown of God's kingdom. To ensure that the year is sweet, fruits such as raisins are often added to the batter. I offer two other options as well: one with oranges and dates and the other with multicolored candy sprinkles, which is called Manna from Heaven Challah (see page 8). If you plan to continue the holiday festivities into lunch the next day, you will want to make an extra challah.

FIRST COURSE

For many Jews, fish is the first course of choice for Rosh Hashanah dinner because it is the ancient symbol of fertility and abundance. Salmon Gefilte Fish, made with salmon and white fish fillets, is a new, lighter, and fresher-tasting version of this traditional dish. Instead of poaching the pureed fish in balls, you bake it in a casserole and cut it into squares. If you're not fond of squiggly gelatin or aspic clinging to your fish, you will happily note its absence from this dish. Best of all, you won't be standing for hours making it. It takes only twenty minutes from food processor to oven. And after that you can refrigerate or freeze it.

ENTRÉE

One of my very favorite holiday entrées, Herb-Encrusted Roast Chicken, is beautifully bronzed, crispy-skinned, and permeated throughout with fresh herbs. Roasting a chicken whole, instead of

Menu

*Raisin Challah,
Manna from Heaven
Challah, or
Orange-Date Challah
(see page 8)*

Salmon Gefilte Fish

◆

*Herb-Encrusted
Roast Chicken*

*Rice Pilaf with
Fideo Nests
or
Double Apple
Noodle Kugel*

*Sugar Snap Peas with
Carrot Coins*

◆

*Shanah Tovah
Apple Puffs* with
*Vanilla Sauce
and/or
Date-Walnut
Shofar Cookie*

in pieces, produces more moist and flavorful meat. I like to embellish the chicken with a sherry and herb mushroom gravy, but you
may choose to omit it. If you wish to make a substitution, Cornish
Hens with Apricots and Prunes (see page 137) would be an appropriate one for the holiday. In parts of the Middle East, apricots are
known as "golden apples," so they make a symbolic addition to
Rosh Hashanah dishes.

SIDE DISHES

For a savory dish to complement any poultry recipe, serve Rice
Pilaf with Fideo Nests. Fideo pasta, which comes coiled in a round
like the challah, bakes with the rice and turns an ordinary dish into
an elegant one. If you desire something sweeter and that repeats the
apple theme, try the Double Apple Noodle Kugel. If you don't own
two ovens and prefer not to cook a starch in the same oven with the
chicken, make Barley and Bow-tie Pilaf (see page 79) ahead and
reheat it in the microwave. Sugar snap peas, as their name implies,
are naturally sweet, and carrots are the sign of prosperity because
the slices resemble gold coins.

DESSERT

Continuing the apple theme, serve Shanah Tovah Apple Puffs,
individual, warm flaky pastries filled with juicy chunks of apples
and served with a *pareve* (nondairy) Vanilla Sauce.

I also offer a Date-Walnut Shofar Cookie, which is made by shaping an entire batch of dough into a life-size ram's horn. You can
incorporate the cookie into the centerpiece, then remove it and
serve it to accompany fresh fruit. Orange Honey Cake (see page 49)
and/or Tayglach (see page 50) from the luncheon menu, as well as
Crowned Apple Cake (see page 57) are also options.

GAME PLAN

As Far Ahead As Desired	Make challah and freeze
	Make gefilte fish and freeze or refrigerate up to 2 days
	Make cookie and freeze or store at room temperature up to 3 days
2 Days Ahead	Make Vanilla Sauce
1 Day Ahead	Defrost gefilte fish, if frozen
	Defrost cookie, if frozen
	Prepare chicken
	Make gravy
	Sauté pilaf, if serving
	Make kugel, if serving
	Cook vegetables

DAY OF DINNER

8 Hours Ahead	Make apple puffs
6 Hours Ahead	Decorate cookie
2 Hours Before Serving (or Longer, Depending on Size)	Bring challah to room temperature
	Roast chicken
1¼ Hours Before Serving	Bake kugel, if serving
	Bake pilaf, if serving
20 Minutes Before Serving	Reheat challah
Shortly Before Serving	Dish out gefilte fish
	Carve chicken
	Reheat gravy
	Sauté vegetables
	Remove Vanilla Sauce from refrigerator, if serving at room temperature
Before Sitting Down to Dinner	Bake apple puffs

I remember my mother standing for hours (it seemed like days) grinding gefilte fish with her hand grinder, shaping it into balls, and poaching it in broth on the stove. You won't need to do any of that with this version. A food processor simplifies the pureeing tremendously, and for easier cooking, the fish is baked in a shallow casserole, then cut into squares. This treasured recipe was given to me by Mina Cohen, who got it from her mother-in-law, May Georges. My deepest thanks to both for sharing this pinker, sweeter, and superior version of a classic.

Prep Time: 20 minutes

Bake Time: 1 hour

Advance Prep: Fish may be refrigerated up to 2 days or frozen.

Salmon Gefilte Fish

Photograph, page 5

2 medium onions, peeled and cut into chunks
5 carrots, peeled and cut into 1-inch pieces
2 stalks celery, cut into 1-inch pieces
1 cup parsley sprigs
1 pound salmon fillets, skinned and cut into 2-inch pieces
2 pounds white fish fillets, such as cod, sole, carp, or red snapper, cut into 2-inch pieces
3 large eggs
½ cup vegetable oil
¼ cup sugar or to taste
2 teaspoons salt or to taste
2 teaspoons freshly ground black pepper
Lettuce leaves, cooked carrot slices and horseradish, for serving (optional)

Place rack in center of oven and preheat to 350°F.

To Make Fish: In food processor with metal blade, process onions until minced. Remove to a very large bowl. Process carrots, celery, and parsley until ground. Add to onions. Process salmon until ground. With motor running, add white fish through feed tube, 1 piece at a time, until ground. Add to vegetables. Add eggs, oil, sugar, salt, and pepper to processor, and mix until well blended. Add to fish mixture and mix with hands or a spoon until thoroughly combined.

To Bake: Transfer mixture to an ungreased 9 × 13-inch glass baking dish. Bake, uncovered, for 1 hour, or until firm to the touch. Remove from oven and cool. (Fish may be refrigerated up to 2 days or frozen. Defrost in the refrigerator.)

To Serve: Cut into squares and place on lettuce leaves. Garnish with carrot slices and serve with horseradish, if desired. Serve chilled or at room temperature.

Makes: 16 servings

Herb-Encrusted Roast Chicken

Photograph, page 4

1 roasting chicken, 7 to 8 pounds
Sprigs of fresh rosemary, thyme, and tarragon
2 tablespoons chopped fresh rosemary
2 tablespoons chopped fresh thyme
2 tablespoons chopped fresh tarragon
1 teaspoon salt
2 teaspoons freshly ground black pepper
1 tablespoon vegetable oil
2 tablespoons nondairy margarine, melted
1 cup chicken broth

Herbed Mushroom Gravy (optional)

¼ cup all-purpose flour
½ cup dry sherry
2 tablespoons nondairy margarine or vegetable oil
8 ounces fresh button or shiitake mushrooms, stemmed and sliced
2 teaspoons chopped fresh rosemary
2 cups chicken broth or pan drippings and enough chicken broth
   to measure 2 cups
1 teaspoon chopped fresh thyme
1 teaspoon chopped fresh tarragon
1 tablespoon Worcestershire sauce

To Prepare Chicken: Remove giblets and neck, and save for another use. Rinse chicken inside and out, pull off and discard fat, and pat chicken dry. Place sprigs of herbs in cavity. Tie legs together loosely. In a small bowl, mix rosemary, thyme, tarragon, salt, and pepper. Brush chicken with oil. Rub herb mixture all over chicken. Place breast side up on a rack in a shallow roasting pan. The pan should hold the chicken comfortably; if it is too large, the drippings in the bottom will burn. (Chicken may be refrigerated, covered, overnight, if desired.)

To Roast: Preheat oven to 450°F. Drizzle melted margarine over chicken. Pour chicken broth into pan. Cover chicken loosely with foil. Roast for 20 minutes. Reduce oven temperature to 350°F. Remove foil and roast, uncovered, for 80 to 90 more minutes, basting occasionally with pan juices. Chicken is done when a meat thermometer inserted into thickest part of thigh registers 180°F. Remove to a cutting board or platter. Let stand 15 minutes before carving. If using pan drippings, pour into a gravy separator or bowl and place in freezer for fat to rise to the top.

To Make Gravy: In a small bowl, mix flour and sherry until smooth; set aside. In a medium saucepan over medium-high heat, heat margarine or oil until hot. Sauté mushrooms and rosemary until mushrooms begin to

A mixture of fresh herbs permeates this golden bird, adding a myriad of provocative flavors. Your family will be enticed to the table by the tantalizing aromas wafting from your oven. Purchase plenty of herbs, so you'll have enough for the cavity and extra for garnishing.

Prep Time: Chicken, 15 minutes; gravy, 15 minutes

Bake Time: 1 hour and 50 minutes plus 15 minutes standing time

Advance Prep: Chicken may be assembled 1 day ahead and roasted before serving. Gravy may be made with chicken broth and refrigerated overnight; stir in pan drippings before serving.

soften, about 3 minutes. If using pan drippings, spoon off fat. Add enough chicken broth to measure 2 cups. Stir into mushrooms. Whisk in flour paste and bring to a boil, whisking until smooth. Boil slowly until thickened to a light gravy, about 10 minutes. Stir in thyme, tarragon, Worcestershire sauce, and salt and pepper to taste. (Gravy may be refrigerated overnight. Reheat before serving.)

To Carve Chicken: Using poultry shears or a carving knife, cut off the wings. Remove each leg with the thigh by carving between the breast and the leg; twist loose at the thigh socket. Separate the drumstick and thigh by cutting between the bones. Remove each breast half by cutting down next to the breastbone. Remove breast meat by cutting it away from the breastbone and removing it in one piece. Slice the breast meat. Scrape off any remaining meat from the bones. Arrange the chicken on a platter and serve with gravy.

Makes: 8 servings

Roasting Time Table for Whole Chicken

(Be sure to allow at least 15 minutes extra time for the chicken to rest before carving.)

Weight	Covered at 450°F	Uncovered at 350°F	Total Time
3 to 4 pounds	20 minutes	50 to 65 minutes	70 to 85 minutes
4 to 6 pounds	20 minutes	60 to 70 minutes	80 to 90 minutes
6 to 8 pounds	20 minutes	80 to 90 minutes	1 hour 40 minutes to 1 hour 50 minutes

Rice Pilaf with Fideo Nests

6 tablespoons nondairy or regular margarine or butter
6 fideo pasta nests
1 cup uncooked long-grain rice
2 cans (10½ ounces each) beef consommé (not broth), undiluted
1½ cups chicken broth
1½ cups water

Preheat oven to 350°F.

To Prepare Rice: Melt margarine in a large skillet (preferably nonstick). Add fideos and sauté over moderate heat until golden on each side. Remove from heat. With tongs or a slotted spoon, remove fideos to an 8- to 12-cup round casserole dish. Add rice to remaining margarine in skillet and stir to coat. Spoon rice over fideos. (The sautéed fideos and rice may be refrigerated overnight, if desired. Bring to room temperature before proceeding with recipe.)

To Bake: Pour undiluted consommé, broth, and water over rice. Bake at 350°F, covered, for 75 minutes, or until all liquid is absorbed. To serve, with a large spoon cut down through the pasta.

Makes: 8 servings

This dish is the result of many years of collaboration between Joanne Neuman's mom, Riva Wohl, and her neighbor Lillian Bogas. Each time they made this pilaf, they found ways to improve it. Finally, after dozens of trials, they both agreed it was perfect. Fideos (pronounced fih-DAY-ohs) are thin, vermicelli-type noodles, coiled into nests. They can be found in the supermarket among the other dried pastas. They are sautéed and placed in a casserole under the rice, but end up on top in a lovely swirled pattern. This recipe is proof that if at first you don't succeed . . .

***Prep Time:** 10 minutes*

***Cook Time:** 1¼ hours*

***Advance Prep:** Rice and fideos may be sautéed 1 day ahead.*

Double Apple Noodle Kugel

Photograph, page 4

16 ounces wide or extra-wide egg noodles
4 tablespoons (½ stick) nondairy or regular margarine or butter, melted
1 cup natural applesauce without sugar added
4 whole large eggs
2 large egg whites
¾ cup sugar
1 teaspoon vanilla extract
1½ teaspoons ground cinnamon
½ cup raisins
4 medium green apples, such as Pippin or Granny Smith, peeled, quartered thinly sliced
Nonstick cooking spray

Preheat oven to 350°F. Grease or spray a 9 × 13-inch casserole with nonstick spray.

To Make Kugel: Cook noodles several minutes less than package directions until barely tender. Drain and return to saucepan. Add melted margarine and applesauce, and toss to coat. In a medium bowl, whisk whole eggs, whites, sugar, vanilla, and cinnamon until blended. Stir into noodles with raisins and apples. Mix well. Pour into casserole; spread evenly. Spray a sheet of foil with nonstick spray and place on top of noodles. (Unbaked kugel may be refrigerated overnight.)

To Bake: Bake, covered, at 350°F for 45 minutes. Increase oven temperature to 375°F. Remove foil, spray top with nonstick spray, and bake for 15 to 20 more minutes, or until lightly golden. Let sit at least 15 minutes before serving. Serve warm or at room temperature.

Makes: 12 servings

*A*pplesauce makes such a good substitute for fat in muffins, quick breads, and cakes that I use it here to replace most of the butter or margarine found in traditional kugels. I also substitute egg whites for several of the whole eggs. The results are superb—no one will miss the fat. The kugel is first baked covered, so the top noodles remain tender, and then uncovered to crisp them up.

Prep Time: 25 minutes

Bake Time: 1 hour plus 15 minutes standing time

Advance Prep: Kugel may be assembled 1 day ahead and baked before serving.

Sugar Snap Peas with Carrot Coins

Photograph, page 5

1 pound sugar snap peas
2½ to 3 cups chicken broth
4 medium carrots, peeled and sliced ¼ inch thick (about 2 cups)
1 tablespoon nondairy or regular margarine
Salt and freshly ground black pepper to taste

To Prepare Sugar Snaps: Rinse peas, cut off stem ends, and string them, if necessary.

To Cook: Add enough chicken broth to a 10- to 12-inch skillet to fill ¾ inch. Bring to a boil over moderate heat. Add carrots, cover, and boil gently for 4 minutes, or until barely tender. Add sugar snap peas, cover, and boil gently for 2 to 3 minutes, or until tender, tossing once. If not serving immediately, drain and place in ice water to stop the cooking. Drain well. (If desired, vegetables may be wrapped in paper towels, sealed in a plastic bag, and refrigerated, covered, overnight.)

Before Serving: Melt margarine in large wok or skillet. Add vegetables and toss over moderately high heat until heated through. Season with salt and pepper.

Makes: 8 servings

Sugar snap peas are a cross between common garden peas and snow peas. These delightfully sweet, plump, crisp legumes are entirely edible— pod and all. When combined with sweet carrot rounds, they are a token of a Happy New Year. Either cook them in chicken broth and serve immediately or refrigerate them overnight and sauté before serving.

Prep Time: 10 minutes

Cook Time: 6 to 7 minutes

Advance Prep: Sugar snaps and carrots may be cooked 1 day ahead. Sauté before serving.

Shanah Tovah Apple Puffs

1 package (17¼ ounces) frozen puff pastry, thawed until pliable but still
  very cold
3 medium Golden Delicious apples, peeled, cored, and chopped into ½-inch
  pieces
¾ cup dried apples, chopped into ½-inch pieces
⅓ cup raisins
¼ cup plus 2 tablespoons sugar
2 tablespoons all-purpose flour
1 teaspoon ground cinnamon
1 egg mixed with 1 tablespoon water, for glaze
Cinnamon sticks, for garnish
Nonpoisonous garden leaves, such as apple, lemon, or camellia, for garnish
Vanilla Sauce (see page 41)

Place oven rack in center of oven and preheat to 375°F. Grease or spray a
heavy or cushioned baking sheet.

To Make Puffs: On a lightly floured board, roll one pastry sheet into a 13-
to 14-inch square. It will be very thin. Cut into 4 equal squares. In a medium
bowl, toss apples with dried apples, raisins, sugar, flour, and cinnamon.
Spoon a scant ¾ cup apple mixture into center of squares. Brush edges
with egg glaze. Pull corners of pastry up over filling like a money bag and
twist to seal. Pull back corners. Place 2 inches apart on greased baking
sheet. Repeat with remaining pastry and filling. Brush tops and sides of
pastry with egg glaze. (Puffs may be refrigerated up to 8 hours.)

To Bake: Bake for 25 to 30 minutes, or until pastry is golden brown. Cool
15 minutes before serving. Top each puff with a piece of cinnamon stick for
a stem and a garden leaf. Serve warm with Vanilla Sauce.

Makes: 8 servings

*W*hat could be a
    more fitting
finale for a Rosh
Hashanah meal than
individual puff
pastries filled with
apples and shaped into
applelike rounds? A
cinnamon stick stem
and garden leaf
complete the picture.

Prep Time: 30 minutes

Bake Time: 25 to 30
minutes

Cool Time: 15 minutes

*Advance Prep: Puffs
may be refrigerated up
to 8 hours before
baking.*

Vanilla Sauce

2 egg yolks
2 whole large eggs
⅓ cup sugar
2¼ cups light nondairy creamer
2 teaspoons cornstarch
1 tablespoon vanilla extract

In a medium, heavy saucepan off the heat, whisk together yolks, eggs, and sugar. In a small bowl, stir nondairy creamer and cornstarch together, and whisk into eggs. Cook over moderate heat, whisking constantly, until mixture comes to a boil and thickens slightly. Reduce heat to low and simmer 2 minutes, stirring constantly. Sauce will continue to thicken as it cools. Remove from heat and stir in vanilla. If sauce is lumpy, press it through a strainer. Place a sheet of plastic wrap directly on surface of sauce and cool to room temperature. Refrigerate until chilled. (Sauce may be refrigerated up to 2 days.) Serve chilled or at room temperature.

Makes: 2¼ cups

This is such a simple sauce, but it is so elegant. The cornstarch allows it to come to a boil without scrambling the eggs. For dairy meals, substitute whole milk for the nondairy creamer.

Prep Time: *5 minutes*

Cook Time: *7 to 10 minutes*

Chill Time: *At least 1 hour*

Advance Prep: *Sauce may be refrigerated up to 2 days.*

Here a moist date-raisin-nut batter is shaped and baked into a gigantic shofar for a centerpiece that is both symbolic of the season and fun. After you've shown it off, slice it into pieces and watch your guests devour it.

Prep Time: *15 minutes*

Bake Time: *35 to 40 minutes*

Advance Prep: *Cookie may be stored at room temperature up to 3 days or frozen.*

Date-Walnut Shofar Cookie

1 cup sugar
¼ pound (1 stick) nondairy or regular margarine or butter, cut into small pieces
1 teaspoon vanilla extract
2 large eggs
2 cups all-purpose flour
1½ teaspoons ground cinnamon
½ teaspoon salt
2 tablespoons orange juice
1 package (8 ounces) pitted dates, chopped
1 cup raisins, chopped
1 cup chopped walnuts
White decorating icing in tube with writing tip

Place rack in center of oven and preheat to 350°F. Grease or spray a large baking sheet.

To Make Dough: In a mixing bowl with electric mixer, beat sugar and margarine on moderately high speed until light and fluffy. Add vanilla and eggs, and mix until blended. The mixture will look curdled. Add flour, cinnamon, salt, and orange juice, and mix until incorporated. Mix in dates, raisins, and walnuts.

To Shape: Remove dough to prepared baking sheet and shape into a shofar about 17 inches long, 6 inches at thickest end and 2 inches at narrowest.

To Bake: Bake for 35 to 40 minutes, or until lightly browned. Cookie will feel soft in the center, but will firm up as it cools. Cool completely. (Cookie may be wrapped in foil and stored at room temperature up to 3 days or frozen.)

To Decorate: Several hours before serving, write "L'Shanah Tovah" with white decorating icing across shofar.

Makes: 16 servings

Change of Pace: To make Date-Walnut Slices, divide dough into 4 portions and shape each into 12 × 2 × ½-inch logs. Bake at 375° for 15 minutes, or until lightly browned. They will be soft but will firm up as they cool. Cool 15 minutes and cut into ¾-inch diagonal slices. Dust with powdered sugar. Makes 64 slices.

Happy New Year Luncheon

It is customary for the family to return from synagogue and enjoy a festive lunch together, all of it prepared before the holiday begins. If time permits, allow the stuffed salmon to come to room temperature or if you prefer, reheat it in the microwave or serve it chilled. Sautéed potatoes and mushrooms sandwiched in the middle of the fish help keep it moist while it bakes. Creamy Emerald Sauce offers a piquant contrast to the salmon's mild flavor. The recipe can be multiplied for any number, as long as you have a baking pan and oven that will accommodate a large fish.

Caesar Pasta Salad with Romaine Ribbons fills both the salad and starch categories. After the pasta absorbs the pungent dressing, it is tossed with shreds of lettuce, Parmesan cheese, and croutons before serving. Should you wish to include a vegetable, Green Beans in Lemon Wine Sauce are delicious served either hot or at room temperature.

For dessert, here are two classics: Orange Honey Cake and/or Tayglach. For many families, Rosh Hashanah (and Yom Kippur as well) wouldn't be complete without a slice of dark, dense honey cake. My version is moister, lighter, and more aromatically flavored than most. Tayglach, small pieces of dough that cook in a caramel-honey glaze, are a cross between a cookie and a candy. Lithuanian Jews traditionally serve tayglach on all happy occasions—Rosh Hashanah, Sukkot, Hanukkah, weddings, and brit milahs. At Rosh Hashanah, some bakeries turn them into a glorious golden center-piece, piling them one on top of the other, like a French *croquembouche*.

THE RITUALS

1 cup wine with the blessing (the same as for Erev Rosh Hashanah, see page 29)

1 round challah with the blessing (see page 30)

Menu

Raisin Challah, Manna from Heaven Challah, or Orange-Date Challah (see page 8)

◆

Salmon Stuffed with Mushrooms, Potatoes, and Dill with Emerald Sauce

Caesar Pasta Salad with Romaine Ribbons

Green Beans in Lemon Wine Sauce

◆

Orange Honey Cake or Tayglach

GAME PLAN

As Far Ahead As Desired	Make challah and freeze
	Make honey cake and freeze or store at room temperature up to 4 days, if serving
	Make Tayglach and freeze or store at room temperature up to 2 weeks, if serving
1 Week Ahead	Prepare Emerald Sauce
	Make vinaigrette
1 Day Ahead	Bake salmon
	Defrost honey cake, if serving
	Defrost Tayglach, if serving
	Prepare green beans
	Cook pasta for salad

DAY OF LUNCH

3 Hours Before Serving	Bring challah to room temperature
1 Hour or More Before Serving	Bring salmon to room temperature
	Bring green beans to room temperature
15 Minutes Before Serving	Bake green beans
	Reheat challah
Shortly Before Serving	Assemble salad

Salmon Stuffed with Mushrooms, Potatoes, and Dill

2 to 4 tablespoons vegetable or olive oil
1 onion, peeled and chopped (about 1 cup)
1 White Rose potato, peeled and chopped (about 1 cup)
8 ounces sliced mushrooms (about 1¼ cups)
½ cup regular, low-fat, or nonfat sour cream
¼ cup chopped fresh dill
Salt and freshly ground black pepper
1 (3- to 4-pound) whole or center-cut salmon, skin and center bone removed
1 to 2 cups dry white wine or imported dry vermouth
Juice of 1 lemon
Emerald Sauce (see page 46)

To Make Stuffing: Heat 2 tablespoons oil in a large skillet, preferably non-stick, over moderately high heat. Add onion and potato and sauté, turning often, until golden brown and potato is nearly done. Add mushrooms and sauté until soft. If mixture is too dry, add more oil. Remove from heat and stir in sour cream, dill, and salt and pepper to taste. Cool to room temperature. Oil or spray with nonstick spray a large sheet of heavy foil and place salmon in center. Open salmon out, sprinkle with salt and pepper, and spread stuffing over half the fish. Fold the other half over to enclose it.

To Bake: Preheat oven to 350°F. To determine the cooking time, measure the height of the fish by holding a ruler perpendicular against it at its thickest point. The salmon should be cooked for 20 minutes per measured inch. Transfer salmon to a shallow roasting pan and turn the foil up around it to hold in juices. Pour in enough wine to come 1 inch up sides of fish. Squeeze lemon juice over. Fold edges of foil together to seal. Bake fish as directed; it is done when the flesh looks opaque when flaked with the tip of a sharp knife. Remove fish from pan, open foil, and cool slightly. Pour off juices and remove fish to platter. (Salmon may be refrigerated, covered, overnight.) Serve warm, chilled, or at room temperature with Emerald Sauce.

Makes: 6 to 8 servings, allowing ½ pound fish per person

This lean and luscious entrée is a snap to prepare if you ask the fishmonger to remove the skin and center bone from the fish. To stuff it, open the fish out like a book, spread the filling over half the fish, and fold the other half over. Wrap in foil, bake until flaky, and serve warm or chilled with a creamy spinach-based Emerald Sauce.

Prep Time: 25 minutes

Bake Time: About 40 minutes

Advance Prep: Baked salmon may be refrigerated overnight.

This bright-tasting, vivid-hued sauce of pureed spinach, watercress, and parsley complements any grilled or baked fish.

Prep Time: *10 minutes*

Advance Prep: *Sauce may be refrigerated up to 1 week.*

Emerald Sauce

½ **package (10 ounces) frozen chopped spinach,**
  thawed and squeezed dry (½ cup)
5 **sprigs fresh parsley**
¼ **cup watercress leaves**
2 **tablespoons chopped green onions**
2 **tablespoons fresh lemon juice**
¼ **teaspoon dry mustard**
1 **teaspoon dried basil**
½ **cup regular, light, or nonfat sour cream**
½ **cup regular, light, or nonfat mayonnaise**
Salt and freshly ground black pepper to taste
2 **tablespoons capers, rinsed and drained (optional)**

In a food processor with the metal blade, process spinach, parsley, watercress, green onions, lemon juice, dry mustard, and basil until pureed. Add sour cream and mayonnaise, and process until blended. Remove to a bowl and, if desired, season with salt and pepper. Stir in capers, if using. (Sauce may be refrigerated up to 1 week.)

Makes: 2 cups sauce; about 10 servings

Caesar Pasta Salad
with Romaine Ribbons

Caesar Vinaigrette
1 large clove garlic, peeled
2 to 3 anchovy fillets, rinsed (optional)
¼ cup fresh lemon juice
1 tablespoon plus 1 teaspoon Worcestershire sauce
2 teaspoons Dijon mustard
⅓ cup grated Parmesan cheese
⅓ cup olive oil
⅓ cup orange juice
½ cup regular, low-fat, or nonfat sour cream
Salt and freshly ground black pepper

Salad
8 ounces fusilli pasta, broken in half if long
½ cup chopped red onion
2 large tomatoes
⅓ cup grated Parmesan cheese
1 large head romaine lettuce, thinly sliced crosswise into ¾-inch-long strips
¾ cup croutons

To Make Vinaigrette: In a food processor with the metal blade, process garlic until minced. Add anchovies, if using, and process until pureed. Add lemon juice, Worcestershire sauce, mustard, Parmesan cheese, oil, and orange juice, and process until mixed. Transfer to a bowl and whisk in sour cream by hand. Season with salt and pepper to taste. (Vinaigrette may be refrigerated up to 1 week.) Makes 1¼ cups.

To Make Salad: Cook pasta as package directs. Drain, run under cold water, and drain again. Place in a large bowl. Add onion and 1 cup vinaigrette. Toss well. (Pasta may be refrigerated overnight. Refrigerate remaining vinaigrette separately.)

Before Serving: Core tomatoes, cut in half crosswise (not through stem end), and squeeze out seeds. Chop into ½-inch pieces and add to pasta. Add Parmesan cheese, romaine, and remaining dressing. Toss well. Add croutons, toss again, and serve immediately.

Makes: 4 main-dish or 8 side-dish servings

Faster: Substitute 1¼ cups bottled creamy Caesar dressing for the Caesar Vinaigrette.

*F*usilli pasta shares the limelight with slivers of romaine, croutons, diced tomatoes, and Parmesan cheese for an exciting and lusty rendition of a classic salad.

Prep Time: Salad, 15 minutes; vinaigrette, 10 minutes

Advance Prep: Vinaigrette may be refrigerated up to 1 week. Pasta may be refrigerated overnight. Add vegetables and croutons before serving.

Green Beans in Lemon Wine Sauce

T̶o shorten preparation time, boil the beans the day before and reheat them in a conventional oven before serving. They will remain bright green and crisp. Refrigerate any leftovers; they are great for noshing.

Prep Time: 10 minutes

Cook Time:
10 minutes

Advance Prep: Sauced beans may be prepared 1 day ahead and baked before serving.

1½ pounds green beans
1 tablespoon olive oil
3 cloves garlic, minced
2 teaspoons fresh lemon juice
3 tablespoons dry white wine
Salt and freshly ground black pepper to taste
3 tablespoons chopped fresh basil

To Cook Beans: Trim ends off beans. Fill a deep saucepan with water and bring to a boil. Add beans, bring back to a boil, and boil for 4 to 6 minutes, or until tender but still crunchy. Drain and run under cold water with ice to stop the cooking. Blot dry. (Blanched beans may be refrigerated overnight.)

To Make Sauce: In a large skillet, heat oil over moderately high heat. Add garlic, lemon juice, and wine. Cook for 1 minute. Stir in beans, salt, pepper, and basil and, if serving immediately, sauté 2 minutes, or until heated through. If not serving right away, remove from heat, cool, cover, and refrigerate. (Sauced beans may be refrigerated overnight. Place beans in a shallow casserole or baking dish and bring to room temperature before baking.)

To Reheat: Preheat oven to 400°F. Bake beans, covered, for 8 to 12 minutes, or until hot, stirring once. Season with additional lemon juice, if desired. Serve hot or at room temperature.

Makes: 6 servings

Traditional Challah
(page 5)

A Sabbath Dinner in Provence

Pear Salad with Mixed Greens and Sesame-Pear Vinaigrette

(page 10)

Lamb Shanks with Portobello Mushrooms and Dried
Cranberries with Cooked Noodles; Peas with Leeks

(pages 11–12)

3

Crowned Apple Cake

(page 57)

Break-the-Fast Buffet

Clockwise: Bubbly Fruit Salad; Lox and Cream Cheese Pizza; Orzo Salad
with Feta and Sun-Dried Tomatoes; Artichoke and Mushroom Bread Pudding

(pages 61–64)

Chocolate Cherry Dreidel Cake
(page 94)

Latkes (Potato Pancakes)
(page 90)

Hamantashen with potato, dried apricot, prune-raisin, and chocolate peanut–butter fillings

(pages 110, 116, 117)

Double Apricot Strudel

(page 102)

Chicken Vegetable Soup with Matzah Balls
(page 129)

Top: Traditional Seder Plate; Cornish Hens with Apricots and Prunes;
Broccoli Farfel Dressing; Bouquet of Baked Spring Vegetables

(pages 137–139)

Passover Cookies: Double Chocolate Meringue Kisses, Chocolate Chip Cookies,
Tangy Lemon Bars, Fudgy Coconut Macaroons, Rocky Road Brownies

(pages 149, 151–154)

Bubbe's Matzah Brei with Lox and
Onions, Jam-Filled Streusel Muffins

(pages 156 and 161)

Tournedos of Salmon with Dill Piccata Sauce; White and Wild Rice
Timbales; Stir-fry Carrots, Zucchini, and Mushrooms

(pages 186–189)

Erev Rosh Hashanah Dinner

Clockwise: Herb-Encrusted Roast Chicken,
Double Apple Noodle Kugel, Sugar Snap
Peas with Carrot Coins, Salmon Gefilte Fish

(pages 34, 35, 38, 39)

Orange Honey Cake

2 large eggs
¾ cup sugar
½ cup honey
3 tablespoons vegetable oil
2 teaspoons instant coffee granules
⅓ cup (3 ounces) frozen orange juice concentrate, thawed
1¾ cups all-purpose flour
1 teaspoon baking powder
1 teaspoon baking soda
½ teaspoon ground cinnamon
½ teaspoon ground allspice
⅛ teaspoon salt

Place rack in center of oven and preheat to 300°F. Grease or spray a 9 × 5 × 3-inch loaf pan with nonstick spray.

To Make Batter: In a large mixing bowl with electric mixer on moderately high speed, beat eggs, sugar, honey, and oil until blended. Dissolve coffee in ½ cup warm water. Mix into batter with orange juice concentrate. Add flour, baking powder, baking soda, cinnamon, allspice, and salt. Mix on low speed until incorporated. Increase speed to high and mix for 1 minute, or until smooth. Pour into prepared pan.

To Bake: Bake for 65 to 75 minutes, or until a toothpick inserted in center comes out clean. Remove from oven to rack and cool in pan for 10 minutes. Invert on rack and cool completely. (Cake may be wrapped in foil and stored at room temperature up to 4 days or frozen. Defrost, wrapped, at room temperature.)

Makes: 12 servings

Lekakh, Yiddish for honey cake, is a traditional East European cake served on Rosh Hashanah, Yom Kippur, and other happy occasions to ensure a sweet year. I've adapted the idea of incorporating orange juice concentrate into the batter from The Jewish Holiday Cookbook *by Gloria Kaufer Greene. This cake could be a cousin to gingerbread—dark and moist, slightly sweet, slightly sticky, and lightly spiced—but it has no ginger.*

Prep Time: 15 minutes

Bake Time: 65 to 75 minutes

Advance Prep: Cake may be stored at room temperature up to 4 days or frozen.

Tayglach (Honey-Glazed Cookies)

These sweet confections have been a Rosh Hashanah specialty with both Ashkenazic and Sephardic Jews for generations. (Sephardic Jews call them pinyonati.) Traditionally, the dough was cooked in a honey syrup on top of the stove, a very tedious, time-consuming, and messy procedure. I've simplified the technique by baking the cookies in the syrup in the oven. The honey coating remains a little sticky, so it's a good idea to serve them in paper candy cups.

Prep Time: 20 minutes

Bake Time: 50 minutes to 1 hour

Advance Prep: Cookies may be stored at room temperature up to 2 weeks or frozen.

Cookies
3 large eggs
2 tablespoons vegetable oil
1 tablespoon grated orange peel
2 cups all-purpose flour
1 teaspoon baking powder

Syrup and Topping
¾ cup honey
½ cup sugar
1 teaspoon ground ginger
¾ cup coarsely chopped walnuts
½ cup shredded coconut, toasted, and/or colored sprinkles (optional)
Paper candy cups

To Make Cookies: Preheat oven to 375°F. In a mixing bowl with electric mixer, beat eggs, oil, and peel until blended. Add flour and baking powder, and mix until incorporated. With hands, shape into seven 2-inch balls. Roll each into a 10 × ¾-inch rope. Cut into ½-inch pieces.

To Make Syrup: In a large, wide saucepan or Dutch oven, bring honey, sugar, and ginger to a boil. Add cookies and stir to coat. Remove from heat.

To Bake: Place pan in oven and bake, covered, for 20 minutes. Add nuts and stir well, separating pieces of dough. Return to oven and bake, covered, for 30 to 40 minutes longer, stirring every 10 minutes, until browned and crisp and syrup is bubbly. Syrup will thicken as it cools.

Meanwhile, line a baking sheet with foil and spray the foil with nonstick spray. Pour the baked cookies and syrup onto baking sheet, spreading into 1 layer. It will be sticky. If desired, sprinkle with coconut and/or sprinkles. Cool completely. Form cookies into little mounds, using about 4 to 5 cookies for each. (Tayglach may be stored, covered, at room temperature up to 2 weeks or frozen.)

Serve in paper candy cups.

Makes: about 75 cookies

Yom Kippur

✦

According to Jewish tradition, God's judgment of a person and his or her fate for the coming year is made on Rosh Hashanah. The final verdict is given ten days later, on Yom Kippur, the most solemn holiday of the Jewish calendar. The period between the two holidays is devoted to prayers, charitable acts, repentance, and self-evaluation in the hopes of receiving a positive verdict. Jews not only atone for their sins against God, they also seek forgiveness from anyone they have wronged. Even those who do not attend services throughout the year often do so on Yom Kippur. While the greetings exchanged on Rosh Hashanah express wishes for a Happy New Year, on Yom Kippur, the Day of Atonement, the greeting is "May your final verdict be favorable."

We fast from sundown to sundown to prove that we can abstain from temptations and pleasure, to ask for forgiveness for our wrongdoings, and to devote ourselves to spirituality and introspection. After a solemn day of fasting and prayer, the shofar is sounded, and we leave the synagogue filled with renewed confidence and hope. Starting the new year with a clean slate, we are ready to eat, drink, and celebrate with a break-the-fast.

THE RITUALS

Two candles are lit at sundown with the following blessing:

We praise You, Eternal God,
Sovereign of the universe:
You hallow us with Your Mitzvot,
and command us to kindle the
lights of the (Sabbath and)
Day of Atonement.

*Ba-ruch a-ta Adonai, Eh-lo-hei-nu
meh-lech ha-o-lam, a-sher
ki-d'sha-nu b'mitz-vo-tav
v'tzi-va-nu l'had-lik ner shel
(Shabbat v'shel) yom tov.*

This is followed by one of the most important Jewish blessings, the She-heh-cheh'yanu, which is recited on every new occasion or event in the cycle of the year, including the first night of holidays:

We praise You, Eternal God,
Sovereign of the universe
for giving us life, for sustaining us,
and for enabling us to reach
this season.

*Ba-ruch a-ta Adonai, Eh-lo-hei-nu
meh-lech ha-o-lam, sheh-heh-
cheh-ya-nu, v'ki-y'manu,
v'higi-anu la-z'man ha-zeh.*

The leader lifts a glass of wine and everyone recites the following blessing:

We praise You, Eternal God,
Sovereign of the universe,
Creator of the fruit of the vine.

*Ba-ruch a-ta Adonai, Eh-lo-hei-nu
meh-lech ha-o-lam, bo-rei p'ri
ha-ga-fen.*

A round challah is covered with a decorated cloth. Everyone breaks off a piece of bread and says the following blessing:

We praise You, Eternal God,
Sovereign of the universe,
for You cause bread to come
forth from the earth.

*Ba-ruch a-ta Adonai, Eh-lo-hei-nu
meh-lech ha-o-lam, ha-mo-tzi
leh-chem min ha-a retz.*

Extra Points

Before Yom Kippur begins, it is customary to donate money to a favorite charity, especially one concerned with social causes. Children can make and decorate an attractive money box to keep throughout the year as a reminder that charity is not limited to one day, but should be performed regularly.

EREV YOM KIPPUR DINNER

The table: This is a simple family meal before the Kol Nidre synagogue services, so keep the decorations simple. A vase of fresh flowers or a bowl with fresh red and green apples is appropriate.

YOM KIPPUR BREAK-THE-FAST

The table: After a day of fasting, decorations should be simple and casual. Drape a tallit (prayer shawl) and/or fabric down the buffet table. Add green vines and branches (search your garden) and a shofar, if you have one.

Menu

*Raisin Challah,
Manna from Heaven
Challah, or
Orange-Date Challah
(see page 8)*

◆

*Spinach Salad with
Mandarin Orange
Dressing*

◆

*Chicken in the Pot
with
Feather Dumplings*

◆

Crowned Apple Cake

Family Dinner Before the Fast

First, the blessings are said over the same round, sweetened challah as on the eve of Rosh Hashanah (see page 30). It is traditional around the world to begin the meal with chicken soup. Here the soup becomes part of the entrée, Chicken in the Pot, a sampling of country cooking at its best. Whole pieces of chicken and vegetables simmer in a rich broth imbued with a little white wine. If you expect it to taste like boring boiled chicken, you are in for a pleasant surprise. The Feather Dumplings are mixed and cooked in the soup right before serving so they remain deliciously light and airy. Everything is then ladled into soup bowls to make clean-up a breeze. Spinach Salad with Mandarin Orange Dressing can be served along with the chicken or as a first course. Crowned Apple Cake makes the ideal ending for this meal. Not only is it sweet and round but it's so large you'll have leftovers for the next evening when you break-the-fast. This dinner is customarily underseasoned, to prevent undue thirst.

GAME PLAN

As Far Ahead As Desired	Make challah and freeze
	Make apple cake and freeze or refrigerate up to 2 days
4 Days Ahead	Make vinaigrette
1 Day Ahead	Make soup with chicken
	Defrost apple cake, if frozen

DAY OF DINNER	
3 Hours Before Serving	Bring challah to room temperature
30 Minutes Before Serving	Bring soup to a boil and cook dumplings
	Reheat challah
Shortly Before Serving	Assemble salad

Spinach Salad with Mandarin Orange Dressing

Mandarin Dressing
8 mandarin orange segments, reserved from salad
¼ cup vegetable oil
1 tablespoon plus 1 teaspoon sugar
½ teaspoon salt or to taste
2 tablespoons balsamic or red wine vinegar
2 or 3 dashes hot pepper sauce, such as Tabasco sauce

Salad
10 ounces washed and trimmed spinach (baby leaves preferred)
¼ cup toasted sunflower seeds
1 can (11 ounces) mandarin orange segments, drained (reserve 8 segments for dressing)
½ red onion, thinly sliced

To Make Dressing: In a food processor with the metal blade or a blender, puree orange segments. Add oil, sugar, salt, vinegar, and hot pepper sauce, and process until pureed. (Dressing may be refrigerated up to 4 days.) Makes ½ cup.

To Make Salad: In a medium bowl, toss spinach, sunflower seeds, oranges, and onion slices with dressing. Serve immediately.

Makes: 4 to 6 servings

Now that spinach leaves are available cleaned, prepped, and ready to dress, this refreshingly light salad can be made in a jiffy. Choose the youngest, smallest leaves because they are the most tender.

Prep Time: 10 minutes

Advance Prep: Dressing may be refrigerated up to 4 days.

When you taste this soul-warming soup brimming with tender pieces of chicken and topped with light-as-air dumplings, you'll understand why people crave the homey taste of Bubbe's slow-cooked dishes. The Feather Dumplings are adapted from Marion Cunningham's Fannie Farmer Cookbook.

Prep Time: *20 minutes*

Cook Time: *Soup, 1 hour; dumplings, 20 minutes*

Advance Prep: *Chicken and soup may be refrigerated overnight. Dumplings should be cooked in soup before serving.*

Note: *To make fresh bread crumbs, remove crusts from bread and process in food processor or blender until crumbly. (Crumbs may be stored in a heavy plastic zipper bag and refrigerated overnight or frozen.)*

Chicken in the Pot with Feather Dumplings

Chicken and Broth
2 pounds chicken drumsticks and thighs
2 pounds skinless, boneless chicken breasts, cut in thirds
1 cup dry white wine or imported dry vermouth
8 to 10 cups chicken broth (regular or low sodium)
3 leeks, white part only, cut in half lengthwise, cleaned, and sliced ½ inch thick
3 stalks celery with ribs, sliced
4 carrots, peeled and sliced diagonally 1 inch thick
2 tablespoons finely minced fresh thyme or 2 teaspoons dried thyme
Salt and freshly ground black pepper to taste

Feather Dumplings
1 cup all-purpose flour
½ cup fresh white or egg bread crumbs (see Note)
2 teaspoons baking powder
¾ teaspoon salt
1 large egg
2 tablespoons nondairy or regular margarine, melted
¼ cup finely chopped green onion with tops
⅓ cup chicken broth
2 teaspoons finely minced fresh thyme or ½ teaspoon dried thyme
1 tablespoon finely minced parsley

To Prepare Chicken and Broth: Using your hands and a towel to facilitate your grip, pull the skin off the legs and thighs and discard. Place chicken, wine, and enough broth to cover chicken by 1 inch in a large, wide saucepan or Dutch oven. Bring to a boil over high heat. Skim the foam off the top. Reduce heat to moderate and simmer, partially covered, for 10 minutes. Add leeks, celery, carrots, and thyme and simmer, covered, for 45 minutes. (Chicken and broth may be refrigerated overnight. Place a sheet of wax paper on the surface to keep the top from drying out. Skim off fat and bring to a boil before adding dumplings.)

Before Serving, Make Dumplings: In a medium bowl, stir together flour, bread crumbs, baking powder, and salt. In another bowl, whisk egg. Stir in margarine, onion, and broth. Stir into flour to make a stiff batter. Stir in thyme and parsley. Drop scant tablespoons of the batter on top of bubbling broth. Cover, reduce heat to moderately low, and simmer until dumplings are cooked through, about 20 minutes, without lifting the lid.

To Serve: Ladle soup into bowls with chicken, vegetables, and dumplings. Serve with fork, knife, and soup spoon.

Makes: 6 to 8 servings

Crowned Apple Cake

Photograph, page 6

Apple Mixture
4 large green apples (about 2½ pounds), such as Granny Smith or Pippin
⅓ cup honey
1 tablespoon ground cinnamon

Cake
3 cups all-purpose flour
2 cups sugar
1 cup vegetable oil
4 large eggs
⅓ cup orange juice
3 teaspoons baking powder
2½ teaspoons vanilla extract
1 teaspoon salt
½ cup chopped walnuts or pecans (optional)
About ½ cup walnut or pecan halves (optional)

Place oven rack in lower third of oven and preheat to 350°F. Grease or spray a 10-inch tube pan with a removable bottom.

To Prepare Apples: Peel, quarter, core, and slice apples ¼ inch thick. Place in a medium bowl with honey and cinnamon. Toss to coat and set aside while preparing cake.

To Make Cake: In a large mixing bowl with electric mixer on low speed, mix flour, sugar, oil, eggs, orange juice, baking powder, vanilla, and salt until combined. Increase to moderately high speed and mix until well blended, about 2 minutes. Pour ⅓ the batter into prepared pan. Arrange ⅓ of the apple slices over and sprinkle with chopped nuts, if using. Cover with ½ the remaining batter. Arrange ½ the remaining apple slices over batter and top with remaining batter, spreading the top evenly. Overlap remaining apple slices around tube of the pan, extending out like petals. Pour any juices that remain in bowl over apples. If desired, arrange nut halves along the outer edge to encircle top of cake.

To Bake: Place cake on a rimmed baking sheet and bake for 80 to 90 minutes, or until a toothpick or skewer inserted into center comes out clean. If top gets too brown, cover loosely with foil. Remove cake from oven and cool 10 minutes. Go around inside edges of pan with a knife and remove sides of pan. Cool cake to room temperature. Cut around tube and bottom and with a spatula, lift cake from pan to a serving plate. (Cake may be stored, covered, at room temperature up to 2 days or frozen.)

Makes: 14 servings

Symbolic of a round, sweet year and the crown of God's kingdom, this heavenly cake has a garland of caramelized apple slices around the top. Its texture is similar to a moist pound cake, with slices of honey-drenched apples scattered throughout the center.

Prep Time: *25 minutes*

Bake Time: *80 to 90 minutes*

Advance Prep: *Cake may be stored at room temperature up to 2 days or frozen.*

Menu

*Round Challah
(see page 6)*

◆

*Herring, Egg, and
Apple Spread*

*Artichoke and
Mushroom Bread
Pudding*

*Lox and Cream
Cheese Pizza*

*Orzo Salad with Feta
and
Sun-Dried Tomatoes*

Bubbly Fruit Salad

◆

*Banana–Chocolate
Chip Coffee Cake*

*Meshuganah
Mandelbrot
(see page 81)*

Break-the-Fast Buffet

Because this meal is eaten after synagogue services, it includes recipes that can be made at least one day ahead. In many American homes, break-the-fast has become synonymous with lox and bagels. Here's a delectable spin-off of that deli breakfast tradition—Lox and Cream Cheese Pizza. Simply substitute a prebaked Italian pizza crust for the bagels, then stand back and await the kudos.

Begin the meal with Herring, Egg, and Apple Spread to help restore the loss of salt after a day of fasting. Dairy foods are easy to digest on an empty stomach, making Artichoke and Mushroom Bread Pudding a good choice. Assemble the casserole a day ahead and place it in the oven while you put the finishing touches on the other dishes. There is nothing prettier or more refreshing than a beautiful bowl of mixed fresh fruit, especially when enhanced with a splash of lemon-lime soda and raspberry-flavored Chambord. Banana–Chocolate Chip Coffee Cake and Meshuganah Mandelbrot are terrific make-ahead desserts that will satisfy everyone's sweet tooth after a day of deprivation.

THE RITUALS

1 round challah with the same blessing as for dinner (see page 6).

GAME PLAN

As Far Ahead As Desired	Make challah and freeze
	Make banana cake and freeze or store at room temperature up to 2 days
	Make mandelbrot and freeze or store airtight for 1 week
1 Day Ahead	Assemble bread pudding
	Defrost banana cake, if frozen
	Defrost mandelbrot, if frozen
	Make herring spread
	Make orzo salad
	Cut fruits for salad

DAY OF BREAK-THE-FAST

8 Hours Before Serving	Prepare toppings for pizza
3 Hours Before Serving	Bring challah to room temperature
75 Minutes Before Serving	Bake bread pudding
20 Minutes Before Serving	Reheat challah
Shortly Before Serving	Bake pizza shells
	Complete fruit salad

erring helps
replenish the body's
salt after the fast. Here,
it's blended with
apples, hard-boiled
eggs, and crunchy bell
peppers into a finely
chopped salad for
spreading on bread
rounds. Sour cream
and mayonnaise make
it smooth enough to
mold—a fish shape is
appropriate.

Prep Time: *15 minutes*

Chill Time: *At least
3 hours*

Advance Prep: *Spread
may be refrigerated
overnight.*

Herring, Egg, and Apple Spread

1 (1-pound) jar herring fillets
2 green apples, peeled, cored, and coarsely chopped
½ onion, peeled and chopped
½ cup chopped green or red bell pepper
2 hard-boiled eggs, coarsely chopped
½ cup regular or low-fat mayonnaise
½ cup regular or light sour cream
Cocktail rye or pumpernickel bread rounds, for serving

Garnish *(optional)*
2 egg yolks, finely minced
2 egg whites, finely minced
½ cup finely minced parsley

To Make Spread: Line a 4-cup mold or bowl with plastic wrap. Drain herring, reserving onion slices from jar. Place herring, onion slices, and apples in food processor with the metal blade. Pulse until chopped. Transfer to a medium-size bowl and stir in chopped onion, bell pepper, and hard-boiled eggs. Stir in mayonnaise and sour cream. Pour into mold. Cover and refrigerate for at least 3 hours. (Spread may be refrigerated overnight.)

Before Serving: Invert mold onto serving plate. Remove plastic wrap. Garnish spread with finely minced egg yolks, whites, and parsley, if desired. Serve with bread rounds.

Makes: 4 cups; about 12 servings

Artichoke and Mushroom Bread Pudding

Photograph, page 7

6 whole large eggs
2 egg whites
2½ cups regular or low-fat milk
1 cup sliced mushrooms
1 (6-ounce) jar marinated artichoke hearts, well drained and coarsely
  chopped
4 green onions, sliced
1 teaspoon dried basil
½ teaspoon dried oregano
½ teaspoon salt
Freshly ground black pepper to taste
6 slices sourdough, white, or egg bread (sliced ½ inch thick)
1½ cups (6 ounces) shredded jalapeño Jack cheese or regular Jack cheese
  with 1 teaspoon finely minced jalapeño

Grease a 9 × 13-inch baking dish or spray with nonstick spray; set aside.

To Make Pudding: In a medium bowl, lightly mix eggs, whites, and milk.
Stir in mushrooms, artichokes, onions, basil, oregano, salt, and pepper.

Remove crusts from bread. Place in baking dish, cutting to fit. Sprinkle
with cheese. Pour egg mixture over bread. Cover with foil. Refrigerate at
least 12 hours or overnight.

To Bake: Place rack in center of oven and preheat to 325°F. Bake dish,
uncovered, for 65 to 75 minutes, or until top is puffed and brown.

Makes: 8 servings

This is an updated Italian rendition of those layered bread, cheese, and egg stratas that were so popular back in the '70s. Be sure to allow enough time for the assembled casserole to chill, at least 12 hours or overnight. Don't be afraid to use jalapeño Jack cheese—even the mildest palate won't find it too spicy.

Prep Time: 20 minutes

Chill Time: At least 12 hours or overnight

Bake Time: 65 to 75 minutes

Advance Prep: Pudding may be assembled 1 day ahead and baked before serving.

Lox and Cream Cheese Pizza

Photograph, page 7

1 (16-ounce) baked Italian bread shell, such as Boboli
4 ounces soft cream cheese
½ red onion, chopped
¼ hothouse cucumber, sliced
3 ounces lox, cut crosswise into thin strips
¼ cup dill, cut into small sprigs
2 tablespoons capers, rinsed and drained (optional)
Lemon slices, for garnish (optional)

Bake bread shell as package directs. Spread with cream cheese. Top with onion, cucumber, lox, dill, and capers, if using. Garnish with lemon, if desired. Slice and serve.

Makes: 8 slices

Change of Pace: To serve at a buffet, spread pizzas with cream cheese and put out toppings for guests to help themselves.

*W*hy serve bagels, lox, and cream cheese when the same ingredients make such a dynamic topping for pizza that your guests will compliment you on your ingenuity? This recipe makes enough topping for one 16-ounce prebaked crust. Multiply recipe as desired.

Prep Time: *10 minutes*

Bake Time:
10 minutes

Advance Prep:
Topping ingredients may be cut and refrigerated up to 8 hours ahead.

Orzo Salad with Feta and Sun-Dried Tomatoes

Photograph, page 7

1 pound orzo
⅓ cup balsamic vinegar
6 ounces feta cheese, coarsely crumbled (1½ cups)
¾ cup chopped fresh basil leaves
¾ cup rehydrated sun-dried tomatoes, sliced (about 20 tomatoes)
1 cup tightly packed fresh spinach leaves, cut into strips (about 3 ounces trimmed)
½ red onion, chopped
1 small red bell pepper, chopped
1 teaspoon salt or to taste
1 teaspoon ground seasoned pepper or rainbow peppercorns
⅓ cup olive oil
¼ cup pine nuts, toasted at 350°F for 10 minutes or until golden

Cook orzo as directed. Drain well and place in a large bowl. Add balsamic vinegar and stir well. Add feta, basil, tomatoes, spinach, onion, red bell pepper, salt, pepper, and oil. Toss well. Refrigerate until serving. (Salad may be refrigerated overnight.)

Before Serving: Stir in pine nuts.

Makes: 12 to 14 servings

Lynn Firestone, a wonderfully creative cook and hostess, created this dynamic salad. Her great sense of humor is evident in its title. Balsamic vinegar is poured over the rice-shaped pasta immediately after cooking, so that it can absorb its sweet, pungent flavor.

Prep Time: *20 minutes*
Advance Prep: *Salad may be refrigerated overnight.*

The effervescence comes from lemon-lime soda, enhanced with a splash of black raspberry liqueur. To cut the melons decoratively, use a rippled cutter especially designed for fruits and vegetables or a French-fry cutter.

Prep Time: *20 minutes*

Advance Prep: *Melons and kiwis may be cut ahead and refrigerated overnight.*

Bubbly Fruit Salad
Photograph, page 7

1 cantaloupe, cut into 1-inch pieces
1 honeydew, cut into 1-inch pieces
2 cups seedless red grapes
2 firm kiwis, peeled, quartered, and sliced
2 apples, peeled, cored, and chopped into 1-inch pieces
1 pint strawberries, stemmed and sliced
1 basket (6 ounces) fresh raspberries (optional)
6 ounces (¾ cup) lemon-lime soda
2 ounces (¼ cup) Chambord liqueur

In a large bowl, toss together cantaloupe, honeydew, grapes, and kiwis. (The fruit may be refrigerated overnight, layered with paper towels and covered tightly.)

Before Serving: Stir in apples and berries. Pour soda and Chambord over and toss lightly. Serve immediately.

Makes: 12 servings

Faster: Purchase fruits already cut up from the refrigerator case in the supermarket.

Banana–Chocolate Chip Coffee Cake

Streusel
½ cup firmly packed light brown sugar
¼ cup all-purpose flour
4 tablespoons (½ stick) butter or margarine, melted
½ cup chopped pecans or walnuts

Cake
¼ pound (1 stick) butter or margarine, at room temperature
1 package (8 ounces) cream cheese, at room temperature
1¼ cups granulated sugar
2 large eggs
2 very ripe bananas, mashed (1 cup)
1 teaspoon vanilla extract
2¼ cups all-purpose flour
2 teaspoons baking powder
1 teaspoon baking soda
¼ teaspoon salt
¼ cup whole or low-fat milk
1 package (6 ounces) semisweet chocolate chips

Preheat oven to 350°F. Grease or spray a 12-cup tube pan with a removable bottom.

To Make Streusel: In a small bowl, stir brown sugar, flour, butter, and nuts until thoroughly moistened. Set aside.

To Make Cake: In a large bowl with electric mixer on high speed, beat butter and cream cheese until smooth. Add sugar and mix until light and fluffy, about 2 minutes. Mix in eggs, one at a time, beating well after each addition. Mix in banana and vanilla. On low speed, mix in flour, baking powder, baking soda, salt, and milk until incorporated, about 1 minute. Mix in chocolate chips. Pour into prepared pan. Crumble Streusel over top.

To Bake: Bake for 60 to 70 minutes, or until a toothpick inserted in center comes out clean and top is deeply browned. Remove from oven and cool 15 minutes.

To Remove from Pan: Remove sides of pan and cool completely. To remove the tube, go around inside edge of cake with a sharp knife and loosen the bottom with a knife or spatula. Lift cake off tube. (Cake may be stored, well wrapped, at room temperature for 2 days or frozen.)

Makes: 12 servings

Cakes made with cream cheese in the batter always have a rich, moist crumb. This one is flavored with bananas and chocolate chips, and blanketed with a crunchy walnut streusel topping. Be sure to buy the bananas early enough for them to ripen fully.

Prep Time: 20 minutes

Bake Time: 60 to 70 minutes

Advance Prep: Cake may be stored at room temperature up to 2 days or frozen.

Sukkot and Simhat Torah

✧

The joyful holiday of Sukkot is celebrated exactly two weeks after the first day of Rosh Hashanah, and it lasts for seven days. Over 3,500 years ago, when the Jews made the journey from slavery in Egypt to freedom in the land of Israel, they wandered in the desert for forty years. Throughout that time they slept in huts or trellis-roofed sheds, which they made out of branches. Later, during the harvest, farmers lived in the same type of huts while they gathered their crops. The word *sukkah* (the singular of the word *sukkot*) means a small booth or hut.

In remembrance of the hardships our ancestors suffered in their flight from freedom and in celebration of the harvest, it is customary to build a sukkah, both in the synagogue and at home. This hut can be constructed of any material; the walls are most commonly covered with tarpaulin, burlap, canvas, and wood. The ceiling should be made of greens through which you can view the sky and stars. The space should be large enough to accommodate a table for family and friends to gather together to talk, eat, laugh, sing, and rejoice.

To show gratitude for a successful harvest, the sukkah is decorated with fruits and vegetables that reach maturity in autumn, such as apples, pears, cranberries, pomegranates, pumpkins, squash, and eggplant. Children especially enjoy decorating this ancestral hut. There are four specific plants of the harvest that are held in the hands each evening during the blessings. One is the *etrog*, or citron, a sour fruit that looks like a large, elongated lemon. The other three consist of a willow, palm, and myrtle, tied together into one branch called the *lulav*.

When the Pilgrims wanted to give thanks to God for the harvest, they looked in the Bible for inspiration, found the lovely holiday of Sukkot, and used it as a model for the American Thanksgiving. Many of the ingredients used in Thanksgiving recipes are popular for Sukkot, as well.

Sukkot is followed by Simhat Torah, when a full year of reciting the Torah comes to an end and a new one begins. In the synagogue, the last verses of Deuteronomy and the first verses of Genesis are read, to symbolize that the study of Torah is never ending. It is a holiday filled with merriment. The sacred scrolls are carried around the synagogue in a procession and passed among the adults so that everyone gets a chance to hold it. The children follow the procession waving Israeli flags and carrying apples. In some synagogues, the children hold paper bags, which the adults fill with candy to symbolize the sweetness of the Torah. Because Simhat Torah is primarily celebrated in the synagogue, a menu is not included for it.

THE RITUALS

Two candles are lit at sundown with the following blessing:

We praise You, Eternal God, Sovereign of the universe: You hallow us with Your Mitzvot, and command us to kindle the (Sabbath and) Festival lights.

Ba-ruch a-ta Adonai, Eh-lo-hei-nu meh-lech ha-o-lam, a-sher ki-d'sha-nu b'mitz-vo-tav v'tzi-va-nu l'had-lik ner shel (Shabbat v'shel) yom tov.

We thank You, O God, for the joy of Yom Tov, and for the opportunity to celebrate it in the company of those we love.

A glass of wine is lifted, and the following blessing is recited:

We praise You, Eternal God, Sovereign of the universe, Creator of the fruit of the vine.

Ba-ruch a-ta Adonai, Eh-lo-hei-nu meh-lech ha-o-lam, bo-rei p'ri ha-ga-fen.

Extra Points

THE INVITATION

Tie a note around a mini pumpkin, mail in a small box, or leave on your neighbor's doorstep.

THE SUKKAH

Children, adults, family, and friends can all help decorate the sukkah by hanging fruit, vegetables, gourds, and Indian corn from the roof. The walls can be decorated with the children's art projects— drawings, strung cranberries and popcorn, paper chains—as well as family photos and Rosh Hashanah cards.

THE TABLE

For the centerpiece, make the Breadstick Sukkah (see page 69).

Have the kids gather green, yellow, and orange leaves or purchase paper ones. Line the center of the table with the leaves and place the Breadstick Sukkah in the center.

The blessing for the holiday and Sukkot, the She-heh-cheh'yanu, is then recited:

We praise You, Eternal God, Sovereign of the universe, for giving us life, for sustaining us, and for enabling us to reach this season.

Ba-ruch a-ta Adonai, Eh-lo-hei-nu meh-lech ha-o-lam, sheh-heh-cheh-ya-nu, v'ki-y'manu, v'higi-anu la-z'man hazeh.

We praise You, Eternal God, Sovereign of the universe: You hallow us with Your Mitzvot, and command us to celebrate in the Sukkah.

Ba-ruch a-ta Adonai, Eh-lo-hei-nu meh-lech ha-o-lam, ah-sher ki-d'sha-nu b'mitz-vo-tav v'tzi-va-nu lei-sheiv ba-su-kah.

One or two challot (plural for challah) are covered with a decorated cloth. Everyone breaks off a piece of bread and recites the following blessing:

We praise You, Eternal God, Sovereign of the universe, for You cause bread to come forth from the earth.

Ba-ruch a-ta Adonai, Eh-lo-hei-nu meh-lech ha-o-lam, ha-mo-tzi leh-chem min ha-aretz.

Breadstick Sukkah

Items Needed
2 packages (4½ ounces each) long breadsticks (about 8 inches long)
1 package (6½ ounces) deli-style breadsticks (about 2½ inches long)
1 recipe Hummus (see page 74) or about 2 tablespoons peanut butter,
 for "glue"
1 large zucchini, sliced into long strips
1 long yellow squash, sliced lengthwise into strips
Greens, such as dill, parsley, or small garden leaves
Small clusters of red and green grapes
Flowers (optional)

Prep Time: 20 minutes

Advance Prep: This sukkah will last for about 10 days, but the herbs and fresh fruits should be added before using.

On a large cutting board or platter, place 2 long breadsticks next to each other. Leaving a 4½-inch space in the middle, lay down 2 more breadsticks, parallel to the first (see illustration 1). Place 2 deli-style breadsticks perpendicularly across the front of each pair of long breadsticks (see illustration 2). Attach in place using hummus or peanut butter as "glue." Lay 1 long breadstick across the back of the 2 long pieces (see illustration 3). Spread hummus or peanut butter on each corner of the structure. Place 2 long breadsticks on top, log-cabin style. Repeat until you've used 27 long breadsticks and 8 deli-style breadsticks.

To Create the Thatch Roof: Lay 1 long breadstick across the back, 1 across the middle, and 1 across the front, attaching them with hummus or peanut butter (see illustration 4). (Sukkah may be assembled several days ahead.)

Before Using: Lay zucchini and squash strips across the top. Garnish the top with dill and/or parsley, leaves, and grapes. Arrange the flowers, if desired, leaves, fruits, and herbs around the bottom.

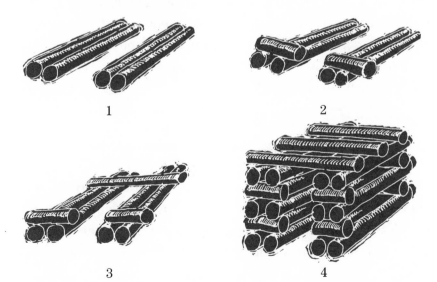

1

2

3

4

Menu

✧

Eggplant Salsa

Hummus

◆

*Pear Salad with Mixed
Greens and Sesame-
Pear Vinaigrette
(Double the recipe
on page 10)*

*Grilled Turkey Breasts
with Wild Mushrooms*

◆

*Marinated Vegetables
on Brochettes or
Carrot Tzimmes*

*Barley and Bow-tie
Pilaf*

◆

Cranberry-Apple Crisp

*Meshuganah
Mandelbrot*

A Harvest Dinner in the Sukkah

APPETIZERS

To reflect the autumn harvest, begin the festivities with Eggplant Salsa, a variation of the popular Israeli and Middle Eastern dip, which is so full of vegetables and spices it literally bursts with flavor. It's a great choice for a crowd, as it can be made ahead, goes a long way, is economical, and you can let it sit out for several hours. Creamy, white, and mild hummus spread makes a terrific counterpoint for the chunky, dark, and spicy eggplant. Accompany both spreads with a basket of pita triangles, bagel chips, and/or crackers. Streamlined Chopped Liver (page 206) would also make a welcome appetizer.

ENTRÉE

If you are eating outside in the sukkah, you might as well cook out there, too. So I offer Grilled Turkey Breasts with Wild Mushrooms. (Stuffed foods are traditionally served on Sukkot because they are considered to be extravagant enough for this opulent holiday.) It is not necessary to wait till the last minute to cook the breasts. Grill them one or two hours ahead and slice them before serving. They are equally tasty and succulent served at room temperature. If you are having young children, consider marinating plain turkey breasts without the stuffing or making Kid's Crusty Baked Chicken (see page 18).

SIDE DISHES

To make things easy, double the recipe for the turkey marinade and reserve half to soak the Marinated Vegetables on Brochettes. The brochettes are a colorful reminder of autumn's best offerings. Carrot Tzimmes is another vegetable option. If you are having a large crowd, serve both vegetables—they pair well together.

Barley and Bow-tie Pilaf is a nutritious and stalwart side dish that can be baked ahead and reheated. Or try Rice Pilaf with Fideo Nests (see page 37). Festive Pear Salad with Mixed Greens and Sesame-Pear Vinaigrette can be served as a first course or alongside the turkey. You will need to double the recipe and either toss it in a bowl or arrange the dressed greens on a platter garnished with pear and avocado slices.

DESSERT

In the spirit of Thanksgiving, I offer a homey Cranberry-Apple Crisp that warms the soul along with the body. An alternative to this *pareve* (nondairy) dessert would be Lemon Yogurt Cake (see page 27). Lemon represents the citron, or *etrog*, the fruit brought to the synagogue to be blessed.

GAME PLAN

As Far Ahead As Desired	Make Eggplant Salsa and freeze or refrigerate up to 3 days
	Make Hummus and freeze or refrigerate up to 1 week
	Make mandelbrot and freeze or store airtight for 1 week
1 Week Ahead	Make marinade for turkey and vegetables
2 Days Ahead	Make pilaf
	Make vinaigrette for salad
1 Day Ahead	Marinate turkey
	Make stuffing for turkey
	Make tzimmes
	Defrost salsa, if frozen, and assemble
	Defrost hummus, if frozen
	Defrost mandelbrot, if frozen
	Prepare streusel and syrup for crisp

DAY OF DINNER

8 Hours Ahead	Marinate vegetables
6 Hours Ahead	Marinate onions for salad
5 Hours Ahead	Assemble and bake crisp
4 Hours Ahead	Stuff turkey and refrigerate
45 Minutes Ahead	Prepare coals
	Bring pilaf to room temperature
20 Minutes Before Serving	Grill turkey and vegetables
Shortly Before Serving	Assemble salad
	Reheat tzimmes
	Reheat pilaf in microwave

Eggplant Salsa

1 large eggplant (about 1½ pounds)
¼ cup olive oil
1 green bell pepper, seeded and chopped
1 onion, peeled and chopped
2 cloves garlic, minced
8 ounces sliced mushrooms
1 can (8 ounces) tomato sauce
½ cup water
2 tablespoons red wine vinegar
1½ teaspoons sugar
1 teaspoon salt
½ teaspoon pepper
½ teaspoon dried oregano
½ teaspoon ground cumin
¼ teaspoon cayenne or to taste
½ cup sliced pimiento-stuffed olives

For Garnish and Serving
2 romaine lettuce leaves
1 tablespoon chopped parsley
Pita or bagel chips, for serving

To Prepare Eggplant: Cut a 2-inch lengthwise slice off top of eggplant. Scoop the pulp out of the bottom to make a shell for serving. Cut a small slice off the bottom so it stands securely. Wrap in plastic wrap and refrigerate until needed. Chop the pulp into 1-inch cubes.

To Cook: In a large, deep skillet or Dutch oven, heat oil over medium-low heat. Add eggplant, green pepper, onion, and garlic and cook, covered, stirring occasionally, for 15 minutes. Add mushrooms, tomato sauce, water, wine vinegar, sugar, salt, pepper, oregano, cumin, and cayenne and simmer, uncovered, stirring occasionally, for 10 to 15 minutes, or until vegetables are tender and sauce has thickened. Stir in green olives. Cool and refrigerate. (Salsa may be refrigerated, covered, up to 3 days or frozen. Defrost in refrigerator.)

To Serve: Line eggplant shell with lettuce leaves and spoon in dip. Sprinkle with parsley. Serve chilled with pita wedges or bagel chips.

Makes: about 3 cups; serves 12 to 14

Faster: Purchase already cleaned and sliced mushrooms

There are so many provocative vegetables and spices in this dip that even people who aren't fond of eggplant like it. My friend and colleague Debbie Shahvar adapted this recipe from her sister-in-law, Sandra. Serve it mounded in a lettuce-lined eggplant shell.

Prep Time: 20 minutes

Cook Time: 25 to 30 minutes

Advance Prep: May be refrigerated up to 3 days or frozen.

Hummus (Chick-pea and Sesame Dip)

This golden puree of garbanzo beans (chick-peas) and sesame seed paste, hummus is traditionally spread on triangles of pita bread, but I like to serve it as a dip with cut-up vegetables, too.

Prep Time: 10 minutes

Chill Time: At least 2 hours

Advance Prep: Hummus may be refrigerated up to 1 week or frozen.

Hummus
3 to 4 cloves garlic, to taste, peeled
2 cans (15½ ounces each) garbanzo beans, rinsed and drained
⅓ cup fresh lemon juice or to taste
6 tablespoons olive oil
¼ cup tahini (sesame seed paste)
Salt and freshly ground black pepper to taste

Garnish (optional)
1 teaspoon olive oil
Paprika
1 tablespoon chopped fresh parsley
1 tablespoon pine nuts, toasted

For Serving
Pita bread, cut into triangles
Fresh vegetables, such as carrots, celery, jicama, broccoli, cauliflower, zucchini, cut into bite-size pieces for dipping

To Make Hummus: In a food processor with the metal blade, process garlic until minced. Add garbanzo beans, lemon juice, oil, tahini, salt, and pepper. Process until pureed. Season to taste with additional lemon juice, garlic, salt, and pepper. Refrigerate for at least 2 hours for flavors to blend. (Hummus may be refrigerated up to 1 week or frozen.)

To Garnish: Spoon into a shallow bowl and drizzle top with olive oil. Sprinkle with paprika, parsley, and pine nuts, if desired.

To Serve: Serve chilled or at room temperature with pita wedges and/or vegetables.

Makes: 4 cups; serves 16 or more

Grilled Turkey Breasts with Wild Mushrooms

2 boneless turkey breast halves (1½ pounds each)

Balsamic Marinade
½ cup olive oil
⅓ cup balsamic vinegar
3 tablespoons soy sauce
4 cloves garlic, minced
1 tablespoon dried basil
1 tablespoon Dijon mustard

Mushroom-Spinach Stuffing
1 tablespoon vegetable or olive oil
1 onion, peeled and chopped
½ pound assorted fresh mushrooms, such as button, shiitake, porcini, portobello, coarsely chopped
4 medium-size tomatoes
⅓ cup chopped fresh basil leaves
2 tablespoons reserved Balsamic Marinade
Salt and pepper to taste
10 ounces washed and stemmed spinach (about 10 cups)
2 tablespoons pine nuts, toasted at 350°F until lightly golden
Metal turkey lacers or toothpicks

To Butterfly Turkey Breasts: Cut each half breast in half lengthwise, making 4 pieces. Using a sharp knife, cut a horizontal slit ¾ of the way through each half breast and open out like a book. Cover with wax paper or plastic wrap and pound lightly to about ½-inch thickness.

To Make Marinade: Mix all ingredients together in jar or bowl. (Marinade may be refrigerated up to 1 week.) Place turkey in shallow dish; the slices may be layered. Reserve 2 tablespoons marinade for stuffing and pour remainder over meat. Turn to coat both sides. Cover and refrigerate for 6 hours or overnight, turning once.

To Make Stuffing: Heat oil in a large skillet. Add onion and sauté 1 minute. Reduce heat to low, cover, and cook until onion is very soft, stirring occasionally, about 10 minutes. Add mushrooms and sauté, uncovered, over moderate heat, stirring frequently, until almost tender. Core tomatoes and cut in half horizontally, not through stem end. Squeeze out seeds and chop into small pieces. Add to mushrooms and sauté until almost all liquid evaporates, about 10 minutes. Stir in basil and marinade. Cool. Place spinach in a large microwave-safe bowl and microwave, covered, on high

This recipe calls for boneless turkey breast halves, sometimes called tenderloins or roasts. Each half breast should weigh about 1½ pounds (about 2¾ pounds with the bones). Each breast is cut in half, butterflied, and pounded lightly. If you don't want to do this yourself, ask your butcher to prepare them. The breasts are first infused with an aromatic balsamic marinade and then stuffed with a medley of mushrooms, tomatoes, spinach, and basil.

Prep Time: 45 minutes

*Marinade Time:
6 hours or overnight*

Grill Time: 15 to 20 minutes

*Advance Prep:
Marinade may be refrigerated up to 1 week. Stuffing may be refrigerated overnight.*

(100%) for 1 to 2 minutes, or until just beginning to wilt. Cool. Stir in pine nuts. (Stuffing and spinach may be refrigerated separately overnight.)

To Stuff Turkey Breasts: Remove turkey from marinade. Lay flat on work surface, skin side down. Sprinkle with salt and pepper. Place a thin layer of spinach over half of each breast. Spread ½ cup stuffing over spinach. Fold meat over filling to enclose. Skewer closed with metal turkey lacers or toothpicks.

To Grill: Prepare coals. Oil grill rack and place it 3 to 4 inches from coals. If using gas, heat on highest setting. Grill, turning once, for 7 to 10 minutes per side, or until cooked through.

Remove skewers and carve meat into ½-inch slices.

Makes: 10 servings

Marinated Vegetables on Brochettes

1 recipe Balsamic Marinade (see page 75)
3 medium zucchini (about 1½ pounds), sliced ½ inch thick
4 medium yellow squash (about 1½ pounds), sliced ½ inch thick
5 Japanese eggplant (about 1¼ pounds), sliced ½ inch thick
1 red bell pepper, cut into 1¼-inch pieces
1 red onion, cut into 1½-inch pieces
10 bamboo or metal skewers

To Marinate: Make marinade as directed. Place all vegetables in a large plastic zipper bag. Pour marinade over, turning to coat all sides. Marinate at room temperature for at least 1 hour or refrigerate up to 8 hours.

To Assemble: Alternate vegetables on skewers. (Skewers may be refrigerated up to 4 hours.)

To Grill: Prepare coals. Oil grill rack and place it 3 to 4 inches from coals. For gas grill, heat on highest setting. Grill vegetables, turning to cook all sides, until cooked through, about 15 minutes.

Makes: 10 servings

The vegetables used here are so porous that a simple balsamic marinade packs a powerful punch. If you serve them with the turkey breasts in this menu, double the marinade and use half for the turkey and the remainder for the vegetables. The brochettes can be either grilled or broiled.

Prep Time: 20 minutes

Marinade Time: 1 to 8 hours

Grill Time: 15 to 20 minutes

Advance Prep: Marinade may be refrigerated up to 1 week. Marinated vegetables may be arranged on skewers up to 4 hours ahead.

*T*zimmes literally means mixture. I'd never met one I liked before I developed this one. Too often they are a real production (or tzimmes) of too many ingredients—meats, sweet potatoes, carrots, squash, honey, spices, and whatever else the cook wants to throw in, usually dried fruits. In this version carrots simmer with orange juice, ginger, and honey—with some dried apricots thrown in for authenticity.

Prep Time: 10 minutes

Cook Time: 15 to 18 minutes

Advance Prep: Tzimmes may be cooked 1 day ahead and reheated.

Carrot Tzimmes

2 pounds carrots
1 cup orange juice
4 tablespoons (½ stick) nondairy or regular margarine or butter
3 tablespoons honey
1 teaspoon ground ginger
1 teaspoon salt
½ cup coarsely chopped dried apricots
2 teaspoons cornstarch, dissolved in 2 teaspoons cold water

Peel, trim, and slice carrots into ¼-inch rounds in food processor or by hand. In a large skillet over moderately high heat, bring orange juice, margarine, honey, ginger, and salt to a boil, whisking until blended. Add carrots, reduce heat to medium low, cover, and simmer 10 minutes. Stir in apricots, cover, and cook until carrots are tender, 5 to 8 more minutes. Remove from heat. Stir in cornstarch mixture. Return to heat and cook until thickened, stirring constantly. (Carrots may be cooled and refrigerated overnight. Reheat in microwave or on top of stove.)

Makes: 10 servings

Barley and Bow-tie Pilaf

3 tablespoons nondairy or regular margarine or butter
1 cup pearl barley
4¼ cups chicken broth
1½ cups sliced green onions, including tops (about 2 bunches)
3 cups bow-tie noodles, also called farfalle, not cooked
½ teaspoon salt or to taste
¼ teaspoon freshly ground black pepper or to taste

Preheat oven to 350°F.

In a large skillet over moderately high heat, melt margarine. Sauté barley until lightly toasted, about 5 minutes. Slowly stir in broth and bring to a boil. Transfer to an ungreased 3-quart (12-cup) round or 9 × 13-inch rectangle casserole. Bake covered for 20 minutes. Stir in green onions, noodles, and salt and pepper. Continue baking, covered, for 20 minutes or until barley is tender. Uncover and bake for 5 to 10 more minutes, or until all liquid is absorbed. (Pilaf may be refrigerated up to 2 days, brought to room temperature, and reheated in the microwave.)

Makes: 6 to 8 servings

Here, I borrow the bow-tie noodles from kasha varnishkas (buckwheat groats) and cook them instead with barley. This is such a tasty dish, and it's effortless to prepare because the dried noodles bake right along with the barley. It makes a nice change of pace from rice and potatoes with any meat, poultry, fish, or vegetarian entrée.

***Prep Time:** 15 minutes*

***Bake Time:** 55 to 60 minutes*

***Advance Prep:** Pilaf may be refrigerated up to 2 days.*

Cranberry-Apple Crisp

Streusel
1 cup all-purpose flour
⅔ cup granulated sugar
⅔ cup firmly packed dark brown sugar
4 teaspoons ground cinnamon
1 teaspoon ground nutmeg
12 tablespoons (1½ sticks) nondairy or regular margarine or butter, cut into pieces
⅔ cup coarsely chopped walnuts or pecans

Orange Syrup
1½ cups orange juice
2 teaspoons grated orange peel
1 cup sugar
1½ teaspoons ground cinnamon
¼ teaspoon ground nutmeg
2 packages (12 ounces each) 4 cups fresh or frozen cranberries

Filling
8 medium-size tart green apples, such as Pippin or Granny Smith, peeled, cored, and sliced ¼ inch thick
2 teaspoons ground cinnamon
Nondairy topping, whipped cream, or ice cream, for serving

Preheat to 350°F. Grease or spray a 9 × 13-inch baking dish.

To Make Streusel: In a food processor with the metal blade, pulse flour, granulated sugar, brown sugar, cinnamon, and nutmeg to blend. Add margarine and pulse until mixture is the texture of wet sand; do not form a ball. Pulse in nuts. (Streusel may be refrigerated, covered, overnight.)

To Make Syrup: In a medium saucepan, stir together orange juice and sugar, cinnamon, and nutmeg. Bring to a boil, stirring, until sugar dissolves. Add cranberries and cook until they begin to pop, about 5 minutes. Drain berries, reserving syrup. Boil syrup over moderately high heat until reduced to 1 cup, about 15 minutes, stirring occasionally. (Cranberries and syrup may be refrigerated separately overnight.)

To Make Filling: In a large bowl, combine cranberries, apples, and cinnamon. Pour half the fruit into prepared pan. Crumble half of streusel on top. Cover with remaining fruit. Crumble remaining streusel.

To Bake: Bake for 40 to 50 minutes, or until apples are tender and streusel is golden. (Crisp may be held at room temperature up to 4 hours.)

To Serve: Cool crisp slightly. Rewarm orange syrup. Spoon crisp into bowls, top with whipped cream or ice cream, and drizzle with syrup.

Makes: 12 servings

Meshuganah Mandelbrot
(Orange–Chocolate Chip Cookie Slices)

½ **cup sugar**
½ **cup vegetable oil**
1 **large egg**
2 **tablespoons frozen orange juice concentrate, thawed**
1 **teaspoon orange extract (optional)**
1½ **cups all-purpose flour**
1 **teaspoon baking powder**
½ **teaspoon salt**
2 **teaspoons finely grated orange peel**
½ **cup chopped walnuts**
½ **cup dried cranberries, cherries, or blueberries**
½ **cup chocolate chips**

Place rack in center of oven and preheat to 350°F. Grease or spray with nonstick spray a large, heavy baking sheet, preferably a cushioned one.

To Make Batter: In food processor with the metal blade or mixing bowl with electric mixer, process or mix sugar, oil, egg, orange juice concentrate, and extract, if using, until blended. Add flour, baking powder, salt, and orange zest, and pulse or mix until incorporated. Add nuts, berries, and chips and pulse or mix to combine.

To Shape: Divide dough into thirds and spoon into 3 rectangular mounds on prepared baking sheet. With wet hands, shape each into a log, about 10 inches long × 1½ inches wide × ¾ inch high.

To Bake: If not using a cushioned baking sheet, double-pan by placing 1 sheet on top of the other. Bake for 20 to 25 minutes, or until lightly browned. Remove from oven and loosen bottoms of logs with a spatula. Cool 5 minutes and cut diagonally into ¾-inch slices. Rearrange on baking sheet about ½ inch apart. Bake for 8 to 10 minutes, or until golden. They will firm up as they cool. If you prefer a softer cookie, bake the minimum amount of time. (Mandelbrot may be stored airtight up to 1 week or frozen.)

Makes: about 36 cookies

Mandelbrot is a Yiddish word meaning almond bread. I call this a "meshuganah" version because it has no almonds. Instead, it is filled with all kinds of goodies—orange zest, orange juice, walnuts, dried berries, and chocolate chips. The dough is shaped into a log, or loaf, and then sliced. Like their Italian cousin, biscotti, these cookies are twice-baked and great for dunking.

Prep Time: 20 minutes

Bake Time: About 35 minutes

Advance Prep: Cookies may be stored airtight for 1 week or frozen.

Hanukkah

✦

For children the happiest and most memorable holiday of the Jewish calendar is Hanukkah. And why not? It's eight days of lighting candles, eating latkes, singing songs, opening presents, playing games, and having fun. Although the weather may be cold and dismal outside, the excitement and glow of the candles create a warm and cozy feeling inside. What, in its origins, was a minor festival, a late celebration of Sukkot, has become a major celebration for the Jews of North America.

Two thousand years ago in Syria, Jews were ruled by a cruel king, Antiochus. He drove the Hebrews out of the Temple in Jerusalem and ordered them to worship Greek gods. Anyone who refused was killed. The Jews, led by a father and his five sons, called the Maccabees, banded together to fight the Syrians. When they won the Temple back, they found it filled with altars and Greek idols. They worked hard to repair it, but when it was ready for services, they could find only enough oil to light the Eternal Light for one day. When the oil burned for eight days, it was considered a miracle.

This miracle is remembered each year on Hanukkah by lighting a candlestick with eight branches, called a *menorah*. Presents and Hanukkah *gelt*, or coins, are all part of the merriment of the holiday. The children use their recently received "gelt" to bet on a game played with a *dreidel*, or spinning top. The dreidel is spun and when it falls, the Hebrew letter on the top determines the amount won or lost. The Hebrew letter *Gimmel* ג means take all; *Heh* ה means take half; *Nun* נ means take nothing, and *Shin* ש means put in a coin.

THE RITUALS

On each of the eight nights an additional candle is inserted into the menorah from right to left. The candles are lit by the _Shamos_ (helper candle) from left to right. The following blessings are recited:

We praise You, Eternal God,
Sovereign of the universe:
You hallow us with Your Mitzvot,
and command us to
kindle the Hanukkah lights.

_Ba-ruch a-ta Adonai, Eh-lo-hei-nu
meh-lech ha-o-lam, a-sher
ki-d'sha-nu b'mitz-vo-tav
v'tzi-va-nu l'had-lik ner shel
Hanukkah._

We praise You, Eternal God,
Sovereign of the universe:
You showed wonders to our
fathers/mothers in days of old,
at this season.

_Ba-ruch a-ta Adonai, Eh-lo-hei-nu
meh-lech ha-o-lam, sheh-a-sa
ni-sim la-a-vo-tei-nu/l'i-mo-tei-nu
ba-ya-mim ha-heim ba-z'man
ha-zeh._

On the first night only the following blessing, the She-heh-cheh'yanu, is said:

We praise You, Eternal God,
Sovereign of the universe,
for giving us life, for sustaining us,
and for enabling us to reach
this season.

_Ba-ruch a-ta Adonai, Eh-lo-hei-nu
meh-lech ha-o-lam, sheh-heh-
cheh-ya-nu, v'ki-y'manu,
v'higi-anu la-z'man hazeh._

Extra Points

INVITATIONS

Write a note and insert it inside a plastic dreidel. Mail in a padded envelope.

THE TABLE

Make the Menorah Centerpiece or place the Chocolate Cherry Dreidel Cake in the center of the table. Scatter Jewish-star confetti made out of Mylar, baby dreidels, and foil-wrapped chocolate gelt around the table.

For napkin rings, wrap blue garlands and ribbons around napkins.

Menorah Centerpiece

Items Needed
Styrofoam, about 2½ feet long × 5 inches wide × 1 inch high
Blue foil paper
9 doughnuts, preferably sprinkled with multicolored sprinkles
8 dripless candles, about 12 inches high × ¾ inch in diameter
1 dripless candle, about 14 inches high × ¾ inch in diameter
Curly ribbon or metallic star garlands

Wrap Styrofoam in blue foil.

Glue doughnuts on Styrofoam. Place on table.

Insert 12-inch candles into eight of the doughnut holes. If holes are too small, cut to fit.

Insert 14-inch candles into center doughnut. Intersperse ribbon or garlands around candles and Styrofoam.

Hanukkah Candle-Lighting Party

LATKES

The traditional foods for Hanukkah are related to the miracle of the oil (see page 82), such as potato pancakes (in Yiddish, the word for pancake is *latke*) and doughnuts fried in oil. (Doughnuts are incorporated into the Menorah Centerpiece.) The best method for shredding potatoes is often debated among cooks. Purists believe it can be done only on a hand grater (I call this the bleeding-knuckle method). I much prefer the ease of the shredding blade on the food processor. If the shreds are too long, simply pulse them a few times with the steel blade. Another source of dispute is freezing the latkes. Of course, they are best served hot and crisp right out of the pan, but that's not always possible. If you follow my directions for freezing and reheating, you will have excellent results. The slight loss in texture may be worth the gain in composure.

This menu offers a variety of latkes, in addition to traditional ones. The Giant Potato–Carrot Pancake is made in a large skillet, browned on top of the stove, baked in the oven, turned out, and cut into wedges. It is easier and faster to make one large pancake, because it cooks in less oil and while it bakes, you can do other chores. I often serve two kinds of latkes, one made with white potatoes and the other with sweet potatoes. If you like the crispness of potato pancakes, but don't want to fry them, Crisp Potato Kugel (see page 132) offers yet another option.

APPETIZER

You'll want to serve an appetizer that can sit out while you light the candles and open the presents, but nothing heavy, because the meal is filling. Hummus dip (see page 74) fills the bill and looks sensational with its Menorah Garnish. Other appetizer options are

Menu

*Hummus
(see page 74)* with
*Menorah Garnish
for Dip*

◆

*Brisket with
Burgundy-Orange
Sauce*

◆

*Latkes
or
Sweet Potato Latkes
or
Giant Potato–Carrot
Pancake
or
Crisp Potato Kugel
(see Change of Pace,
page 132)*

◆

Zucchini Gelt

◆

*Chocolate Cherry
Dreidel Cake*

Dreidel Sundaes

Confetti Tuna Mousse (see page 197) and Streamlined Chopped Liver (see page 206).

ENTRÉE AND SIDE DISHES

There is no religious basis for serving brisket on Hanukkah, but the tender, juicy slices saturated in a rich, brown sauce go so well with crispy latkes, it has become the most popular Hanukkah entrée. Brisket with Burgundy-Orange Sauce is a new item in my repertoire. Last year my daughter Margi went to four Hanukkah parties and had brisket at all of them. She says this version far surpassed all the others in moistness and flavor. Zucchini Gelt, with the squash sliced into rounds like coins, is a light and simple vegetable that complements this robust meal.

DESSERT

Bring dinner to a spinning close with a show-stopping Chocolate Cherry Dreidel Cake festive enough to be the table centerpiece as well as the dessert. Accompany it with individual Dreidel Sundaes, assembled and served in plastic dreidels, ready and waiting in your freezer.

GAME PLAN

As Far Ahead As Desired	Make brisket and freeze or refrigerate up to 2 days
	Make and freeze white or sweet potato latkes, if serving
	Make Hummus and freeze or refrigerate up to 1 week
	Make cake and freeze or refrigerate up to 2 days
	Fill and freeze sundaes
1 Day Ahead	Defrost brisket, if frozen
	Defrost Hummus, if frozen
	Defrost cake, if frozen, and frost and decorate it

DAY OF DINNER

6 Hours Ahead	Make Menorah Garnish for dip
4 Hours Ahead	Make giant potato pancake, if serving
	Slice zucchini
2 Hours Ahead	Bring brisket to room temperature
45 Minutes Before Serving	Add mushrooms to brisket and bake
10 to 20 Minutes Before Serving	Reheat white or sweet potato latkes or giant potato pancake, if serving
Shortly Before Serving	Sauté zucchini

Prep Time: 10 minutes

*Advance Prep: Dip
may be garnished up to
6 hours ahead.*

Menorah Garnish for Dip

1 recipe Hummus (see page 74) or desired dip
1 medium zucchini, trimmed
1 large carrot, peeled
2 to 3 radishes or 1 red bell pepper

Make dip and place in a bowl that measures approximately 6 to 7 inches across the top. Smooth top.

Cut zucchini in half lengthwise. Cut a piece with the peel into a 5-inch strip about ¼ inch wide. To make menorah, place the strip horizontally across dip, slightly below the center. Cut another piece with peel into a 1-inch triangle. Place under the middle of the strip for base of menorah.

Cut carrot into eight 1-inch × ¼-inch strips for candles. For the *Shamos* candle, cut a strip 1½ inches long × ¼ inch wide and place in center of menorah. Place 4 carrot candles to the right and 4 to the left.

Cut radishes or red bell pepper into 9 small triangular shapes to resemble flames. Place on top of each candle. (Dip with garnish may be covered with plastic wrap and refrigerated up to 6 hours.)

Brisket with Burgundy-Orange Sauce

1 envelope (about 1 ounce) onion soup mix
1½ cups Burgundy wine
¼ cup water
2 tablespoons flour
1 tablespoon dried basil
2 teaspoons dried thyme
⅓ cup orange marmalade
1½ teaspoons grated orange peel
2 teaspoons sugar
4 cloves garlic, minced
¼ to ½ teaspoon pepper to taste
1 (4-pound) brisket of beef, trimmed of as much fat as possible
1 pound mushrooms, cleaned; if large, cut in halves or quarters

Preheat oven to 300°F.

To Make Brisket: In a roaster into which the brisket fits comfortably, stir together soup mix, wine, water, and flour until blended. Stir in basil, thyme, marmalade, orange peel, sugar, garlic, and pepper. Add brisket, spooning some of the sauce over the top. Cover and bake for 4 hours, basting every hour until tender when pierced with a fork. If sauce bubbles rapidly, reduce oven to 275°F. Remove from oven and place brisket on a sheet of heavy foil. Pour sauce into a bowl, cover, and refrigerate. When brisket is cool, wrap in foil and refrigerate. (Brisket and sauce may be refrigerated separately overnight.)

To Carve: Remove solidified fat from sauce and discard. Slice brisket thinly against the grain. Overlap slices in a shallow, ovenproof dish that is just large enough to hold them. Pour sauce over meat. (Brisket may be refrigerated, covered, up to 2 days or frozen. Defrost in refrigerator overnight. Bring to room temperature before reheating.)

To Reheat: Preheat oven to 325° or 350°F. Add mushrooms to meat, basting with sauce. Bake, covered with foil, for 40 to 50 minutes, basting once, until heated through and mushrooms are tender.

Makes: 8 servings

The secret to tender, juicy, cut-with-a-fork brisket is long, slow cooking. By roasting the meat ahead and refrigerating it, you can remove all the solidified fat before slicing. The stalwart brown sauce, accented with orange peel and marmalade, is poured over the sliced meat and then refrigerated or frozen. All you need do before serving is reheat it.

Prep Time: 10 minutes

Bake Time: 4 hours

Advance Prep: Brisket is best prepared at least 1 day ahead. It may be refrigerated up to 2 days or frozen.

Latkes (Potato Pancakes)

Photograph, page 8

1 vitamin C tablet
2½ pounds baking potatoes, peeled (about 4 large potatoes)
1 onion, peeled
2 eggs, lightly beaten
1 teaspoon salt
¼ teaspoon baking powder
2 tablespoons flour or matzah meal
Vegetable oil
Applesauce and/or nondairy or regular sour cream, for serving (optional)

To Prepare Batter: Place vitamin C tablet in a small bowl with 2 tablespoons hot water to dissolve. Shred potatoes, using shredding blade of food processor or hand shredder. Place in a bowl. If shreds are large, return to food processor with metal knife and pulse in batches to chop slightly. Remove to bowl and stir in dissolved vitamin C. Shred or finely chop onion. Add to potatoes. Stir in eggs, salt, baking powder, and flour or matzah meal until incorporated. Use immediately.

To Cook: In a large skillet, heat ½ inch oil over medium-high heat. Using a slotted spoon, spoon about 2 tablespoons batter into hot oil for each pancake. Do not crowd. Flatten slightly with the back of a spoon. Fry pancakes until golden on both sides, turning once. When you reach the end of the batter, squeeze it lightly to remove excess liquid. After frying, remove pancakes to paper towels to drain. Pancakes may be kept warm in a low oven on a baking sheet in a single layer for 1 hour.

To Freeze and Reheat: Freeze on baking sheets in single layers. When solid, layer in airtight container with wax paper between each layer. Before reheating, return the frozen pancakes to baking sheets. Reheat in a single layer without crowding at 450°F for 5 to 10 minutes if thawed, 15 to 20 minutes if frozen, or until crisp and bubbling.

Serve with applesauce and/or sour cream, if desired.

Makes: about 24 pancakes

---

*E*ver since I first published this recipe in 1982, I've been experimenting with variations. But none have surpassed the original, so I'm reprinting it. I don't advise doubling it because the last of the raw potato batter turns starchy and brown as it sits. It's not much more time-consuming to make two or three batches. Ascorbic acid, vitamin C, is added to the potatoes to prevent them from turning brown.

Prep Time: 15 minutes

Cook Time: About 20 minutes

Advance Prep: Pancakes may be kept warm in a low oven for 1 hour or frozen.

Sweet Potato Latkes

1 pound sweet potatoes or yams (about 2 medium), peeled
1 piece peeled fresh ginger (about 2 × 1 inch) or 2 tablespoons minced
  ginger
2 eggs
½ cup regular or low-fat milk
½ cup all-purpose flour
1 tablespoon sugar
1 teaspoon baking powder
1 teaspoon salt or to taste
Vegetable oil
Applesauce, for serving (optional)

To Make Batter: Shred sweet potatoes with shredding disk of food processor or by hand. Place in a large bowl. Using steel blade, chop ginger. Measure 2 tablespoons and stir into potatoes. Process eggs, milk, flour, sugar, baking powder, and salt to combine. Add to potatoes and toss together until mixed.

To Cook: In large skillet, heat ½ inch oil over medium-high heat until it registers 365°F on a thermometer or sizzles instantly when a small amount of batter is added. Drop ⅓ cup batter into oil for each pancake, making 3- to 4-inch pancakes. Cook until golden on the bottom, 3 to 4 minutes. If pancakes cook too fast or slow, decrease or increase the heat. Turn and brown on other side, 3 to 4 minutes. Remove to a tray lined with paper towels. Serve with applesauce, if desired. (Pancakes may be refrigerated overnight, layered with wax paper, tightly covered.)

To Freeze and Reheat: Freeze on baking sheets in single layers. When they are solid, layer in airtight container with wax paper. To reheat, do not defrost. Arrange in a single layer on baking sheets and bake at 400°F for 10 minutes, or until hot and crisp.

Makes: about 10 pancakes

A thick batter binds these crisp, ginger-infused pancakes together, making them easy to cook. They also reheat beautifully. Once you taste them, you may begin a sweet new tradition.

Prep Time: 15 minutes

Cook Time: About 15 minutes

Advance Prep: Pancakes may be refrigerated overnight or frozen.

Making one large pancake saves so much time and uses much less oil. My son-in-law, Jim, has another reason: It's the best potato pancake he's ever eaten.

Prep Time: 15 minutes

Cook Time: 15 to 20 minutes

Advance Prep: Pancake may be made up to 4 hours ahead and reheated.

Giant Potato–Carrot Pancake

½ **cup finely chopped green onions with tops**
2 **tablespoons chopped parsley**
3 **medium carrots, peeled (about 8 ounces)**
4 **medium baking potatoes, peeled (about 2 pounds)**
1½ **teaspoons salt**
¼ **teaspoon freshly ground black pepper**
3 **tablespoons vegetable oil**
3 **tablespoons nondairy or regular margarine or butter**
Applesauce and/or sour cream, for serving (optional)

Place oven rack in upper third of oven and preheat to 450°F.

To Make Batter: Place the green onions and parsley in a large bowl. Shred the carrots and potatoes with the shredding disk of the food processor or by hand and add to the onions. Add salt and pepper, and toss until well combined.

To Cook on Stove: Heat the oil and margarine in a 12-inch skillet (preferably nonstick) over moderately high heat. If the handle is not ovenproof, cover it with a double thickness of heavy foil. Add the potato mixture, pressing down and smoothing the top with your hands or a spatula. Cover and cook for 7 to 10 minutes, or until bottom is golden brown. Lift with a spatula from time to time to loosen the bottom and make sure it does not burn. If the pancake browns too quickly or slowly, lower or increase the heat.

To Bake: When the bottom is golden, place pan in oven. Bake for 7 to 10 minutes, or until the top is firm. If desired, place under broiler and brown top. Remove from the oven and loosen the bottom with a spatula. Slide the pancake onto a platter or place the platter over the top and invert it. If not serving immediately, invert onto a baking sheet sprayed with nonstick coating. The pancake may be cooled and held at room temperature, loosely covered, up to 4 hours. Reheat, uncovered, at 400°F for 10 minutes, or until crisp.

To Serve: Cut into wedges and serve with applesauce and/or sour cream, if desired.

Makes: 8 servings

Zucchini Gelt

8 medium zucchini (about 2 pounds), trimmed
2 tablespoons olive oil
2 cloves garlic, minced
1 bunch green onions, sliced (about 1 cup)
½ cup seasoned dried bread crumbs

Slice zucchini into ⅛-inch rounds. In a large skillet over medium-high heat, heat olive oil. Add garlic, zucchini, and green onions. Sauté until vegetables begin to soften, about 5 minutes. Sprinkle with bread crumbs. Cook for 1 to 2 minutes for crumbs to adhere, turn with a spatula, and cook on other side for 2 minutes. Serve immediately.

Makes: 8 servings

Rounds of zucchini, lightly sautéed and coated with bread crumbs, make delicious Hanukkah gelt, or coins. Al Neuman created this simple recipe, and I'd put my money on it any time.

Prep Time: 10 minutes

Cook Time: 10 minutes

Advance Prep: Zucchini may be sliced ahead and refrigerated up to 4 hours. Cook before serving.

When devil's food cake mix is enhanced with cocoa powder and cherry pie filling, then slathered with a rich fudgy frosting, it tastes as if you made it from scratch. Cutting and decorating the cake like a dreidel makes it the talk of the table.

Prep Time: Cake, 10 minutes; frosting, 5 minutes

Bake Time: 35 to 40 minutes

Frost and Decorate Time: 20 minutes

Advance Prep: Unfrosted cake may be refrigerated up to 2 days or frozen. Frosted cake may be held at room temperature overnight.

Chocolate Cherry Dreidel Cake

Photograph, page 9

Chocolate Cherry Cake
1 package (18½ ounces) regular or reduced-fat devil's food cake mix
Eggs, amount called for on cake mix box
Oil, amount called for on cake mix box
1 can (16 ounces) cherry pie filling
⅓ cup Chambord liqueur or water
3 tablespoons unsweetened cocoa powder

Fudge Frosting
4 tablespoons (½ stick) nondairy or regular margarine or butter
4 squares (1 ounce each) unsweetened chocolate, chopped
2 tablespoons unsweetened cocoa powder
2 tablespoons light corn syrup
1½ cups powdered sugar
4 to 5 tablespoons very hot water

Decorations
2 tubes chocolate decorating icing with rosette or star tip
Multicolored sprinkles or chocolate jimmies

Place oven rack in center of oven and preheat to 350°F. Spray a 9 × 13-inch baking pan with nonstick spray.

To Make Cake: In a mixing bowl with electric mixer, beat cake mix, eggs, oil, half the cherry pie filling, Chambord, and cocoa on low speed until blended. Do not add water called for on box. Increase speed to medium and beat 2 minutes. Fold in remaining pie filling. Pour into prepared pan and spread evenly.

To Bake: Bake for 35 to 40 minutes, or until toothpick comes out clean. Cool in pan 15 minutes and invert onto a cutting board or sheet of foil. Cool completely. (Cake may be wrapped in foil and refrigerated up to 2 days or frozen. Defrost, covered, at room temperature.)

To Cut Cake: Cut into dreidel shape. Using 2 spatulas, remove cake to a large platter. Cut scraps of cake to make a "Chai" (see illustrations.)

To Make Frosting: In a large microwave-safe bowl, microwave margarine and chocolate, uncovered, on high (100%) until melted, about 1 minute. Stir in cocoa, corn syrup, powdered sugar, and 3 tablespoons hot water. Stir until smooth. Add enough additional water to make a spreading consistency. Use immediately.

To Frost and Decorate: Frost top and sides of cake with about ¾ the frosting. Using chocolate decorating icing, pipe a border around bottom edge of cake. Frost top and sides of the "Chai" with remaining frosting and sprinkle with multicolored sprinkles or chocolate jimmies. Using a spatula, place on top of cake. (Cake may be held, uncovered, at room temperature overnight.)

Makes: 14 servings

Dreidel Sundaes

Desired flavor ice cream, frozen yogurt, or sorbet
One plastic dreidel per person, with a top that opens
Fudge or caramel ice cream topping (optional)
Mini chocolate chips, nuts, or sprinkles (optional)

Leave ice cream at room temperature until soft enough to spoon. Wash and dry dreidels. Fill the bottom of each dreidel with ice cream, yogurt, or sorbet, alternating with topping and sprinkling with candies or nuts, if using. Mound the top slightly and place top of dreidel over ice cream on a slant, allowing some of the ice cream to show. Place on a tray, cover with foil, and freeze for at least 6 hours. (Sundaes may be frozen up to 2 weeks.)

*F*ill plastic dreidels with ice cream, frozen yogurt, or a fruity sorbet. You might make some cream-laden and others low-fat or nonfat. Let your taste buds and diet be your guide.

Prep Time: 3 minutes per dreidel

Freeze Time: At least 6 hours

Advance Prep: Sundaes may be frozen up to 2 weeks.

Tu B'Shevat

✧

Tu B'Shevat is known as the New Year of the Trees, a minor holiday but a joyous one, marking the beginning of spring in Israel. After the barren winter, Tu B'Shevat celebrates the awakening of nature and the blossoming of meadows, orchards, and vineyards.

It is customary on this holiday for the children in Sunday school to purchase leaf stickers and paste them onto a drawing of a tree. When the tree is filled, the money is sent to Israel in the child's name and a new tree is planted.

To celebrate Tu B'Shevat, Jews worldwide eat fruits and nuts indigenous to ancient Israel. Nowadays the holiday is celebrated with a Seder, meaning order, with four different types of wines (or fruit juice), and a wide variety of fruits; some with an inedible shell, like nuts and oranges; some with pits or a seed, like dates and peaches; and others that are totally edible, like berries and raisins. In the olden days, few fresh fruits were available at this time of year, so the dried varieties were used. During the Seder, alternate tastings of wine and fruit are sampled with selected readings and singing.

THE RITUALS

The leader lifts a glass of wine and all present recite the following blessing:

We praise You, Eternal God,
Sovereign of the universe,
Creator of the fruit of the vine.

Ba-ruch a-ta Adonai,
Eh-lo-hei-nu meh-lech ha-o-lam,
bo-rei p'ri ha-ga-fen.

The two principal blessings of the Seder are recited over the fruit:

We praise You, Eternal God,
Sovereign of the universe,
Creator of the fruit of the tree.

Ba-ruch a-ta Adonai,
Eh-lo-hei-nu meh-lech ha-o-lam,
bo-rei p'ri ha-eitz.

We praise You, Eternal God,
Sovereign of the universe,
Creator of the fruit of the earth.

Ba-ruch a-ta Adonai,
Eh-lo-hei-nu meh-lech ha-o-lam,
bo-rei p'ri ha-a-dama.

Extra Points

THE INVITATIONS

Glue a note onto a seed packet and mail it in a padded envelope.

THE TABLE

Carry out nature's theme with green paper plates or ones with a fruit or flower motif. Decorate the table with potted plants of various sizes and put out bowls of fresh fruits and nuts.

FOR THE KIDS

For each child, fill a small plastic cup with dirt and plant the seed of a green bean in it. (A green bean is the easiest to grow.) The seed will begin to sprout in 3 to 5 days, and in about a month, it should grow into a full-size bean.

Menu

*Tomatillo-Avocado
Salsa (see page 111)*

◆

*Black Bean Chili
(see page 114)*

Tuna Hye Roller

PB&J Hye Roller

Tabbouleh

◆

Double Apricot Strudel

*Fresh and dried
fruits, such as apples,
melons, oranges,
grapes, and berries*

Casual Buffet Supper

Celebrate this festive holiday with a relaxed, informal, anything-goes get-together. The food is uncomplicated and easy to eat off your lap—no knives needed. For starters, put out a bowl of Tomatillo–Avocado Salsa and/or Eggplant Salsa (see page 73). Black Bean Chili is the only dish in the menu that needs heating. Because the chili will be eaten with sandwiches, serve it from an earthenware crock instead of a bread bowl. America is seeing a resurgence of roll-up sandwiches. Wraps, so popular in ancient times, are back in vogue. Tuna Hye Roller features layers of fresh vegetables and canned tuna rolled up in a large, round cracker bread called a Hye Roller. This bread was originally sold as a big, crisp cracker. It needed to be soaked in water in order to become soft enough to roll. Now you can find Hye Rollers already softened in the refrigerator case of most supermarkets. For the youngsters, spread the bread with peanut butter, strawberry jam, sliced bananas, and plump raisins.

Tabbouleh, a flavorful mix of bulgur wheat, chopped vegetables, parsley, and mint, makes the perfect partner for these sandwiches. You can supplement this salad with leafy Mixed Greens with Apples, Blue Cheese, and Sweet 'n' Spicy Walnuts (see page 175), Orzo Salad with Feta and Sun-Dried Tomatoes (see page 63), or Caesar Pasta Salad with Romaine Ribbons (see page 47).

Few dishes have more significance for this celebration of fruits and nuts than Double Apricot Strudel with its luscious layers of preserves, walnuts, dried apricots, and coconut. Dried Fruits Stewed in Cinammon and Port (see page 148) would also be appropriate. Recipes may be multiplied to serve any size group.

GAME PLAN

As Far Ahead As Desired   Make strudel and freeze or store at room
                                     temperature up to 1 week
                                     Make chili and freeze or refrigerate up to
                                     3 days

2 Days Ahead   Make salsa

1 Day Ahead   Make tabbouleh
                                     Defrost strudel, if frozen
                                     Defrost chili, if frozen

DAY OF PARTY

4 Hours Before Serving   Make Hye Rollers

Shortly Before Serving   Reheat chili
                                     Slice Hye Rollers

This sandwich gives you a lot of flexibility. If you don't like avocado, leave it out. If you like sliced cheese, add it. Just don't make the sandwich too full or it will be difficult to roll up and eat. Look for soft Hye Roller cracker-bread sheets in the refrigerator case of your supermarket.

Prep Time: *20 minutes*

Advance Prep: *Sandwich may be refrigerated up to 4 hours.*

Tuna Hye Roller

4 to 5 ounces creamy spiced cheese, such as Alouette or Rondelé
1 soft, round sheet Hye Roller cracker bread (from 17-ounce package)
About 15 spinach leaves, stemmed
1 can (6⅛ ounces) tuna packed in water, drained
2 tablespoons unflavored yogurt or mayonnaise
Seasoned salt and freshly ground black pepper to taste
3 plum tomatoes, thinly sliced
¼ hothouse or European cucumber, thinly sliced
1 avocado, peeled, pitted, and sliced
¾ cup fresh basil leaves
¼ red onion, thinly sliced

Spread a thin layer of spiced cheese over Hye Roller to cover completely. Beginning with edge closest to you, arrange overlapping leaves of spinach over cheese, leaving 4 inches of cheese uncovered at opposite end. In a small bowl, mix tuna and yogurt or mayonnaise. Season with salt and pepper. Spread tuna in a 2½-inch strip across center of spinach. Top with a layer of tomatoes, cucumber, avocado, basil, and red onion. Beginning with filled end closest to you, roll up as tightly as possible. Serve immediately or wrap in plastic and refrigerate. (Sandwich may be refrigerated up to 4 hours.) Before serving, cut off ends of roll and slice remainder into 1½-inch pieces.

Makes: six 1½-inch sandwiches; serves 3

Here's a sandwich for kids of all ages.

Prep Time: *10 minutes*

Advance Prep: *Sandwich may be refrigerated up to 4 hours.*

PB&J Hye Roller

¾ cup creamy peanut butter
1 soft, round sheet Hye Roller cracker bread
⅓ cup strawberry or other flavor jam or preserves
1 banana, sliced
½ cup raisins

Spread a thin layer of peanut butter over Hye Roller. Spread jam over peanut butter, leaving 4 inches of just peanut butter at end opposite you. Place 2 rows of bananas over jam, one about 2 inches from one edge and the other across the center. Sprinkle with raisins. Beginning with jam end, roll sandwich up tightly. (Sandwich may be wrapped in plastic wrap and refrigerated up to 4 hours.) Before serving, cut off ends of roll and slice remainder into 1½-inch pieces.

Makes: six 1½-inch sandwiches; serves 3

Tabbouleh
(Bulgur Wheat and Vegetable Salad)

2 cups cracked bulgur wheat
4 cups boiling water
2 cups finely chopped parsley
½ cup finely chopped fresh mint or 2 tablespoons dried mint, crumbled
1 cup finely sliced green onions, including tops
4 medium tomatoes (preferably vine ripened), finely chopped
2 stalks celery, finely chopped (about 1 cup)
2 medium cucumbers (preferably hothouse), finely chopped
½ cup olive oil
⅔ to ¾ cup fresh lemon juice
1½ teaspoons salt
½ teaspoon freshly ground black pepper
Small romaine lettuce leaves, for serving

To Make Salad: Place bulgur in a large bowl, pour boiling water over, and let stand for 1 hour, or until tender. Drain well and squeeze out excess water. Return to bowl and stir in parsley, mint, green onions, tomatoes, celery, and cucumbers. Stir in olive oil, ⅔ cup lemon juice, and salt and pepper. The flavor should be tangy; if not, add remaining lemon juice to taste. If the fresh mint is not flavorful, you can supplement it with some dried mint. Stir well and refrigerate for at least 2 hours. (The salad may be refrigerated, covered, overnight.)

To Serve: Stir well. Serve with lettuce leaves for scooping.

Makes: 12 servings

This popular Middle Eastern salad is made with bulgur, precooked and dried wheat kernels, which requires no cooking. The grains are soaked in water to reconstitute before being mixed with finely chopped vegetables, mint, and lemon juice. For the most attractive presentation, dice the vegetables by hand, but it's fine to mince the herbs in the food processor. Tabbouleh is traditionally served with romaine lettuce leaves for scooping; pita bread works well, too.

Prep Time: 20 minutes

Soak Time: 1 hour

Chill Time: At least 2 hours

Advance Prep: Salad may be refrigerated overnight.

Double Apricot Strudel
Photograph, page 10

A search through my timeworn recipe files turned up a vintage temple sisterhood strudel recipe with, of all things, ice cream in the pastry. At first I was skeptical, but I tried it. To my surprise, the pastry makes an ideal wrap for jam, dried fruits, and nuts. It's substantial enough to have character when bitten into, sturdy enough to pick up and eat, but still soft and tender. This strudel ranks right up there with the best.

Prep Time: 30 minutes

Bake Time: 35 to 40 minutes

Advance Prep: Strudels may be stored airtight for 1 week or frozen.

Ice Cream Pastry
½ pint (1 cup) vanilla ice cream, not defrosted
¼ pound (1 stick) butter or margarine, at room temperature
2 cups all-purpose flour
¼ teaspoon salt

Filling
⅓ cup plus ⅓ cup apricot jam or preserves
½ cup plus ½ cup chopped dried apricots
½ cup plus ½ cup shredded coconut
¼ cup plus ¼ cup raisins
½ cup plus ½ cup chopped walnuts

Topping
1 tablespoon butter or margarine, melted
2 tablespoons sugar mixed with ¼ teaspoon ground cinnamon

To Make Pastry: In mixing bowl with electric mixer, beat ice cream and butter on medium speed until smooth and blended. Add flour and salt, and mix on low until incorporated. Mix on medium until dough holds together. Remove to a floured board, divide in half, and shape into 2 logs. Flatten each slightly. Use immediately or wrap in plastic wrap and refrigerate. (Pastry may be refrigerated overnight.)

To Roll Pastry: Place oven rack in middle of oven and preheat to 350°F. Line a heavy or cushioned baking sheet with heavy foil. Spray with non-stick spray or grease the foil. If you don't have a cushioned sheet, double-pan by placing 1 baking sheet on top of the other. On a heavily floured sheet of wax paper, using a floured rolling pin, roll pastry into a 15 × 7-inch rectangle. Pick pastry up often to make sure it doesn't stick and reflour as needed.

To Assemble: Spread ⅓ cup jam evenly over center third of pastry, leaving a 1½-inch border unspread on each long end. Sprinkle jam with ½ cup dried apricots, ½ cup coconut, ¼ cup raisins, and ½ cup nuts. Beginning with a long end, fold pastry up over filling and then roll up jelly-roll fashion. Press seam together securely and close ends. Place seam side down on prepared baking sheet. Repeat with remaining pastry and filling. (Strudels may be refrigerated overnight or frozen up to 2 weeks. If freezing, wrap in a sprayed sheet of heavy foil. Do not defrost. Before baking, open foil and place on baking sheet.)

To Bake: Brush tops with melted butter and sprinkle with sugar-cinnamon mixture. Bake for 35 to 40 minutes (40 minutes if frozen), or until the strudels begin to color lightly. They will still be pale. Remove from oven and immediately loosen bottoms with a spatula. Cool 10 minutes, remove to a cutting board, and cut with a serrated knife into 1-inch slices. (Strudels may be stored, covered, at room temperature up to 1 week or frozen.) Serve at room temperature or reheat at 350°F for 10 minutes and serve warm.

Makes: 2 strudels, about 14 slices each

Purim

✦

The most fun-filled and exuberant of all Jewish holidays, Purim celebrates the triumph of Jews over their archenemy Haman in Persia (modern Iran) in the fifth century B.C.E.

According to the biblical story, Haman was an ambitious and deceitful minister who gained enormous power by taking advantage of the easily influenced King Ahasuerus. When the king commanded that everyone bow down to Haman, Mordechai, a Jew who had once saved the king's life, refused. This infuriated the anti-Semitic Haman, who convinced the king that all the Jews were disloyal and should be killed. Lots were drawn to decide on what date the Jews would be annihilated (the word Purim means "lots").

Neither Haman nor the king knew that his wife, the beautiful and much-beloved Queen Esther was a Jew and also Mordechai's cousin. When Esther learned of the plot, she risked her life by telling the king she was Jewish and that Haman was going to have her and all her people killed. When the king realized that Haman was the real danger, he had him hung on the gallows that had been prepared for Mordechai.

After Haman's death, Mordechai insisted that the day be com-memorated as a celebration of life and survival by all people, rich and poor alike. Thus began the custom of exchanging food and sweets with friends and relatives and giving food and money to the poor. The most popular of these foods are filled three-cornered cookies called *hamantashen*, which resemble Haman's hat or ears.

On Purim the Book of Esther is written in a scroll called the Megillah, which is read in the synagogue. Every time Haman's name is read, the congregants twirl *gragers* (noisemakers), stamp their feet, boo, and hiss to drown out his evil name. Children and adults dress in costumes, march in parades, and participate in their synagogue's joyful carnival. Adults continue the festivities with Mardi Gras–like masquerade parties. In Israel a huge parade of costumed merrymakers takes place annually.

Purim also marks the founding of the Women's Zionist Organization in 1912 by Henrietta Szold. She named the group Hadassah, which means Esther in Hebrew, in honor of the heroine of the Purim story.

Extra Points

THE INVITATIONS

Write a note and attach it to a grager *(noisemaker) or mask. Mail in a bubble envelope.*

THE TABLE

The more color and glitz the better. Decorate the table with masks, gragers, *feathers, sequins, boas, beaded necklaces, streamers, and Mylar confetti. Fill champagne flutes with marbles and colorful feathers.*

FOR THE KIDS

Plan a Hamantashen Party. Have the dough ready and, depending on the age group, either roll it out yourself or supply small rolling pins or bottles and let the children roll it out. Supply cookie cutters or water glasses, and let them cut out, fill, and bake the cookies.

Make costumes of Purim characters (Esther, Mordechai, Haman) using old clothes, crepe paper, cardboard, makeup, and some imagination.

Menu

Appetizers

*Mushroom,
Goat Cheese, and Pine
Nut Hamantashen*

*Potato Knish
Hamantashen*

*Tomatillo-Avocado
Salsa*

*Artichoke and Red
Pepper Torta*

*Apricot Brie in Puff
Pastry*

*Black Bean Chili in a
Bread Bowl*

◆

Desserts

*Flo Braker's Cookie-
Dough Hamantashen
with Dried Apricot or
Prune-Raisin Filling*

*Chocolate–Peanut
Butter Hamantashen*

Rugelach Bar Cookies

Shikker Cake

◆

Beverages

*Blushing Champagne
Punch with Fruited
Ice Mold*

*Sparkling Citrus
Punch*

Appetizer and Dessert Masquerade Gala

For a fun and frolicsome party, serve appetizers and desserts instead of an entire meal. You only need to set a buffet table. This menu includes dishes that are easy to multiply and are hassle-free. They can all be made ahead, and only a few of the appetizers should to be served warm. The desserts are all room temperature and can safely sit out the entire party. In keeping with kosher dietary laws, the menu is dairy and vegetarian. According to the Purim story, Queen Esther became a vegetarian while living in the court of King Ahasuerus, because she could not obtain kosher food.

APPETIZERS

I have taken some liberty with hamantashen, traditionally a dessert, and developed two triangular-shaped appetizers—Mushroom, Goat Cheese, and Pine Nut Hamantashen and Potato Knish Hamantashen. The pastry for both recipes is made from separated layers of flaky refrigerator biscuits. Fill some with the mushroom mixture and the others with mashed potatoes. Don't hesitate to freeze them ahead—they taste just as good as those freshly made. Although they are best served warm, they can be reheated throughout the party and are also fine at room temperature.

Apricot Brie in Puff Pastry can sit out for about an hour before it gets too firm to spread, but I guarantee it won't last that long. If you're having a very large crowd, make two or three and stagger the baking times.

When appetizers are served in place of an entrée, one should be substantial, so I suggest Black Bean Chili in a Bread Bowl. Of course, you don't need to serve it in the bread; I offer it merely as a decorative option. The dark chili looks pretty garnished with rings of colorful condiments, but you might offer bowls of condiments as well. Serve with small plates and forks or as a dip with chips.

Here also are two cold appetizers that can sit out safely for several hours. Artichoke and Red Pepper Torta is a spread to be served on crackers. If your party is large, instead of doubling or tripling the recipe in one large mold, make two or three single molds. When one is finished or looks messy, you can bring out a fresh one. No jarred salsa from the grocer's shelf tastes as fresh and vibrant as Tomatillo-Avocado Salsa. But if time is short, substitute your favorite bottled salsa. You might also consider Eggplant Salsa (see page 73) or Confetti Tuna Mousse (see page 197).

DESSERTS

Hamantashen are as synonymous with Purim as matzah is with Passover. For a soft, buttery, tender cookie, try Flo Braker's Cookie-Dough Hamantashen. But you'll also want to try Chocolate–Peanut Butter Hamantashen. They are rich, crumbly chocolate cookies filled with creamy peanut butter and strawberry jam. Rugelach, crescent-shaped cookies filled with cinnamon, nuts, and raisins, are America's most popular Jewish cookie. They are very time-consuming to prepare, so I've incorporated their sensational taste into bar cookies.

On Purim you're commanded to get so drunk you can't tell the difference between Mordechai and Haman. While I don't recommend this, I do recommend Shikker Cake. (In Yiddish the word *shikker* means drunk.) This buttery pound cake is drenched with a generous dose of rum. Generally, I don't care much for desserts made with liquor, but this one is irresistible.

BEVERAGES

For a large group, I suggest Blushing Champagne Punch with Fruited Ice Mold and nonalcoholic Sparkling Citrus Punch. They are far more economical and easier to serve than opening bottles of wine or champagne. Be sure you have enough glasses on hand; plastic ones are fine. Plan on 2 to 3 glasses per person for a 3- to 4-hour party. You can also offer some plain sparkling and still waters.

GAME PLAN

As Far Ahead As Desired
Make and freeze mushroom hamantashen
Make and freeze potato hamantashen
Make chili and freeze or refrigerate up to
    2 days
Make cookie hamantashen and freeze or
    store airtight for several days
Make chocolate hamantashen and freeze
    or store airtight for several days
Make cake and freeze or refrigerate up to
    3 days
Make and freeze ice mold

3 Days Ahead
Make rugelach bars

2 Days Ahead
Make salsa

1 Day Ahead
Make torta
Prepare brie
Defrost chili, if frozen
Defrost cookie and chocolate
    hamantashen, if frozen
Defrost cake, if frozen
Make champagne punch
Make base for citrus punch

DAY OF PARTY

Morning of Party
Bring rugelach bars, cake, and chili to
    room temperature

2 Hours Before Serving
Unmold torta

1 Hour Before Serving
Bake brie

15 Minutes Before Serving
Bake bread shell for chili, if using

Shortly Before Serving
Reheat chili
Complete champagne punch
Complete citrus punch
Reheat frozen mushroom and potato
    hamantashen

Mushroom, Goat Cheese, and Pine Nut Hamantashen

1 tablespoon olive oil, butter, or margarine
2 cups chopped mushrooms (about 6 ounces)
1 large tomato, seeded and diced
⅓ cup chopped green onions with tops
2 tablespoons regular, low-fat, or nonfat sour cream
⅓ cup crumbled goat cheese
2 tablespoons pine nuts, toasted at 350°F until golden, about 5 minutes
Freshly ground black pepper to taste
1 package (12 ounces) refrigerated flaky-layers buttermilk biscuits

Place oven rack in upper third of oven and preheat to 375°F. Grease or spray 2 heavy-duty or cushioned baking sheets with nonstick spray.

To Make Filling: Heat oil or butter in a medium skillet over moderately high heat. Sauté mushrooms and tomato, stirring frequently, until most of the liquid has evaporated. Remove from heat and stir in green onions, sour cream, goat cheese, pine nuts, and pepper. Cool completely. (Filling may be refrigerated overnight.) Makes 1½ cups.

To Make Hamantashen: Separate 1 roll into 3 or 4 rounds and place them on a work surface. Keep remainder chilled while you work or they will be difficult to separate. Don't be concerned if some tear; just patch them back together. Spoon a heaping teaspoon of filling in the center of each biscuit round. Pinch 3 edges together tightly to form a triangle; the filling will not be covered. (See illustrations, page 110) Repeat with remaining rolls.

To Bake: Place on prepared baking sheets about 1½ inches apart. Bake for 12 to 16 minutes, or until bottoms are very brown. If baking 2 pans in one oven, rotate their positions after 6 minutes. (Hamantashen may be refrigerated overnight or frozen. If frozen, do not defrost. Bake frozen at 375°F for 7 minutes; 4 to 5 minutes, if refrigerated.)

Makes: about 36 hamantashen

Faster: Purchase mushrooms already cleaned and sliced so all you have to do is chop them.

Change of Pace: Substitute blue cheese for the goat cheese.

These bite-size morsels, smaller than dessert hamantashen, are made by separating flaky refrigerated biscuits into thin rounds and topping them with a savory vegetarian filling. The edges are then pinched together to form a triangle in the shape of Haman's hat.

Prep Time: 30 minutes

Bake Time: 12 to 16 minutes

Advance Prep: Hamantashen may be refrigerated overnight or frozen.

Potato Knish Hamantashen

Photograph, page 11

2 cups warm instant mashed potatoes, made according to
   package directions
2 teaspoons dried minced onions
1 clove garlic, minced
Salt and pepper to taste
1 egg yolk, lightly beaten
1 package (12 ounces) refrigerated flaky-layers buttermilk biscuits

Place oven rack in upper third of oven and preheat to 375°F. Grease or spray with nonstick spray 2 heavy-duty or cushioned baking sheets.

To Make Filling: While potatoes are still warm, mix in onions, garlic, salt, pepper, and egg yolk.

To Make Hamantashen: Separate 1 biscuit roll into 3 or 4 rounds and place them on a work surface. Keep remainder chilled while you work or they will be difficult to separate. Don't be concerned if some tear; just patch them back together. Pipe a rosette through a star tip or spoon a heaping teaspoon of filling in the center of each biscuit round. Press 3 edges together tightly to form a triangle, leaving a small opening in the center for the filling to show (see illustrations). Repeat with remaining rolls.

To Bake: Place on prepared baking sheets about 1 inch apart. Bake for 12 to 16 minutes, or until bottoms are very brown, rotating pans after 7 minutes, if baking 2 pans in one oven. (Knishes may be refrigerated overnight or frozen. If frozen, do not defrost. Bake frozen at 375°F for 9 minutes; 6 to 7 minutes, if refrigerated.)

Makes: about 36 knishes

*K*nishes are appetizer pastries that are filled with anything from potatoes to chopped meat or sauerkraut. Traditionally they are made with a baking powder or yeast dough, rolled, cut, filled, folded, and baked. This easy version begins with refrigerated rolls and instant mashed potatoes, which are preferable to fresh in this recipe because they are so creamy. These little appetizers are delightful—smooth, light, and flaky.

Prep Time: 20 minutes

Bake Time: 12 to 16 minutes

Advance Prep: Knishes may be refrigerated overnight or frozen and reheated.

Tomatillo-Avocado Salsa

6 fresh tomatillos or 1 can (13 ounces) tomatillos, drained
2 large cloves garlic, peeled
2 large green onions with tops, coarsely chopped
½ cup packed cilantro leaves
4 teaspoons jarred salsa jalapeño or hot picante salsa or
  minced fresh jalapeños
4 teaspoons fresh lime juice
½ cup vegetable or chicken broth
½ teaspoon sugar
1 large or 2 medium avocados, peeled, pitted, and coarsely chopped
Salt to taste
Tortilla chips, for serving

To Prepare Tomatillos: If using fresh tomatillos, remove husks and wash. Bring a medium pot of water to a boil, add tomatillos, and cook for 5 minutes, or until soft. Drain and cool.

To Make Salsa: In a food processor with the metal blade, mince garlic and onions. Add cilantro, tomatillos, and salsa jalapeño, and process until pureed. Add lime juice, broth, and sugar, and process to blend. Add avocado and pulse until finely chopped but not pureed. Remove to a bowl and add salt to taste. (Salsa may be refrigerated up to 2 days.)

Serve with tortilla chips.

Makes: 2½ cups

This salsa version of guacamole is highly flavored, but not too spicy. It makes a great sauce for fish as well as a dip for tortilla chips.

Prep Time: 15 minutes

Advance Prep: Salsa may be refrigerated up to 2 days.

Artichoke and Red Pepper Torta

This refined, colorful, and simple-to-prepare spread alternates layers of cream cheese, seasoned with dried ranch dressing, with marinated artichoke hearts, green onions, and red bell pepper. The mixture is shaped in a bowl or mold, turned out, and served with crackers.

Prep Time: 20 minutes

Chill Time: At least 4 hours

Advance Prep: Torta may be refrigerated overnight.

2 packages (8 ounces each) regular or light cream cheese, softened
1 package (1 ounce) ranch salad dressing mix
1 jar (6 ounces) marinated artichoke hearts, drained and chopped
⅓ cup finely chopped parsley
3 green onions with tops, chopped
1 medium red bell pepper, chopped (reserve a 1½-inch square for garnish)
Red leaf lettuce, for garnish
Crackers, for serving

To Make Spread: In a mixing bowl with electric mixer, mix cream cheese and dressing mix until blended. In a medium bowl, stir together artichoke hearts, parsley, green onions, and bell pepper.

To Mold: Line a 3-cup bowl or mold with plastic wrap. Beginning with cream cheese mixture, alternate layers of cream cheese and vegetables, ending with cream cheese. (If cheese is difficult to spread, wet your hands and smooth it.) Refrigerate at least 4 hours. (Torta may be refrigerated overnight.)

To Serve: Line a serving plate with lettuce leaves and invert torta onto leaves. Using a canape cutter or knife, cut the reserved red pepper into a small design or triangle and place on top. Serve with crackers.

Makes: 10 to 12 servings

Apricot Brie in Puff Pastry

1 sheet (½ a 12-ounce package) frozen puff pastry, defrosted until soft
   enough to roll but still very cold
⅓ cup chopped dried apricots
1 round Brie (8 ounces)
⅔ cup apricot preserves
1 egg mixed with 1 tablespoon water, for glaze
Thinly sliced baguette, for serving

To Prepare Brie: On a lightly floured board with a lightly floured rolling pin, roll pastry into a 14-inch square. Cut off corners, making an uneven 13-inch circle. Place dried apricots in center of pastry, forming a round the size of the Brie. Place cheese on apricots. Spread preserves over top. Bring sides of pastry up over the top and twist tightly into a knot like a money bag. Pull back edges to open them out. Place in a greased pie dish or on a rimmed baking sheet. Brush pastry with egg. (Cheese may be refrigerated, covered with foil, overnight.)

To Bake: About 1 hour before serving, preheat oven to 400°F. Bake Brie for 30 minutes, or until golden. If top browns too quickly, cover loosely with foil. Let rest 20 to 30 minutes before serving to set up slightly. Remove to a platter and serve with baguette slices.

Makes: 12 servings

When Lynn Firestone gave me this recipe, she warned me to be prepared for utter silence when I served it . . . everyone would be too busy devouring it to talk. She was right. Although the cheese is baked in pastry, it is still spread on thin slices of baguette.

Prep Time: 15 minutes

Bake Time: 30 minutes

Rest Time: 20 to 30 minutes

Advance Prep: Brie may be prepared a day ahead and baked before serving.

This vegetarian chili with its deep, mildly spicy taste and versatility is a great appetizer, vegetable dish, or entrée, and it improves in flavor when made ahead. For an attractive buffet presentation, fill a round French bread with the chili and garnish the top with rings of cheese, sour cream, and chopped tomatoes. Leftovers make terrific burritos rolled up in tortillas.

Prep Time: 10 minutes

Cook Time: 30 minutes

Advance Prep: Chili may be refrigerated up to 2 days or frozen.

Black Bean Chili in a Bread Bowl

Chili
2 to 3 tablespoons olive oil
2 large onions, peeled and finely chopped
1 large green bell pepper, finely chopped (about 1½ cups)
2 cloves garlic, minced
1 tablespoon ground cumin
¼ teaspoon cayenne or to taste
2 teaspoons paprika
2 tablespoons dried oregano
1 teaspoon salt or to taste
1 can (28 ounces) crushed whole tomatoes
3 cans (15 ounces each) black beans, rinsed and drained

For Serving (use any or all as desired)
1 round loaf (about 1 pound) French or sourdough bread
Chopped tomatoes
Shredded Cheddar or Jack cheese or a combination
Sour cream
Chopped green onions
Chopped fresh cilantro
Tortilla chips, for serving (optional)

To Make Chili: In a large skillet, heat 2 tablespoons olive oil over moderate heat until hot. Add onions, bell pepper, garlic, cumin, cayenne, paprika, oregano, and salt. Cook, stirring frequently, until onions are soft, about 10 minutes. If pan is dry, add more oil. Add tomatoes with their juice, black beans, and ¼ cup water. Simmer, uncovered, for 15 to 20 minutes, or until thickened slightly. (Chili may be refrigerated up to 2 days or frozen. Defrost in refrigerator overnight or at room temperature. Reheat on top of stove or in microwave.)

To Make Bread Bowl (if using): Cut a slice off top of bread. Scoop out bread, leaving a ½-inch shell. Reserve scooped-out bread for another use. Use shell at room temperature or, if you plan to eat it, bake it at 425°F for 10 to 15 minutes, or until crisp.

Before Serving: Spoon hot chili into bread shell. Arrange a circle of tomatoes around outer edge of chili, then a circle of cheese. Spoon a dollop of sour cream in the center. Sprinkle green onions and cilantro over all. Serve with tortilla chips for dipping or on plates with a fork.

Makes: 16 appetizer servings or 6 main-dish servings

Change of Pace: For individual entrées, scoop out sourdough rolls. Bake at 375°F for 10 to 15 minutes, or until crisp. Fill with chili. Serve with condiments.

Flo Braker's Cookie-Dough Hamantashen

3 cups all-purpose flour
2 teaspoons baking powder
½ teaspoon salt
¼ pound (1 stick) butter or margarine
1 cup sugar
1 large egg
⅓ cup orange juice
1 teaspoon vanilla extract
1 recipe Dried Apricot or Prune-Raisin Filling (recipes follow)

Place rack in upper third of oven. Preheat oven to 350°F. Line 2 heavy-duty or cushioned baking sheets with parchment paper or grease or spray them.

To Make Dough: Sift flour, baking powder, and salt. In mixing bowl with electric mixer, cream butter and sugar until light and fluffy, about 2 minutes. Add egg and mix 1 minute. Mix in orange juice and vanilla. Add flour mixture and mix until incorporated. Shape into a flat disk, wrap in plastic, and refrigerate until firm enough to roll out, at least 15 minutes. (Dough may be refrigerated up to 2 days.)

To Shape Hamantashen: Divide the dough in half; it will be very sticky. Cover 1 portion with plastic wrap and refrigerate. Place other half between 2 sheets of floured wax paper. Roll from the center out toward the edges into a 13-inch circle, about ⅛ inch thick. If dough is difficult to roll out, place in freezer to firm up. Using a 3-inch floured cookie cutter, cut out circles. (A clean, empty tuna can with both ends removed works well.) Using a floured spatula, pick up circles and flip onto prepared baking sheets. Spoon 1½ teaspoons filling in the center of each circle. Press 3 edges together (see illustration, page 110) to make a triangle, leaving a small opening in the center. Place 1½ inches apart. Repeat with remaining dough. Reroll scraps, cut out, and fill.

To Bake: Bake for 15 to 18 minutes, or until golden on the bottom. If baking 2 sheets in one oven, rotate positions after 7 minutes. Cool 5 minutes and remove to racks. (Hamantashen may be stored, airtight, for several days. They will bake crisp but will soften slightly after storing. They may also be frozen.)

Makes: about 36 hamantashen

Leave it to my dear friend Flo, master baker and author of Sweet Miniatures *and* The Simple Art of Perfect Baking, *to come up with a no-yeast, buttery hamantashen dough that rolls out easily and surpasses its many yeast ancestors. Fill the cookies with either Dried Apricot or Prune-Raisin Filling. Or try thick preserves, canned fruit pie fillings, or canned poppy seed filling.*

Prep Time: 40 minutes

Chill Time: At least 15 minutes

Bake Time: 15 to 18 minutes

Advance Prep: Hamantashen may be stored, airtight, for several days or frozen.

Prep Time: 5 minutes

Cook Time: About
35 minutes

Advance Prep: Filling
may be refrigerated
indefinitely.

Dried Apricot Filling
Photograph, page 11

8 ounces dried apricots
½ cup sugar
2 tablespoons lemon juice

Place apricots in a microwave-safe bowl, cover with water, and transfer apricots with a slotted spoon to a small heavy saucepan. Add 5 tablespoons fruit liquid, sugar, and lemon juice. Bring to a boil over moderate heat. Reduce heat to medium low and simmer, stirring occasionally, until most of the liquid is absorbed and syrupy, about 25 minutes. While the mixture is warm, transfer to a food processor with the metal blade and process until smooth. Cool before using. (Filling may be refrigerated indefinitely.)

Makes: 1⅓ cups; fills about 36 hamantashen

Prep Time: 5 minutes

Soak Time: 10
minutes

Advance Prep: Filling
may be refrigerated
indefinitely.

Prune-Raisin Filling
Photograph, page 11

9 ounces dried prunes
⅓ cup raisins
1 tablespoon firmly packed brown sugar
1 tablespoon honey
½ teaspoon vanilla extract
¼ teaspoon ground cinnamon
2 teaspoons lemon juice
⅓ cup chopped pecans or walnuts, toasted and cooled

Place prunes and raisins in a medium bowl. Pour 2 cups hot water over and allow to soak for 10 minutes, or until soft. Drain water. Place fruit in food processor with metal blade. Add brown sugar, honey, vanilla, cinnamon, and lemon juice. Process until smooth. Transfer to a small bowl and stir in nuts. (Filling may be refrigerated indefinitely.)

Makes: 1⅓ cups; fills about 36 hamantashen

Chocolate–Peanut Butter Hamantashen

Photograph, page 11

Chocolate Dough
6 tablespoons butter or margarine, at room temperature
1 cup powdered sugar
1 large egg
1 teaspoon vanilla extract
2 ounces unsweetened chocolate, chopped, melted, and cooled slightly
1½ cups all-purpose flour
½ teaspoon baking soda
¼ teaspoon salt

Peanut Butter Filling
Scant ¾ cup creamy peanut butter
½ cup strawberry jam or preserves
3 tablespoons whole or low-fat milk
Strawberry jam for topping (optional)

Place rack in upper third of oven and preheat to 350°F. Grease or spray 2 heavy-duty or cushioned baking sheets.

To Make Dough: In mixing bowl with electric mixer, cream butter and powdered sugar on medium-high speed until very light and fluffy, about 2 minutes. Mix in egg and vanilla until well blended. Mix in melted chocolate. Add flour, baking soda, and salt, and mix on low speed until incorporated. Mix on medium speed 1 minute. Shape into a flat disk and wrap in plastic wrap. Refrigerate until cold enough to roll. (Dough may be refrigerated up to 2 days. Leave at room temperature until soft enough to roll but still very cold.)

To Make Filling: In a medium bowl, stir peanut butter and jam together. Stir in milk.

To Shape Hamantashen: Divide dough in half; cover 1 portion with plastic wrap. Roll other half between 2 sheets of wax paper into an 11-inch circle, about ⅛ inch thick. Using a 3-inch round cutter, cut out circles. (A clean, empty tuna can with both ends removed makes an ideal cutter.) Spoon 1½ teaspoons filling in the center of each circle. Press 3 edges together (see illustration, page 110) to make a triangle, leaving a small opening in the center for the filling to show. Place 1 inch apart on prepared baking sheets. Reroll scraps, cut out, and fill. Repeat with remaining dough.

To Bake: If not baking on cushioned baking sheets, double-pan by placing 1 baking sheet on top of another. Bake for 10 to 12 minutes, or until tops are firm. The cookies will firm up slightly as they cool. If you like them

*W*ho ever said hamantashen had to be made with white dough and a fruit filling? Not my friend Joanne Neuman who created these soft, brownie-like peanut-butter and jam-filled ones. If you're not a fan of peanut butter, you can substitute the Dried Apricot Filling (see page 116) or a thick jam with some chocolate chips stirred in.

Prep Time: 25 minutes

Bake Time: 10 to 12 minutes

Advance Prep: Hamantashen may be stored, airtight, for several days or frozen.

Chill Time: At least 15 minutes

soft, bake the minimum time; for crisper cookies, bake longer. If baking 2 sheets in one oven, rotate positions halfway through the baking time. If desired, top each with a small dollop of jam and return to oven for 1 minute to set. Cool 2 minutes and remove to racks. (Hamantashen may be stored, airtight, for several days or frozen.)

Makes: about 24 hamantashen

Rugelach Bar Cookies

Cream Cheese Pastry
6 ounces cream cheese, cold and cut into pieces
¼ pound plus 4 tablespoons (1½ sticks) butter or margarine, cold and cut into small pieces
1½ cups all-purpose flour
⅓ cup granulated sugar
1 teaspoon vanilla extract
¼ teaspoon salt

Topping
3 tablespoons packed light brown sugar,
1½ teaspoons ground cinnamon
2 tablespoons butter or margarine, melted
½ cup chopped walnuts
¼ cup mini chocolate chips (optional)
⅔ cup strawberry or apricot jam or preserves, or ⅓ cup of each

Place rack in center of oven and preheat to 350°F. Grease or spray bottom and sides of a 9 × 13-inch metal pan.

To Make Pastry: In a food processor with the metal blade, process cream cheese and butter until blended. Add flour, sugar, vanilla, and salt, and process until mixture begins to hold together. Transfer to prepared pan and press evenly into bottom. Bake for 25 minutes, or until edges are brown and center is lightly golden.

To Make Topping: Meanwhile, stir together brown sugar, cinnamon, melted butter, walnuts, and chocolate chips, if using. Stir jam to soften it and spread over baked crust. Sprinkle cinnamon mixture over jam. Return to oven and bake 10 minutes, or until edges of jam are bubbling. Remove from oven and cool completely. Cut into 1½ × 1-inch bars. (Cookies may be stored, covered, at room temperature overnight or refrigerated up to 3 days.)

Makes: about 56 bars

*J*ewish rugelach have found their way from Eastern Europe to the American mainstream for a good reason: They are irresistible. But who has time to make them? I take the same delectable ingredients—cream cheese pastry, preserves, cinnamon, brown sugar, and nuts—layer them in a baking pan, and cut them into squares. Note the prep time: 15 minutes for 56 cookies. They may not look like rugelach, but they have the same great taste.

Prep Time: 15 minutes

Bake Time: 35 minutes

Advance Prep: Cookies may be stored at room temperature overnight or refrigerated up to 3 days. They do not freeze well.

Shikker Cake

Cake
½ cup poppy seeds (2.6-ounce jar)
¾ cup half-and-half
¾ cup (1½ sticks) unsalted butter (not margarine), room temperature
1¼ cups plus ¼ cup sugar
4 large eggs, separated
3 teaspoons vanilla extract
¼ cup golden rum
2 cups all-purpose flour
2½ teaspoons baking powder
½ teaspoon salt

Glaze
1 cup sugar
¼ pound (1 stick) butter
½ cup golden rum

To Prepare Poppy Seeds: Place poppy seeds in a small bowl, add half-and-half, and soak for 30 minutes.

With oven rack in center, preheat oven to 350°F. Grease or spray with non-stick spray a 12-cup Bundt pan. Sprinkle with flour, shaking out excess.

To Make Cake: In a mixing bowl with electric mixer on high speed, cream butter until soft. Add 1¼ cups sugar and mix until light and fluffy, 2 to 3 minutes. Add yolks, one at a time, mixing continuously. Add vanilla, poppy seeds with half-and-half, and rum, and mix on medium speed until incorporated. The mixture will look curdled. Add flour, baking powder, and salt, and mix on low speed until incorporated. Mix on high speed for 2 minutes.

In clean mixing bowl with electric mixer, beat egg whites until soft peaks form. Gradually add remaining ¼ cup sugar, 2 tablespoons at a time, until stiff but not dry peaks form. Fold whites into batter. Pour into prepared pan.

To Bake: Bake for 45 minutes, or until cake tester comes out clean.

To Make Glaze: In a small saucepan, combine sugar, butter, and rum. Stir over low heat until sugar dissolves, about 3 minutes. Increase heat to moderately high and boil for 3 minutes, stirring occasionally.

To Glaze Cake: Remove cake from oven; immediately pour half the hot glaze over it. Let sit 7 minutes. Loosen edges and turn out onto a rimmed platter. Reheat remaining glaze to hot and slowly pour and spoon over top of cake. Cool and serve at room temperature.

Makes: 12 servings

T*o keep from consuming this dense, poppy seed–laden, butter-rum–drenched cake in one sitting, I hid it in the freezer. Guess what? It's even terrific frozen.*

Prep Time: 30 minutes

Soak Time: 30 minutes

Bake Time: 45 minutes

Glaze Time: About 15 minutes

Advance Prep: Cake may be refrigerated up to 3 days or frozen.

You don't need to buy an expensive champagne to make this refreshingly light and effervescent beverage. If you plan to serve the punch for an extended time, make 2 or more ice molds.

Prep Time: Ice mold, 10 minutes plus time for water to freeze; punch, 5 minutes

Ice Mold Freeze Time: Overnight

Advance Preparation: Ice mold may be frozen up to 1 month. Punch may be refrigerated overnight.

Blushing Champagne Punch with Fruited Ice Mold

Ice Mold
1 bunch green grapes (preferably seedless), cut into small sprigs
1 bunch red grapes (preferably seedless), cut into small sprigs
1 pint box strawberries
Lemons, limes, and/or oranges, cut in half and sliced
Nonpoisonous garden leaves, such as lemon, rose, or grape leaves

Punch
1 (25.4 fluid-ounce) bottle blush wine or sauterne
1 cup brandy
¼ cup sugar
1 (32-ounce) bottle club soda, chilled
2 (⅕-quart) bottles dry champagne, chilled

To Make Ice Mold: Fill a ring mold, star, or any other shaped mold or cake pan half full of water. Freeze solid. When frozen, place small clusters of grapes over the top. Add strawberries, sliced fruit, and leaves to cover the top completely. Carefully pour in enough water to cover fruit. Return to freezer. Freeze solid. To unmold, dip into warm water and unmold onto a sheet of heavy-duty foil. Wrap in foil and freeze until ready to use, at least overnight. (Ice mold may be frozen up to 1 month.)

To Make Punch: In a large bowl, combine wine, brandy, and sugar, stirring until sugar is dissolved. Refrigerate until chilled or overnight.

Before Serving: Pour wine mixture into a large punch bowl. Pour in soda and champagne. Add ice mold.

Makes: 28 (4-ounce) servings

120 • FAST & FESTIVE MEALS FOR THE JEWISH HOLIDAYS

Sparkling Citrus Punch

1 can (6 ounces) frozen orange juice concentrate, partially thawed
1 can (6 ounces) frozen lemonade concentrate, partially thawed
1 can (6 ounces) frozen limeade concentrate, partially thawed
4 cups cold water
1 bottle (1 liter) lemon-lime carbonated beverage, chilled
Lemon, lime, and orange slices, for garnish (optional)
Mint leaves, for garnish (optional)

In a large pitcher or punch bowl, stir together orange, lemonade, and limeade concentrates and water. (Mixture may be refrigerated overnight.)

Before serving, stir in lemon-lime beverage. Garnish with slices of fruit and mint leaves, if desired.

Makes: 18 (4-ounce) servings

This nonalcoholic punch can be multiplied to serve any size group. It's fizzy and not too sweet, and if someone spills any, it won't stain your carpet.

Prep Time: 5 minutes

Advance Prep: Base may be refrigerated overnight.

Passover

✧

Passover (in Hebrew, *Pesach*) celebrates the ancient Hebrews' escape from slavery in Egypt three thousand years ago. Moses was a messenger of God who pleaded with Pharaoh to let the Hebrews go. When Pharaoh refused, God sent Ten Plagues as punishment. The tenth and ultimate plague was the slaying of the first-born. God "passed over" the Israelites and struck down only the Egyptian first-born. That night Pharaoh finally agreed to free the Hebrews. Since then, we gather together on that same night to remember the ancient Hebrews' time of bondage and to celebrate and contemplate the importance of freedom.

Passover is also called *Hag ha-Aviv*—the holiday of spring. Following the bleakness of winter when the earth is covered with snow, spring bursts forth with new life. Similarly, a people shackled in slavery, doomed to possible extinction, burst forth out of Egypt into a new life's journey leading to a land flowing with milk and honey. Passover's message of freedom reinforces the spirit of renewed optimism aroused by the sights and smells of spring. The holiday reminds us annually that no matter how difficult our situation, we must never lose hope.

Another name for Passover is *Hag ha-Matzot* (plural for matzah)—the holiday of unleavened bread. In their haste to escape from Egypt, the Israelites had no time to let the dough rise for bread, and so they carried with them matzah as their only provision. Throughout the holiday, we do not eat any food with leavening, nor any wheat flour because wheat can leaven. Although matzah is made with wheat flour, it is regulated during baking to ensure that it does not rise or ferment. Matzah symbolizes the complete story of Passover—it is the bread of slavery and also the bread of freedom.

Family and friends gather together for the Seder—a ceremonial feast held on the first and, for many, second evening of the eight-day celebration. The Hebrew word *seder* means order. We read from the Haggadah, a book that describes the order of the Seder and the meaning of the rituals. The reading of the Haggadah and the singing of the songs in it are among the most widely observed practices in Judaism.

Highlights for the children are asking The Four Questions and searching for the *afikomen* (a piece of matzah that has been hidden). It is the adults' role to impress upon children the significance of their Jewish heritage. In this way, each new generation can take its place in the chain of the Jewish people, from the Exodus to the present.

The central object on every table is the **Seder plate,** which contains a variety of symbolic foods:

Roasted Lamb Bone: This represents the lamb that was sacrificed in the Holy Temple at Jerusalem. Such a sacrifice was made on the eve of the Exodus from Egypt, and the blood was used to mark the doorposts of the Israelites. A chicken or turkey neck may be substituted for the lamb, and in vegetarian homes, the rabbis suggest a roasted red beet. The lamb or poultry should be roasted in the oven until done and then scorched over a flame, such as a gas burner, grill, or candle.

Roasted Egg: Another sacrificial offering, the egg represents the most humble of the festival offerings. It is also the symbol of rebirth whose round form reminds us of the perpetual cycle of life. To roast the egg, first boil it and then brown one side of the shell by holding it with tongs over a gas burner or a candle flame.

Greens: Sprigs of parsley or a celery top symbolizes spring and rebirth.

Bitter Herbs (*Maror*): A piece of fresh or ground horseradish, without beets or vinegar, reminds us of the bitterness of slavery.

Haroset: A mixture of chopped apples or fruits, nuts, wine, and spices that represents the mortar or clay the Hebrew slaves used for making bricks for Pharaoh.

Extra Points

THE TABLE

For a centerpiece, fill a shallow bowl or basket with floral foam and cover it with fresh green moss or grass. Make a mock version of a Seder plate by filling the bowl with lots of fern or other leaves and parsley; a stuffed toy lamb; a piece of matzah; crabapples, dates, and walnuts (for haroset); hard-boiled eggs; and a piece of fresh horseradish. Fill spaces with fresh flowers.

PLACE CARDS

Write names on hard-boiled eggs. Have guests peel and eat them with salt water as part of the Seder. Or purchase small clay planters filled with parsley (or other herbs) and write names on them with puffy ink pens.

FOR THE KIDS

To make a matzah cover, use a handkerchief, napkin, or piece of fabric and decorate it using felt markers, puffy paints, glue, beads, ribbons, etc.

To make Elijah's cup, decorate an inexpensive wine goblet with beads, gold or silver twine, jewels, etc.

To keep the young ones occupied during the Seder,

buy or make as many of the Ten Plagues as possible. Cut out pictures or purchase small plastic toys depicting blood, darkness, locusts (grasshoppers), frogs, small clear stones for hail, lice, boils, cattle, flies, and babies.

Let the kids dress up as Elijah the prophet. They can sneak out and when the door is open, come in and surprise the guests.

FESTIVE NOTES

While singing the song "Dayenu," follow the Sephardic Jews' playful "green onion" tradition: Each person is given a green onion. To represent the fact the Israelites were whipped and chained, every time the word dayenu is sung, hit someone (gently!) with the onion.

The table should be set with two candles, the Seder plate, an ornate wine cup for Elijah the prophet, a kiddush cup, a wineglass for each person present, a wine decanter filled with kosher wine, and three matzot, stacked on top of each other under a special layered cover, to represent the three categories of Jews who were slaves.

Parsley sprigs and salt water should be placed around the table for everyone to share.

Wine: During the Seder, the adults are required to drink four glasses of wine. (You may wish to offer the children grape juice.) Until the early 1980s, standard American kosher wines were cloyingly sweet Concord grape or blackberry wines in square bottles. Although these traditional wines are still popular, a wider variety of kosher wines is now available that more closely resemble dry varietal table wines. Some of the more popular kosher-for-Passover wines from California are made by Baron Herzog, Weinstock, and Gan Eden. Herzog Selections imports kosher wines from Israel, France, and Italy. Gamla, Yarden, and Carmel are the main Israeli exporters.

For the order and rituals and blessings of the Seder, see any Passover Haggadah.

Set It and Forget It Seder

In many families, it is traditional to begin the Seder meal with hard-boiled eggs served in salt water. There are several reasons for this custom: Eggs represent spring and new life; they remind us of the Temple sacrifices in Jerusalem and of the destruction of the Temple; they also were served at Roman Seders over two thousand years ago. The salt water symbolizes the tears shed by the Israelite slaves.

For many, fish is *the* Passover appetizer, often followed by chicken soup. If you are a purist who enjoys making everything from scratch and spending hours doing so, you can pass over Gefilte Fish Mousse and make Salmon Gefilte Fish (see page 34) instead. To make the mousse you begin by pureeing jarred gefilte fish and end layering it with colorful rows of red and green vegetables. It takes merely minutes to prepare.

Chicken soup is a very personal thing. We tend to like what we grew up with. I know because my children are so accustomed to Chicken Vegetable Soup with Matzah Balls that they think plain chicken soup is boring. In keeping with my on-the-run philosophy, this soup uses canned broth, but no one can tell. The flavor is thoroughly camouflaged by all the fresh vegetables.

Set It and Forget It Prime Rib Roast is an ideal choice for the Seder if you have two ovens, since it will take 2 hours or longer to cook. You'll need the other oven to bake the Crisp Potato Kugel. Baked Asparagus with Toasted Walnuts can be made ahead and reheated in the microwave. If you don't have two ovens, choose either the Herb-Encrusted Roast Chicken (see page 35), which can sit out for an hour while the kugel bakes, or Brisket with Burgundy-Orange Sauce (see page 89), which can be reheated in the microwave. This regal meal calls for a royal finale like Mocha Fudge Torte, but any of my Passover desserts can be substituted.

Menu

Classic and/or Modern Haroset

◆

Gefilte Fish Mousse

◆

Chicken Vegetable Soup with Matzah Balls

◆

Set It and Forget It Prime Rib Roast

Crisp Potato Kugel

Baked Asparagus with Toasted Walnuts

◆

Mocha Fudge Torte (see page 145)

GAME PLAN

As Far Ahead As Desired	Make unglazed torte and freeze or refrigerate up to 4 days
	Make soup and freeze or refrigerate up to 2 days
2 Days Ahead	Defrost soup, if frozen
	Make Matzah Balls
1 Day Ahead	Make haroset
	Defrost torte, if frozen, and glaze it
	Make fish mousse
	Prepare asparagus and topping

DAY OF SEDER

2 to 3 Hours Before Serving	Roast prime rib
	Unmold fish mousse
	Bring asparagus topping to room temperature
1½ Hours Before Serving	Make kugel
Shortly Before Serving	Reheat soup
	Carve roast
	Reheat asparagus and add topping

Classic Haroset

¼ cup slivered almonds
½ cup walnuts
½ cup raisins
½ cup pitted dates
2 medium apples, unpeeled, halved, cored, and cut into chunks
1 teaspoon ground ginger
1 teaspoon ground cinnamon
¼ cup sweet red Passover wine

In a food processor with the metal blade, pulse almonds and walnuts until finely chopped. Remove to a bowl. Add raisins and dates to processor and pulse until chopped. Add apples, ginger, cinnamon, and wine, and pulse until finely chopped or ground, as you prefer. Stir into nuts, cover, and refrigerate. (Haroset may be refrigerated overnight.)

Makes: 2 cups; about 12 servings

Modern Haroset

1 cup dried cranberries
½ cup shelled pistachios
1 large apple, peeled, halved, cored, and cut into chunks
¾ teaspoon ground cinnamon
¼ cup sweet red Passover wine

In a food processor with the metal blade, pulse dried cranberries and pistachios until chopped. Add apple, cinnamon, and wine, and pulse until finely chopped or ground, as you prefer. Remove to a bowl, cover, and refrigerate at least 1 hour. (Haroset may be refrigerated overnight.)

Makes: 1¾ cups; about 10 servings

Haroset is prepared differently in Jewish communities around the world. This version, which is typical of those served in Central Europe, is made with apples, dates, sweet spices, and red wine. To save time, chop everything in the food processor, as fine or chunky as you like.

Prep Time: 10 minutes

Advance Prep: Haroset may be refrigerated overnight.

Because haroset is a blending of fruits and spices made to resemble mortar, you can mix and match ingredients as you please. In this contemporary version, pistachios are substituted for the almonds and walnuts, and dried cranberries stand in for the dates and raisins.

Prep Time: 10 minutes

Chill Time: At least 1 hour

Advance Prep: Haroset may be refrigerated overnight.

Gefilte Fish Mousse

Fish Mousse
1 jar (24 ounces) gefilte fish, well drained
2 tablespoons regular, low-fat, or nonfat mayonnaise
2 tablespoons nondairy or regular, low-fat, or nonfat sour cream
2 teaspoons prepared white horseradish

Vegetable Layer
2 green onions with tops, thinly sliced
2 tablespoons chopped jarred or fresh roasted red peppers, patted dry
2 tablespoons chopped parsley
3 ounces (½ a 6-ounce jar) marinated artichoke hearts, drained and
  chopped

For Serving
Lettuce leaves
Matzah crackers, such as Tam Tams

To Make Fish Layer: In a food processor with the metal blade, process fish, mayonnaise, sour cream, and horseradish until finely ground. Do not overprocess.

To Make Vegetable Layer: In a medium bowl, mix together green onions, red peppers, parsley, and artichokes.

To Assemble: Line a 3-cup bowl or mold with plastic wrap. Spoon a third of the fish on the bottom, pressing it down with the back of a spoon. Top with half the vegetables. Spread with another third of the fish; press it down. Add remaining vegetables and top with remaining fish. Place a small plate on top to weigh down the mousse. Refrigerate at least 6 hours. (Mousse may be refrigerated overnight.)

To Serve: Line a platter with lettuce leaves, invert mousse onto it, and peel off plastic wrap. Serve with matzah crackers.

Makes: 14 to 16 servings

*H*ere's a thoroughly modernized play on gefilte fish. You begin by pureeing jarred gefilte fish with a little mayonnaise and sour cream until smooth and creamy. Then you layer it with chopped roasted red peppers, artichoke hearts, and green onions, and spread it on matzah.

Prep Time: 15 minutes

Chill Time: At least 6 hours

Advance Prep: Mousse may be refrigerated overnight.

Chicken Vegetable Soup with Matzah Balls

Photograph, page 12

3 tablespoons vegetable oil
2 large onions, peeled and chopped
2 carrots, peeled and chopped into ½-inch pieces
3 large leeks, white parts only, cleaned and chopped
½ cup celery root, peeled and chopped into ½-inch pieces
1 small turnip, peeled and chopped into ½-inch pieces
1 small rutabaga, peeled and chopped into ½-inch pieces
1 small head green cabbage, cored and shredded
11 cups chicken broth
3 peppercorns
1 teaspoon dried thyme
1 teaspoon dried basil
Salt and freshly ground black pepper to taste
2 tomatoes, seeded and chopped
1 recipe Matzah Balls (recipe follows)

To Make Soup: In a large soup pot over medium heat, heat oil until hot. Add onions, carrots, leeks, celery root, turnip, rutabaga, and cabbage. Sauté, stirring often, until soft, about 15 minutes.

Add chicken broth, peppercorns, thyme, and basil. Cover, bring to a boil, reduce heat, and simmer about 2 hours, stirring occasionally. Strain into a clean pot or large bowl. Stir in as many vegetables as desired. (Soup may be refrigerated up to 2 days or frozen.)

Before Serving: Reheat soup and season to taste. Add chopped tomatoes and Matzah Balls and cook until heated through.

Makes: 8 to 10 servings

This recipe was originally published in my second cookbook, now revised as Marlene Sorosky's Cooking for Holidays and Celebrations. *It has been so popular that I felt it was worth repeating. It begins with canned broth, but a myriad of robust root vegetables, cabbage, and herbs adds a wholesome freshness.*

Prep Time: 30 minutes

Cook Time: 2¼ hours

Advance Prep: Soup may be refrigerated up to 2 days or frozen.

Everyone thinks his or her mother's matzah balls are the best. My mother's recipe (which came from her mother) calls for ground almonds and ginger. Try them. They're the best.

Prep Time: 10 minutes

Chill Time: At least 1 hour

Cook Time: 20 minutes

Advance Prep: Matzah balls may be refrigerated in soup up to 2 days.

Matzah Balls

4 large eggs
3 tablespoons vegetable oil or rendered chicken fat
1 cup matzah meal
⅓ cup chicken broth
¼ cup finely ground almonds
1½ teaspoons salt or to taste
2 tablespoons finely chopped parsley
½ teaspoon ground ginger (optional)

To Make Balls: In a medium bowl, whisk eggs and oil until blended. Stir in matzah meal. Add broth, almonds, salt, parsley, and ginger, if using. Stir to combine. Refrigerate 1 hour or more. With wet hands, form into 1½-inch balls.

To Cook: In a soup pot, bring 4 quarts of salted water to a boil. Reduce to a simmer and drop in matzah balls. Cover and cook at a low simmer for 20 minutes. Do not lift lid while cooking. Drain and add matzah balls to soup. (Matzah balls may be refrigerated in soup up to 2 days.)

Makes: about 28 matzah balls

Set It and Forget It Prime Rib Roast

When you buy a rib roast, calculate that one rib will serve 2 persons, so for six, you will need a 3-rib roast, without the short ribs.

The timetable for roasting by the following method is approximately 15 minutes per rib, or 5 minutes per pound of trimmed, ready-to-cook meat. For example, a 3-rib roast, weighing 8 to 9 pounds, will roast for 40 to 45 minutes.

Bring the roast to room temperature. Preheat the oven to 500°F. Place the roast in a shallow roasting pan. Sprinkle with a little matzah cake meal or potato starch and rub it lightly into the fat; this will help seal in the juices. Season generously with salt and coarsely cracked black pepper. To protect your oven from spattering fat, place a tent of aluminum foil loosely over the top of the meat. Roast according to the above timetable, following the minutes exactly. If you have a timer, set it to remind you.

When the cooking time ends, turn off the oven heat, but do not open the door. Allow the roast to remain in the oven for at least 1 hour, or until the oven is lukewarm, about 2 hours.

The roast will be beautifully rare inside and retain a crunchy outside and an internal heat suitable for serving for as long as 4 hours.

To my mind, no holiday entrée yet devised is easier (or more foolproof) than the following technique for roasting beef. This ingenious method came to me from Irene Angelo and her late husband, Steve, proprietors of Angelo's Market and Cooking School in Modesto, California. I couldn't describe it better than they do: "We think if you follow our rule for rare roast beef, you will have the greatest luck in the world with it."

Prep Time: 5 minutes

Bake Time: 15 minutes per rib or 5 minutes per pound

Rest Time: 1 to 2 hours in the oven on "off."

When we think of Jewish foods that have become a mainstay in the American diet, chicken soup, corned beef sandwiches, and bagels come to mind. So what happened to potato kugel? With its soft, moist interior and crispy golden topping, it deserves to be right up there with the rest of them.

Prep Time: 20 minutes

Bake Time: 1 hour

Advance Prep: Potatoes may be peeled and kept in cold water up to 4 hours. Kugel is best made and baked before serving.

Crisp Potato Kugel

6 medium baking potatoes, peeled (about 4 pounds)
1 large onion, peeled
2 large eggs
1 teaspoon salt or to taste
6 tablespoons (⅔ stick) nondairy or regular margarine or butter, melted
2 tablespoons matzah meal
2 tablespoons nondairy or regular margarine or butter

Place rack in upper third of oven and preheat to 400°F.

To Make Kugel: Grate the potatoes and onion in a food processor with the shredding disk or with a hand grater. Place in a colander and drain well, squeezing out excess moisture. In a large bowl, whisk eggs, salt, melted margarine, and matzah meal. Stir in potatoes until well combined.

To Bake: Place 2 tablespoons margarine in a 9 × 13-inch baking dish. Melt in oven or microwave. Tilt dish to coat evenly. Pour potato mixture into dish and spread evenly. Bake, uncovered, at 400°F for 15 minutes. Reduce oven temperature to 375°F and continue baking for 45 more minutes, or until top is crisp. Cut into squares.

Makes: 8 servings

Change of Pace: For year-round potato kugel, substitute 2 tablespoons all-purpose flour for the matzah meal.

Baked Asparagus with Toasted Walnuts

Asparagus
2 to 3 pounds asparagus, the thinnest spears available
Salt and freshly ground black pepper
1 tablespoon nondairy or regular margarine or butter, cut into small pieces

Walnut Topping
3 tablespoons walnut oil or olive oil
1½ tablespoons lemon juice
Salt to taste
Freshly ground black pepper to taste
4 tablespoons finely chopped walnuts, toasted at 350°F until golden, about
  10 minutes

To Cook Asparagus: Preheat oven to 300°F. Break off woody stems of asparagus. If stalks are thick, peel with a vegetable peeler, pulling from stem end toward tip. (Pencil-thin spears do not need peeling.) Place in a greased or sprayed 9 × 13-inch glass baking dish. Sprinkle lightly with salt and pepper. Dot with margarine. Cover with foil and bake for 30 to 35 minutes, or until tender but still crisp. (Asparagus may be baked 1 day ahead and reheated in microwave.)

To Make Topping: In a small bowl, whisk together oil, lemon juice, salt, and pepper. (Topping may be refrigerated overnight. Bring to room temperature before using.)

Before Serving: Spoon topping over asparagus and sprinkle with walnuts.

Makes: 8 to 10 servings

Change of Pace: Substitute hazelnut oil for walnut oil and hazelnuts for the walnuts.

Baking asparagus eliminates all the guesswork, because oven heat is constant and they cook more evenly. Put the spears in a casserole, dot them with margarine, and bake. When crisp-tender, sprinkle on some lemon juice and toasted walnuts.

Prep Time: 10 minutes

Bake Time: 30 to 35 minutes

Advance Prep: Asparagus and topping may be refrigerated, separately, overnight.

Menu

✧

*Classic and/or
Modern Haroset
(see page 127)*

◆

*Warm Baby Potatoes
Stuffed with Egg
Salad*

◆

*Chicken Vegetable
Soup with Matzah
Balls (see page 129)*

◆

*Cornish Hens with
Apricots and Prunes*

*Broccoli Farfel
Dressing*

*Bouquet of Baked
Spring Vegetables*

◆

*Carrot Pecan Cake
with Orange Caramel
Glaze (see page 141)*

A Joyful Spring Seder

Instead of beginning this meal with hard-boiled eggs in salt water, the cooked eggs are chopped into a salad and piled into scooped-out baked baby potatoes. For the soup, I suggest that you make as much of the Chicken Vegetable Soup (see page 129) as needed and serve it at both Seders.

Cornish Hens with Apricots and Prunes are the ultimate party entrée. The hens are golden brown and thickly glazed, and the apricots and prunes are soft enough to enrich the sauce. I like to roast the hens a day ahead and when cool, remove the small breastbones, leaving the wings and drumsticks intact.

For more Passovers than I care to count, I've been stuffing turkey, chicken, and brisket with broccoli and farfel stuffing. Here, I turn the stuffing into a succulent side dish by baking it, covered, in a casserole. If you prefer a crispy topping, uncover the dish for the last half hour of baking. To serve 12, make one and a half times the recipe and bake it in a 9 × 13-inch baking dish. Giant Potato–Carrot Pancake (see page 92) is also an excellent accompaniment.

I find that baking vegetables is so much easier than steaming or boiling them. Bouquet of Baked Spring Vegetables is a wild mélange of colors whose looks belie its simplicity. If you have only one oven, roast the hens a day ahead, and before you reheat them, bake the stuffing. It can sit out for 10 minutes while you reheat the hens. The vegetables can be reheated in the microwave. I've selected Carrot Pecan Cake with Orange Caramel Glaze for dessert simply because I like its fresh orange flavor with the hens. But feel free to substitute any of the other Passover desserts. All of the recipes in this menu can be doubled.

GAME PLAN

As Far Ahead As Desired

Make cake unglazed and freeze or
  refrigerate up to 2 days
Make soup and freeze or refrigerate up to
  2 days

2 Days Ahead

Defrost soup, if frozen
Make Matzah Balls

1 Day Ahead

Make haroset
Defrost cake, if frozen, and glaze it
Roast hens
Bake potatoes and make egg salad
Make vegetables
Make dressing

DAY OF PARTY

1 to 3 Hours Before Serving

Bake dressing
Bring egg salad to room temperature

Shortly Before Serving

Reheat potatoes and stuff with egg salad
Reheat soup
Reheat hens and sauce
Reheat vegetables

Warm Baby Potatoes Stuffed with Egg Salad

15 baby red-skinned potatoes (2 inches in diameter), scrubbed
Nonstick cooking spray
Salt

Egg Salad
6 eggs, hard boiled, peeled, and coarsely chopped
½ cup finely diced celery
¼ cup finely diced onion
3 tablespoons regular, low-fat, or nonfat mayonnaise
2 tablespoons nondairy, regular, low-fat, or nonfat sour cream
¼ teaspoon salt or to taste
Dash of freshly ground black pepper

Red and/or black caviar or poppy seeds, for garnish

To Prepare Potatoes: Place rack in center of oven and preheat to 500°F. Cut potatoes in half crosswise. Cut a small slice off each end so they sit flat. Place on baking sheet and spray with nonstick spray. Sprinkle with salt. Turn potatoes cut side down, spray, and sprinkle with salt. Bake for 15 to 20 minutes, or until soft when tested with a sharp knife. Cool slightly. Using a melon baller or teaspoon, scoop out insides, leaving a ¼-inch shell. (Reserve scooped-out potato for another use.) (Potatoes may be refrigerated, covered, overnight. Bring to room temperature and before filling, bake at 350°F for 8 to 10 minutes, or until warm.)

To Make Egg Salad: In a medium bowl, lightly stir together the eggs, celery, onion, mayonnaise, sour cream, salt, and pepper to taste. (Salad may be refrigerated overnight. Bring to room temperature before serving.)

To Serve: Spoon egg salad into warm potatoes. Top with red and/or black caviar or poppy seeds.

Makes: 30 potatoes

Cornish Hens with Apricots and Prunes

Photograph, pages 12–13

4 Cornish hens (about 1½ pounds each)
Salt and freshly ground black pepper to taste

Sauce
¾ cup apricot jam
1½ cups orange juice
1½ cups dry red wine
1 tablespoon ground ginger
1 teaspoon salt or to taste
2 teaspoons garlic powder
1½ teaspoons dried thyme
2 tablespoons honey
2 teaspoons potato starch, dissolved in 2 teaspoons cold water
6 ounces dried apricots, cut in half if large
6 ounces dried prunes

Preheat oven to 425°F.

To Prepare Hens: Using kitchen shears, cut hens in half by cutting along one side of breastbone. Cut down both sides of backbone and remove row of small bones.

To Make Sauce: In a medium saucepan, melt jam. Whisk in orange juice, wine, ginger, salt, garlic powder, thyme, and honey. Simmer over moderate heat, whisking occasionally, until thickened slightly and reduced to about 3 cups, about 10 minutes. Remove from heat and set aside.

To Roast: Choose a shallow roasting pan or rimmed baking sheet into which the hens fit comfortably with about a 1-inch space between them. If the pan is too large, the juices will evaporate and burn. Line pan with a double thickness of heavy-duty foil. Place hens breast side up. Sprinkle with salt and pepper. Roast for 10 minutes. Remove from oven and brush with sauce. Roast for 30 to 35 minutes more, brushing with sauce every 10 to 15 minutes. (Hens may be refrigerated overnight or held, covered, at room temperature up to 2 hours. If refrigerated overnight, the skin will shrink slightly, but the hens will taste fine. Reheat at 425°F for 7 to 10 minutes.)

While Hens Roast, Complete Sauce: Off the heat, stir potato starch into sauce. Return to moderately high heat and bring to a boil, whisking constantly. Stir in apricots and prunes and simmer 5 minutes, or until softened. When hens are done, stir ½ cup pan juices into sauce. To serve, spoon sauce over hens.

Makes: 8 servings

Crisp mahogany-colored hens are glazed and served with a sumptuous sauce of red wine, orange juice, and apricot jam, more savory than sweet. With the addition of dried apricots and prunes, you could call it a tzimmes sauce. If you wish to serve more than one half hen per person, there is enough glaze and sauce for 5 hens, or 10 halves.

For a leaner version, remove skin from hens with your fingers or a knife and brush the sauce directly on the meat.

Prep Time: 20 to 30 minutes

Bake Time: 40 to 45 minutes

Advance Prep: Hens may be roasted and refrigerated overnight. Sauce may be refrigerated overnight. Reheat before serving. If too thick, thin with orange juice.

Do you know the
difference between
a stuffing and a
dressing? A stuffing is
baked inside the bird,
and a dressing is baked
outside. If you omit the
1 cup chicken broth
from this dressing, you
will have a stellar
stuffing for Cornish
hens, chicken, or
turkey.

Prep Time: 20 minutes

Bake Time: 1 hour

Advance Prep:
Dressing may be
refrigerated overnight
and baked before
serving.

Broccoli Farfel Dressing
Photograph, pages 12–13

2 teaspoons vegetable oil
1 large onion, peeled and chopped (1 cup)
8 ounces mushrooms, coarsely chopped
2 cloves garlic, minced
1 package (10 ounces) frozen chopped broccoli, thawed and drained
1½ cups matzah farfel
1 egg, lightly mixed
1 cup chicken broth
1 teaspoon dried basil or 2 tablespoons chopped fresh basil
1 teaspoon salt
Freshly ground black pepper to taste

Grease or spray an 11 × 7-inch glass baking dish.

To Make Stuffing: In a large skillet over moderate heat, heat oil until hot. Add onion and sauté 1 minute. Reduce heat to moderately low, cover, and cook, stirring often, until very soft, about 10 minutes. Add mushrooms and garlic, and sauté uncovered until most of the liquid has evaporated. Transfer to a medium bowl and cool slightly. Stir in broccoli, farfel, egg, broth, basil, salt, and pepper. Spoon into baking dish. Cover with foil. (Dressing may be refrigerated overnight. Bring to room temperature 1 hour before baking.)

To Bake: Preheat oven to 325°F. Bake, covered, for 1 hour. For a crisp top, bake uncovered for the last 30 minutes. (Dressing may be held at room temperature up to 2 hours and reheated.)

Makes: 8 servings

Bouquet of Baked Spring Vegetables

Photograph, pages 12–13

2 tablespoons nondairy or regular margarine or butter
3 tablespoons olive oil
1½ teaspoons dried basil
1 teaspoon dried thyme
2 cloves garlic, minced
16 to 20 peeled baby carrots
1 large red onion, peeled, halved, and cut into 2-inch chunks
Salt and freshly ground black pepper
1 pound pattypan squash (preferably green and yellow), cut into ¾-inch
  chunks
1½ pounds pencil-thin asparagus, bottoms trimmed (if spears are larger,
  use only 4-inch tips)
1 small red bell pepper, cut into 1-inch chunks or strips

Preheat oven to 475°F.

To Bake Vegetables: In a small microwave-safe bowl, heat margarine, oil, basil, thyme, and garlic until margarine melts. Remove 2 tablespoons oil mixture to a small bowl. Pour remainder into a 9 × 13-inch baking dish. Stir in carrots and onion. Season with salt and pepper. Cover and bake for 15 minutes.

Add squash, asparagus, and bell pepper. Drizzle with remaining oil mixture. (If margarine has hardened, microwave until pourable.) Season with salt and pepper. Cover and bake for 15 minutes, or until vegetables are barely tender. (If not serving immediately, uncover and cool, then cover and refrigerate overnight. Reheat, covered, in microwave or in oven at 475°F for 7 to 10 minutes.)

To Serve: Stir vegetables gently to coat. Serve from baking dish or arrange on platter.

Makes: 8 servings

*S*carlet onions, crimson peppers, orange carrots, emerald asparagus, and gold and green squash bake in one casserole for an ultraglamorous, simple-to-prepare medley of fresh vegetables.

Prep Time: 10 minutes

Bake Time: 30 minutes

Advance Prep: Vegetables may be baked and refrigerated overnight.

Passover Desserts

✧

Carrot Pecan Cake with Orange Caramel Glaze

Double Nut Chocolate Torte

Cantaloupe, Kiwi, and Strawberry Tart

Mocha Fudge Torte

Strawberry, Raspberry, and Rhubarb Crisp

Coconut Chiffon Cheesecake

Dried Fruits Stewed in Cinnamon and Port

Raspberry-Glazed Poached Pears (see page 22)

Desserts Not to Be Passed Over

Because flour and all leavenings are prohibited on Passover, the preparation of pastries, cookies, and desserts is a little more complicated—you might say daunting—than usual. Cakes and cookies must be prepared from potato starch or matzah meal, made from ground matzah. Matzah cake meal, which is finer than matzah meal, is another alternative. In several recipes, I have indicated the optional addition of vanilla extract. According to the laws of *kashrut*, it is not allowed on Passover. People who adhere strictly to the dietary laws will not want to use it.

I have divided the sweets into two categories, desserts and cookies. You'll find that despite the restraints imposed by religious law, these desserts more than hold their own against all other holiday fare. Don't be surprised if you get requests for repeats throughout the year.

Carrot Pecan Cake
with Orange Caramel Glaze

Cake
3 to 4 carrots, peeled
1 medium navel orange
2 tablespoons plus ¾ cup granulated sugar
5 eggs, separated
⅓ cup potato starch
2 cups coarsely chopped pecans
½ cup golden raisins (about 7 ounces)
½ teaspoon salt

Caramel Glaze
¼ pound (1 stick) nondairy or regular margarine or butter
½ cup orange juice
½ cup firmly packed light brown sugar
1 tablespoon potato starch
Orange slices or shredded orange peel, for garnish

Place rack in center of oven and preheat to 350°F. Grease a 9-inch spring-form pan.

To Make Cake: In food processor with the shredding disk, shred carrots. Measure 2 cups and set aside. With a sharp vegetable peeler, remove peel from orange. Cut off all the white pith and place peel in a clean food processor bowl with metal blade. Add 2 tablespoons sugar. Process until finely ground. (Reserve orange segments for garnish.) Add egg yolks and remaining ¾ cup sugar, and process until thick and pale yellow. Add carrots, potato starch, pecans, and raisins, and pulse until just combined. Transfer mixture to a large bowl.

In a mixing bowl with electric mixer, beat egg whites with salt until stiff but moist peaks form. Stir ¼ of the whites into carrot batter. Add remaining whites and fold together until blended. Pour batter into prepared pan, smoothing the top.

To Bake: Bake for 30 minutes. Cover loosely with foil and continue baking for 30 more minutes, or until a cake tester inserted in the center comes out clean and sides pull away from pan. Remove foil and cool on rack for 20 minutes. Run a sharp knife around the edge and remove sides of pan. Invert cake onto a cake plate with rimmed edges or heavy foil and cool to room temperature. (Cake may be refrigerated up to 2 days or frozen, tightly wrapped. Bring to room temperature before glazing.)

This cake, reminiscent of the ever-popular, old-fashioned Passover nut cakes, is similar to one my grandmother made every year for our family Seder. I've sparked it up with orange peel, carrots, raisins, and a delicious caramel glaze. Use the food processor to shred the carrots, chop the orange peel, and mix the batter.

Prep Time: Cake, 20 minutes; glaze, 5 minutes

Bake Time: 1 hour

Advance Prep: Unglazed cake may be refrigerated up to 2 days or frozen. Glazed cake may be refrigerated overnight.

To Make Glaze: In a small saucepan, melt margarine. Remove from heat and stir in orange juice, brown sugar, and potato starch. Cook over low heat, stirring constantly, until smooth. Bring to a boil for 3 to 4 seconds, stirring constantly. Remove from heat and cool until thick enough to glaze the cake.

To Glaze: Pour evenly over top and sides of cake, using a small spatula if necessary to smooth sides. Glaze will form a pool on cake plate. (Cake may be refrigerated, uncovered, overnight. Bring to room temperature before serving.)

To Serve: Garnish top with orange slices or shredded orange peel.

Makes: 8 to 10 servings

Double Nut Chocolate Torte

Torte
8 ounces semisweet chocolate, chopped
¼ pound (1 stick) nondairy or regular margarine or butter, at room temperature and cut into small pieces
2 tablespoons water, orange juice, or coffee
½ cup blanched chopped almonds
½ cup chopped pecans or walnuts
¼ cup plus ¼ cup sugar, divided
⅓ cup potato starch
4 eggs, separated and at room temperature

Chocolate Glaze
6 ounces semisweet chocolate, chopped
6 tablespoons nondairy or regular margarine or butter, cut into small pieces
Whole or sliced almonds for garnish, if desired

Place rack in center of oven and preheat to 375°F. Grease or spray with nonstick spray a 9 × 1½- or 2-inch cake pan. Cut circle of parchment paper or wax paper to fit the bottom and spray or grease the paper.

To Make Torte: In a medium microwave-safe bowl, melt chocolate, margarine, and water on high (100%) for 1½ to 3 minutes, or until melted. Stir until smooth. In a food processor with the metal blade, pulse nuts with ¼ cup sugar until finely ground. Pulse in potato starch. Add chocolate mixture and pulse until incorporated. Mix in egg yolks.

In a large bowl with electric mixer, beat egg whites until soft peaks form. Slowly beat in remaining ¼ cup sugar, 1 tablespoon at a time, until stiff but not dry peaks form. Add chocolate mixture and fold together until blended. Pour into prepared pan.

To Bake: Bake for 20 minutes, or until sides feel firm but middle is still slightly soft. A knife inserted near the center should come out lightly coated. Remove to rack and cool; it will shrink. When cool, turn out of pan by inverting onto a rack or sheet of foil. (Torte may be wrapped in foil and refrigerated up to 3 days or frozen.)

To Make Glaze: Place chocolate and margarine in a 4-quart microwave-safe glass measure. Microwave on high (100%) for 2 to 3 minutes, or until chocolate melts. Stir smooth. If desired, dip half of each almond in glaze and place on wax paper–lined baking sheet. Refrigerate until set. If glaze is very thin, set aside until thick enough to coat the cake.

This torte is so seductively fudgy that it evokes gasps and swoons from delighted guests. It's easy to serve at the table because it cuts into perfect slices.

Prep Time: Torte, 20 minutes; glaze, 5 minutes

Bake Time: 20 minutes

Advance Prep: Unfrosted torte may be refrigerated up to 3 days or frozen. Frosted torte may be stored at room temperature overnight.

To Frost: Line a small baking sheet with wax paper. Place cake on rack over baking sheet. Pour glaze onto middle of cake, tilting cake so glaze runs down the sides. Spread glaze over sides, but do not spread the top or the knife marks will show. Garnish with a border of almonds. Let torte sit at room temperature, uncovered, until glaze is set. (Torte may be held at room temperature, uncovered, overnight.)

Makes: 10 servings

Cantaloupe, Kiwi, and Strawberry Tart

Crust
1 can (10 ounces) soft coconut Passover macaroons (about 26)
2 tablespoons nondairy or regular margarine or butter, melted

Filling
½ cup chopped cantaloupe
¼ cup sugar
8 ounces regular or light cream cheese, softened

Topping
1 small cantaloupe
2 ripe but firm kiwis
1 pint fresh strawberries

To Make Crust: Place rack in center of oven and preheat to 350°F. In food processor with metal blade, process macaroons into crumbs. Add margarine and process until mixture holds together. Press into bottom and sides of a 9-inch tart pan with a removable bottom. Place on a baking sheet and bake for 13 to 15 minutes, or until edges are golden brown. Remove to rack and cool to room temperature.

To Make Filling: In food processor, process cantaloupe and sugar until pureed. Add cream cheese and process until blended. Spread into crust. Cover with plastic wrap and refrigerate for at least 2 hours. (Tart may be refrigerated overnight.)

To Top with Fruit: As close to serving as possible, quarter cantaloupe, remove seeds and rind, and thinly slice. Peel kiwis, cut in half lengthwise, and thinly slice. Set aside 1 pretty strawberry. Stem and slice remaining berries. Beginning with the outer edge, arrange alternate circles of cantaloupe, kiwi, and strawberries over tart, ending with reserved strawberry in the center. Refrigerate until serving.

Makes: 8 servings

I've never understood why cantaloupe is so seldom used in desserts. It is sweet, juicy, colorful, readily available, and inexpensive. Here, it does double duty: it's pureed into a cream cheese filling in a macaroon crust, and sliced over the top along with tart-sweet kiwis and ripe fresh strawberries.

Prep Time: 15 minutes

Bake Time: 13 to 15 minutes

Chill Time: At least 2 hours

Advance Prep: Filled tart base may be refrigerated overnight. Garnish with fruit before serving.

Mocha Fudge Torte

Torte
⅔ cup walnuts, toasted and cooled
¾ cup and ¾ cup sugar
½ cup unsweetened cocoa powder
1 tablespoon instant coffee granules
7 large egg whites
¼ teaspoon salt
½ stick (¼ cup) nondairy or regular margarine or butter, melted and cooled

Glaze
3 ounces semisweet chocolate, chopped
1½ tablespoons water
3 tablespoons nondairy or regular margarine or butter
2 teaspoons instant coffee granules
12 walnut halves, for garnish (optional)

Place rack in center of oven and preheat to 350°F. Grease or spray with nonstick spray an 8 × 2-inch springform pan.

To Make Torte: Toast the walnuts until golden. In a food processor or nut grinder, process or grind the nuts fine (not to a paste) and place in a large bowl. Stir in ¾ cup sugar, cocoa powder, and coffee granules. In a mixing bowl with electric mixer, beat egg whites with salt until they hold soft peaks. Gradually add remaining ¾ cup sugar, beating until whites hold stiff but moist peaks. Gently stir a third of the whites into the nut batter. Drop remaining whites onto batter and partially fold them in. Add margarine and fold together gently until incorporated. Pour batter into prepared pan.

To Bake: Bake for 35 to 40 minutes, or until a cake tester inserted into the center comes out with moist crumbs attached. Remove to rack and cool to room temperature. It will fall as it cools. Run a sharp knife around inside edge and remove springform sides.

To Glaze: In a microwave-safe bowl, microwave chocolate, water, margarine, and coffee, uncovered, at 70% power for 1½ to 3 minutes, stirring every minute until melted and smooth. Or melt in a heavy saucepan over low heat, stirring until smooth. Remove sides of springform and invert torte onto a rack set over a baking sheet. Pour glaze over center of cake, tilting it so the glaze runs down the sides. With a spatula, smooth the sides but do not touch up the top or the spatula marks will show. If desired, garnish with a ring of walnut halves. Refrigerate until glaze is set. (Glazed torte may be refrigerated, uncovered, overnight.) Serve at room temperature.

Makes: 8 servings

*M*ost of us are familiar with those incredibly rich flourless chocolate tortes often known as "Death by Chocolate" or "Chocolate Suicide." In this version I substitute cocoa for most of the chocolate, reduce the butter, and eliminate the egg yolks. It is still rich, moist, and fudgy—but it won't kill you!

Prep Time:
Torte, 15 minutes; glaze, 4 minutes

Bake Time: 35 to 40 minutes

Advance Prep:
Unglazed torte may be refrigerated up to 4 days or frozen tightly wrapped. Glazed torte may be refrigerated overnight.

I am amazed by the number of people who have never cooked rhubarb. It's a shame because it is so tasty and easy to prepare. When buying rhubarb, look for bright red stalks because they are sweeter. They don't even need to be peeled, just sliced. Or, if you prefer, you can always substitute frozen rhubarb. This homespun dessert is a beautiful balance of sweet and tart fruit, blanketed with a chewy macaroon topping.

Prep Time: 10 minutes

Bake Time: 40 to 45 minutes

Cool Time: 30 minutes

Advance Prep: Crisp may be baked up to 8 hours before serving.

Strawberry, Raspberry, and Rhubarb Crisp

Filling
2 cups fresh or frozen rhubarb (about 12 ounces); if fresh, trim ends and slice into ½-inch pieces; if frozen, do not defrost
1 cup (½ pint) fresh or frozen raspberries, not defrosted
2 cups (about 10 ounces) fresh strawberries, cored and halved or quartered, if large
1½ cups sugar
3 tablespoons packed potato starch
Regular or nondairy whipped cream or ice cream, for serving (optional)

Crumb Topping
¾ cup matzah meal
20 soft coconut or almond macaroons, crumbled with fingers (about 1 cup packed)
4 tablespoons nondairy or regular margarine or butter, melted

Place oven rack in center of oven and preheat to 350°F. Grease or spray with a nonstick spray a 9-inch square baking dish.

To Make Filling: In a medium bowl, gently stir together rhubarb, raspberries, strawberries, sugar, and potato starch. Let sit while preparing topping.

To Make Topping: In a medium bowl, stir together matzah meal, macaroons, and melted margarine. Stir fruit to distribute potato starch and sugar, and pour into prepared baking dish. Sprinkle topping over fruit.

To Bake: Bake for 40 to 45 minutes, or until fruit is tender when pierced with a toothpick and sauce is thick and bubbling. Cool at least 30 minutes before serving. (Crisp may be baked up to 8 hours before serving. Serve warm or at room temperature.) If desired, serve with ice cream or whipped cream.

Makes: 8 servings

Coconut Chiffon Cheesecake

Crust
¾ cup matzah meal
¼ pound (1 stick) margarine or butter, at room temperature
2 tablespoons sugar
1 egg yolk

Cheesecake
1 pound regular or light cream cheese, at room temperature
1 tablespoon potato starch
¾ cup sugar
4 large eggs, separated
¼ cup regular or light sour cream
¼ cup whipping cream
1 teaspoon vanilla extract (optional)
1 cup shredded unsweetened coconut
¼ teaspoon salt

For Garnish
1 cup strawberry or seedless raspberry preserves or jam
1 pint fresh strawberries, stemmed, or raspberries

Place rack in center of oven and preheat to 400°F.

To Make Crust: In a food processor with the metal blade, pulse matzah meal and margarine until blended. Add sugar and egg yolk and pulse until incorporated. Press evenly into the bottom of a 9-inch springform pan. Bake for 8 to 10 minutes, or until pale golden. Cool to lukewarm or room temperature. Reduce oven temperature to 350°F.

To Make Cheesecake: In a large mixing bowl with electric mixer, beat cream cheese until soft and fluffy. Add potato starch and sugar, and beat until well combined. Beat in egg yolks, sour cream, whipping cream, and vanilla, if using, until creamy and smooth. Mix in coconut. In a clean mixing bowl, beat egg whites and salt until they hold soft peaks when the beater is lifted. Fold whites into cream cheese batter. Pour into prepared crust.

To Bake: Bake at 350°F for 45 minutes, or until outer 3 inches of cake are set but center trembles slightly. Do not overbake; it will firm up as it cools. Remove from oven to rack and cool to room temperature; cake will fall. (Cake may be refrigerated up to 4 days or frozen.)

To Garnish: Several hours before serving, remove sides of springform pan and place cake on serving plate. Heat preserves and if using strawberry, strain to remove pulp. Spread over top of cake. Garnish with berries. Refrigerate until serving.

continued

*M*arion Cunning-ham's daughter Catherine gets the credit for creating this sublime cake, which I've adapted to comply with Passover dietary laws. You might say this cake is a contradiction in terms: It's rich and creamy as a cheesecake but light and airy as a soufflé. Look for unsweetened desiccated coconut in natural food stores or some specialty food shops and store it in the freezer.

Prep Time: 25 minutes

Bake Time: Crust, 8 to 10 minutes; cake, 45 minutes

Advance Prep: Cake may be refrigerated up to 4 days or frozen.

Change of Pace: For a year-round version, substitute 1 cup all-purpose flour for ¾ cup matzah meal in the crust, and 1 tablespoon flour for 1 tablespoon potato starch in the filling.

*F*or centuries European Jews have prepared all kinds of dried fruit compotes. My mother, being from Germany, served her own rendition every year for the Seder along with a sponge cake. This recipe is so incredibly tasty that even I, who usually don't consider fruit to be dessert, am content to conclude a meal with it. Of course, topping the fruit with a dollop of sour cream sweetened with a little brown sugar or serving it with a slice of Banana Coffee Cake with Cinnamon Streusel (see page 163) doesn't hurt. To comply with Passover dietary restrictions, use a vanilla bean instead of extract.

Prep Time: 5 minutes

Soak Time: 2 hours or overnight

Bake Time: 40 minutes

Advance Prep: Fruits may be refrigerated up to 2 weeks.

Dried Fruits Stewed in Cinnamon and Port

2 bags (6 ounces each) mixed dried fruit
1 cinnamon stick, broken into pieces
1 cup firmly packed light or dark brown sugar
¾ cup port or dry red wine
¼ cup water
½ vanilla bean, split down the middle to expose seeds, or 1 tablespoon vanilla extract
½ lemon, thinly sliced
1 small orange, thinly sliced

Preheat oven to 325°F.

To Assemble: Place dried fruit in microwave-safe bowl. Cover with water. Microwave, covered, on high (100%) for 15 to 20 minutes, or until boiling. Remove and let soak in water for at least 2 hours or overnight. Drain off water. Stir in cinnamon stick, brown sugar, wine, ¼ cup water, vanilla, and lemon and orange slices. Pour into 9-inch square baking dish.

To Bake: Bake, uncovered, for 40 minutes. (Fruit may be covered and refrigerated up to 2 weeks. If desired, reheat in microwave.) Serve warm or at room temperature.

Makes: 8 servings

Double Chocolate Meringue Kisses

Photograph, page 14

1 ounce unsweetened chocolate, chopped
3 tablespoons unsweetened cocoa powder
2 tablespoons plus 1 teaspoon potato starch
½ teaspoon instant coffee granules
3 large egg whites (about ½ cup)
¾ cup sugar
⅓ cup chocolate chips, for decorating (optional)

Preheat oven to 325°F. Line 2 heavy or cushioned baking sheets with parchment paper.

To Make Kisses: In a food processor with the metal blade, process chocolate until very finely chopped. Add cocoa and process until finely ground. Add potato starch and process until incorporated.

In a mixing bowl, stir coffee granules into egg whites and let stand for 5 minutes. With electric mixer on medium speed, beat egg whites until soft peaks form. Increase speed to high and gradually add sugar, 1 tablespoon at a time, until stiff, glossy peaks form, 6 to 7 minutes. Fold chocolate mixture into whites. The mixture will be very stiff, but will deflate as you fold.

Drop by heaping teaspoons, or pipe through a pastry bag fitted with a ½-inch plain tip onto prepared baking sheets, about 2 inches apart.

To Bake: Bake for 15 to 18 minutes, or until tops are firm and set. If baking both sheets in one oven, reverse positions after 8 minutes. Remove from oven and cool to room temperature on baking sheets. Carefully remove kisses from parchment paper.

Optional Decoration: Place chips in a small heavy plastic zipper bag. Microwave at 70% for 40 to 90 seconds, or until chocolate is melted and smooth when pressed with fingers. Cut a small tip off the corner of the bag and through it pipe a Jewish star or other design on the top of each cookie. (Cookies may be stored in an airtight container in dry weather up to 1 week or frozen.)

Makes: about 36 cookies

Passover Cookies

Double Chocolate Meringue Kisses

Brown Sugar Almond Crisps

Chocolate Chip Cookies

Tangy Lemon Bars

Fudgy Coconut Macaroons

Rocky Road Brownies

Because meringues are made without flour, they have been a longtime favorite Passover cookie. This version is in a class by itself. Cocoa, unsweetened chocolate, and instant coffee are folded into egg whites with a little potato starch. The result: an extremely fudgy, crisp, but not brittle cookie.

Prep Time: 20 minutes

Bake Time: 15 to 18 minutes

Advance Prep: Kisses may be stored airtight in dry weather up to 1 week or frozen.

Prep Time: 20 minutes

Bake Time: 15 minutes plus 15 minutes in the oven on "off"

Advance Prep: Cookies may be stored airtight in dry weather for several days or frozen.

Brown Sugar Almond Crisps

3 large egg whites (about ½ cup)
¼ teaspoon salt
1½ teaspoons vanilla extract (optional)
1½ cups firmly packed light brown sugar, forced through a sieve after measuring to remove all lumps
1½ tablespoons potato starch
1½ tablespoons matzah cake meal
1½ cups coarsely chopped almonds

Place rack in upper third of oven and preheat to 300°F. Line 2 cushioned baking sheets with parchment paper.

To Make Cookies: In a mixing bowl with electric mixer, beat egg whites, salt, and vanilla, if using, on high speed until they form soft peaks. Gradually add the sieved brown sugar, continuing to beat for 3 to 5 minutes, or until the mixture stands in stiff peaks. (A stiff meringue will hold its shape better when baked.) Sprinkle the potato starch, matzah cake meal, and almonds on the meringue, and mix on low speed for 3 to 4 seconds until combined.

Drop by heaping teaspoons or pipe through a pastry bag fitted with a ½-inch plain tip into 2-inch mounds, about 1½ inches apart.

To Bake: If not baking on cushioned baking sheets, double-pan by placing 1 baking sheet on top of the other. Bake for 15 minutes. (Do not overbake.) Turn off oven and leave cookies in oven for another 15 minutes. The edges will be crisp but the insides soft. They will firm up as they cool. Remove from oven and carefully peel off parchment paper. Cool to room temperature. (Cookies may be stored in an airtight container in dry weather for several days or frozen.)

Makes: about 36 cookies

Chocolate Chip Cookies

Photograph, page 14

½ **cup shortening**
¾ **cup sugar**
1 large egg
2 teaspoons orange juice
½ **teaspoon vanilla extract (optional)**
¾ **cup matzah cake meal**
1 teaspoon firmly packed potato starch
Scant ½ **teaspoon salt or to taste**
⅔ **cup chocolate chips**

Place rack in upper third of oven and preheat to 350°F. Grease or spray with nonstick spray 2 cushioned or heavy-duty baking sheets.

To Make Batter: In a large mixing bowl with electric mixer, beat shortening and sugar on medium speed until well blended. Add egg and mix well. Add orange juice, vanilla, if using, cake meal, potato starch, and salt. Mix on low until blended. Mix in chocolate chips. Drop by rounded teaspoons onto prepared baking sheets, about 2 inches apart.

To Bake: If not using cushioned baking sheets, double-pan by placing 1 baking sheet on top of the other. Bake for 14 to 17 minutes, or until pale golden. Cool 2 minutes and remove to rack to cool completely. (Cookies may be stored at room temperature up to 2 days or frozen.)

Makes: 24 cookies

Change of Pace: ½ cup chopped pecans or walnuts may be added to the batter with the chocolate chips.

These crispy gems are adapted from a collection of recipes entitled "Passover Treasures" from the Minneapolis Talmud Torah Family. I am always amazed at the outstanding results obtained by substituting matzah cake meal and potato starch for flour. The 1 teaspoon potato starch does make a difference, so don't leave it out.

Prep Time: 10 minutes

Bake Time: 14 to 17 minutes

Advance Prep: Cookies may be stored airtight for up to 2 days or frozen.

Tangy Lemon Bars

Photograph, page 14

Pastry
½ cup granulated sugar
1 cup matzah meal
¼ pound (1 stick) nondairy or regular margarine or butter, melted

Lemon Filling
3 large eggs
¾ cup granulated sugar
2 tablespoons nondairy or regular margarine or butter, melted
⅓ cup fresh lemon juice
2 tablespoons potato starch
Powdered sugar for sprinkling on top

Place oven rack in center of oven and preheat to 350°F. Line an 8-inch square baking pan with heavy foil, letting it extend an inch over the sides. Oil or spray the foil with nonstick spray.

To Make Pastry: In a small bowl, stir together sugar, matzah meal, and margarine. Press into bottom of prepared pan. Bake for 20 to 25 minutes, or until pale golden. Reduce oven temperature to 325°F.

To Make Filling: In a medium bowl, whisk eggs. Whisk in granulated sugar, margarine, lemon juice, and potato starch. Pour over crust and bake at 325°F for 20 to 25 minutes, or until top is lightly golden and set. Remove from oven and cool to room temperature.

To Cut: Remove from pan by lifting out foil. Place on cutting board. Trim edges of pastry and cut into 1½-inch squares or diamonds. (The bars may be refrigerated up to 1 week or frozen.)

Before Serving: Sprinkle with powdered sugar. Serve chilled or at room temperature.

Makes: 25 bars

Fudgy Coconut Macaroons

Photograph, page 14

1 can (15 ounces) regular or low-fat sweetened condensed milk
  (not evaporated)
2 ounces (2 squares) unsweetened chocolate, chopped
2 cups shredded coconut
¼ teaspoon instant coffee granules, dissolved in 1 tablespoon boiling water,
  or 1 tablespoon strong coffee
Dash of salt
1 cup coarsely chopped walnuts or pecans

Preheat oven to 350°F. Grease or spray a cushioned or heavy-duty baking sheet.

To Make Cookies: In a medium microwave-safe bowl, microwave milk and chocolate on high (100%) for 3 to 4 minutes, or until melted and smooth. Be careful not to overcook or the mixture will become granular. Stir in coconut, coffee, salt, and nuts. Drop batter by teaspoonfuls onto prepared baking sheet.

To Bake: If you do not have a cushioned baking sheet, double-pan by placing 1 baking sheet on top of the other. Bake for 10 to 12 minutes, or until bottoms are set. They will be very soft, but will firm up as they cool. Remove from oven and immediately transfer to wax paper–lined trays to cool completely. (Cookies may be refrigerated for 1 week or frozen.)

Makes: 36 cookies

Change of Pace: To make Fudgy Coconut Raisin Macaroons, substitute ½ cup raisins for ½ cup nuts.

Once you taste these macaroons, you won't want to wait until next Passover to make them again. The key to their moist, chewy texture lies in not overbaking them. So, watch carefully and remove them from the oven when the bottoms are set.

Prep Time: 10 minutes

Bake Time: 10 to 12 minutes

Advance Prep: Macaroons may be refrigerated for 1 week or frozen.

When Debbie Shahvar made these for me, I had a hard time believing they didn't have flour in them. But when brownies are crammed with two kinds of chocolate, marshmallows, and nuts, and then topped with more of the same, who needs flour? If you keep kosher, look for kosher-for-Passover marshmallows.

Prep Time: *10 minutes*

Bake Time: *30 to 35 minutes*

Advance Prep: *Brownies may be refrigerated up to 4 days or frozen.*

Rocky Road Brownies
Photograph, page 14

Brownies
4 ounces (4 squares) semisweet chocolate, chopped
½ pound (2 sticks) margarine or butter
1½ cups sugar
4 large eggs
1 cup matzah cake meal
½ teaspoon salt
1 cup chocolate chips
2 cups mini marshmallows, or large marshmallows, cut up
1 cup chopped walnuts

Topping
1 cup mini marshmallows, or large marshmallows, cut up
½ cup chocolate chips
½ cup chopped walnuts

Place oven rack in center of oven and preheat to 325°F. Grease or spray with nonstick spray a 9 × 13-inch baking pan.

To Make Brownies: In a large microwave-safe bowl, melt chocolate and margarine on high (100%) for 1 to 2 minutes, or until melted. Stir well. Stir in sugar and cool slightly. Whisk in eggs, one at a time. Stir in cake meal and salt. Stir in chocolate chips, marshmallows, and walnuts. Pour into prepared pan. Spread evenly.

To Bake: Bake for 30 minutes, or until set.

To Top: After 30 minutes, sprinkle brownies with marshmallows. Return to oven for 3 to 4 minutes, or until puffed but not browned. Remove from oven. Place chocolate chips in a small, heavy plastic bag. Microwave on high (100%) for 60 to 90 seconds, or until melted and smooth when pressed with fingers. Squeeze chocolate into one corner of bag. Cut a small tip off the corner and drizzle chocolate over brownies. Sprinkle with nuts. Cool completely. Cut with a serrated knife into 1¾ × 2¼-inch bars. (Brownies may be refrigerated up to 4 days or frozen.)

Makes: 30 brownies

Wake Up to More Than Matzah Brei

The idea for developing a collection of Passover breakfast recipes stems from the many years I've enjoyed eating and serving matzah brei (the Yiddish term for matzah fried with eggs). As a child it was my most requested recipe and it became my children's as well. Here are some additional morning treats for your family to pass on to their children.

When I began experimenting with matzah, I found that it lends itself wonderfully to egg dishes—in casseroles, in variations of matzah brei, and even in an almost-quiche. I like to accompany these entrées with Dried Fruits Stewed in Cinnamon and Port (see page 148). Because during Passover I miss muffins and coffee cakes the most, I've created some that are so tasty they can almost pass for the real thing.

Menu

Main Dishes
Milanese Matzah Brei

Bubbe's Matzah Brei with Lox and Onions

Mexican Matzah Brei Omelet

You'll-Never-Believe-They're-Passover Banana Pancakes

Matzah Blintz Soufflé Casserole with *Strawberry Sauce*

Spinach Matzah Quiche

◆

Muffins and Coffee Cake
Jam-Filled Streusel Muffins

Carrot Raisin Muffins

Banana Coffee Cake with Cinnamon Streusel

Milanese Matzah Brei

1 matzah, broken into 2-inch pieces
3 eggs
Salt and freshly ground black pepper to taste
1 to 2 teaspoons margarine or butter
½ cup chopped onion
¼ pound mushrooms, chopped
1 teaspoon dried basil or 1 tablespoon chopped fresh basil
2 tablespoons chopped fresh parsley

To Prepare Matzah: Place matzah in a colander in the sink and pour boiling water over. Let soak 2 minutes. Squeeze out liquid. In a medium bowl, whisk eggs. Stir in matzah and salt and pepper to taste.

To Cook: In a medium skillet over moderately high heat, preferably nonstick, heat margarine. Sauté onions until soft. Add mushrooms and herbs, and sauté until tender. Pour in eggs. Cook over moderate heat until set on bottom. Mix gently, like scrambled eggs, until cooked through. Serve immediately.

Makes: 3 servings

When you scramble matzah brei with basil, mushrooms, and onions it becomes part Italian. Mangia matzah—eat and enjoy!

Prep Time: 10 minutes

Cook Time: About 5 minutes

Advance Prep: Ingredients may be prepared ahead and cooked just before serving.

Bubbe's Matzah Brei with Lox and Onions
Photograph, page 15

1 matzah, broken into 2-inch pieces
3 eggs
1 medium green onion with top, chopped
1 tablespoon chopped fresh dill or ½ teaspoon dried dill
1 ounce finely chopped cream cheese (about 2 tablespoons)
¼ cup chopped tomato
Salt and freshly ground black pepper to taste
2 teaspoons margarine or butter
¼ cup shredded lox or smoked salmon

Place matzah in a colander in the sink and pour boiling water over. Let soak 2 minutes. Squeeze out liquid. In a medium bowl, whisk eggs. Stir in green onion, dill, cream cheese, tomato, matzah, and salt and pepper.

Heat margarine in medium skillet, preferably nonstick. Pour in eggs. Cook over moderate heat until set on bottom. Mix gently, like scrambled eggs, until lightly cooked. Sprinkle with lox and fold in gently until incorporated. Serve immediately.

Makes: 3 servings

If you've limited cream cheese, tomatoes, lox, and onions to bagels, you're in for a real treat when you taste them scrambled with matzah and eggs.

Prep Time: 10 minutes

Cook Time: About 5 minutes

Advance Prep: Ingredients may be chopped ahead. Cook just before serving.

Mexican Matzah Brei Omelet

Guacamole Filling
½ avocado, peeled, pitted, and chopped
1 tablespoon chopped green onion
2 tablespoons sour cream
1 teaspoon lemon juice

Omelet
1 matzah, broken into 2-inch pieces
3 eggs
Salt and freshly ground black pepper to taste
1 teaspoon margarine or butter
¼ cup shredded jalapeño Jack cheese or Jack cheese with 1 teaspoon
  chopped jalapeños
Salsa, for serving

To Make Guacamole: In a small bowl, stir together avocado, green onion, sour cream, and lemon juice.

To Prepare Matzah: Place matzah in a colander in the sink and pour boiling water over. Let soak 2 minutes. Squeeze out liquid. In a medium bowl, whisk eggs. Stir in matzah and salt and pepper.

To Make Omelet: In a 10-inch skillet, preferably nonstick, heat margarine over moderate heat until sizzling. Add egg mixture. Cook, pulling eggs toward center of pan with a narrow spatula and tilting pan to allow uncooked portion to flow into empty spaces, until set. Sprinkle with cheese. Spread guacamole filling over half the omelet. Cook on low heat, covered, until top is set. Fold over, slide onto a plate, cut in half, and serve immediately, with salsa.

Makes: 2 servings

Matzah brei travels south of the border when it's cooked like an omelet, filled with guacamole and shredded spicy Jack cheese, and then topped with salsa.

Prep Time: 10 minutes

Cook Time: About 5 minutes

Advance Prep: Ingredients may be prepared ahead and cooked just before serving.

The adjectives light and fluffy aren't usually associated with Passover dishes, but they aptly describe these tender pancakes.

Prep Time: 5 minutes

Cook Time: About 5 minutes

Advance Prep: Pancakes are best made just before serving.

You'll-Never-Believe-They're-Passover Banana Pancakes

3 large eggs
⅓ cup matzah meal
2 tablespoons matzah cake meal
¼ cup regular or low-fat sour cream
¼ cup regular or low-fat cottage cheese
Dash of salt
1 very ripe banana, chopped
1 to 2 teaspoons vegetable oil
Butter and syrup or jam, for serving (optional)

In a medium bowl, whisk eggs. Whisk in matzah meal, cake meal, sour cream, cottage cheese, and salt. Stir in banana. Batter will be very thick. Pour oil onto griddle or large skillet. Heat over moderate heat until hot. Make 3-inch pancakes using about ¼ cup batter for each. Cook until a few bubbles appear on top and underside is golden, about 3 minutes. Turn and brown on other side, about 2 minutes. Serve with butter and/or syrup or jam, if desired.

Makes: 10 pancakes

Matzah Blintz Soufflé Casserole

4 large eggs
1 package (8 ounces) regular or low-fat cream cheese, softened
1 pint regular or low-fat small-curd cottage cheese
⅓ cup regular or light sour cream
⅓ cup sugar
1 tablespoon potato starch
2 tablespoons vanilla extract (optional)
3 matzot
Strawberry Sauce (recipe follows), fresh fruit, or syrup, for serving

Place oven rack in center of oven and preheat to 350°F. Grease or spray with nonstick spray an 8-inch square baking dish.

To Make Batter: In food processor with metal blade, process eggs until light and fluffy, about 1 minute. Add cream cheese, cottage cheese, sour cream, sugar, potato starch, and vanilla, if using. Process until smooth. (Batter may be refrigerated overnight.)

To Assemble: Pour hot water over matzot, being careful not to break them. Drain. Place 1 matzah in baking dish. Cover with a third of the blintz batter. Repeat 2 more layers, ending with batter.

To Bake: Bake for 50 minutes, or until center is set. Serve hot with Strawberry Sauce, sliced fruit, or syrup.

Makes: 6 servings

Strawberry Sauce

1 package (10 ounces) frozen sliced strawberries, slightly defrosted
3 tablespoons frozen undiluted orange juice concentrate or 2 tablespoons orange marmalade
1 tablespoon currant jelly
1 cup sliced fresh strawberries

In food processor with metal blade, process strawberries and orange juice concentrate or marmalade until pureed. Add currant jelly and process until blended. Remove to a bowl. (Sauce may be refrigerated up to 2 days.) Before serving, stir in strawberries.

Makes: 1½ cups sauce

Here's a new twist on blintzes: The cheese filling sandwiches three layers of softened matzah to bake into a puffed and golden custard.

Prep Time: 5 minutes

Bake Time: 50 minutes

Advance Prep: Batter can be made ahead and refrigerated overnight. Assemble and bake just before serving.

This sauce is just as terrific served over ice cream and yogurt as it is drizzled over pancakes and brunch dishes.

Prep Time: 5 minutes

Advance Prep: Sauce may be refrigerated up to 2 days. Stir in fresh strawberries just before serving.

When you start pouring this spinach-laden batter into a 9-inch baking dish, you may think it will never fit. But it will. The spinach shrinks as it cooks and everything bakes into a lovely puffed custard laced with ribbons of green.

Prep Time: 10 minutes

Bake Time: 1 hour

Advance Prep: Quiche may be refrigerated overnight and reheated.

Spinach Matzah Quiche

3 matzot, broken into 2-inch pieces
6 large eggs
4 egg whites
2 cups regular, low-fat, or nonfat cottage cheese
2 cups shredded jalapeño Jack cheese or regular Jack cheese (about 8 ounces)
½ teaspoon salt or to taste
Freshly ground black pepper to taste
1 pound trimmed and stemmed spinach (baby leaves preferred)

Place oven rack in center of oven and preheat to 350°F. Grease or spray with nonstick spray a 9-inch square baking dish.

To Make Quiche: Place matzot in a colander in the sink and pour boiling water over. Let soak 2 minutes. Squeeze out liquid. In a large bowl, whisk eggs and whites. Stir in cottage cheese, Jack cheese, matzot, salt, and pepper. Stir in spinach. Pour into prepared pan. It may seem like too much; just pack it in tightly.

To Bake: Bake, uncovered, for 1 hour, or until puffed and golden. (Quiche may be cooled and refrigerated, covered, overnight. Before serving, bring to room temperature. Reheat at 350°F, uncovered, about 10 minutes, or until heated through.)

Makes: 8 servings

Jam-Filled Streusel Muffins

Photograph, page 15

Streusel Topping
⅓ cup packed light brown sugar
3 tablespoons potato starch
1½ teaspoons ground cinnamon
¾ cup chopped pecans
2 tablespoons vegetable oil

Muffins
6 large eggs
¾ cup vegetable oil
1 cup packed light brown sugar
½ cup matzah meal
1 cup matzah cake meal
2 teaspoons vanilla extract (optional)
1 teaspoon ground cinnamon
¼ teaspoon salt
2 tablespoons orange juice
6 teaspoons cherry or strawberry jam or preserves (do not use jelly)

Place oven rack in center of oven and preheat to 350°F. Grease or spray with nonstick spray 12 muffin cups.

To Make Streusel Topping: In a small bowl, stir together brown sugar, potato starch, cinnamon, and pecans. Add oil and toss with fingers until crumbly; set aside.

To Make Muffins: In a large bowl, whisk eggs until blended. Whisk in oil, brown sugar, matzah meal, cake meal, vanilla, if using, cinnamon, salt, and orange juice until incorporated. Spoon into muffin cups, filling ¾ full. Spoon ½ teaspoon preserves into the center of each muffin. Lightly press preserves into batter. Sprinkle streusel over tops.

To Bake: Bake for 25 minutes, or until a toothpick comes out clean. Cool 10 minutes, go around edges of muffin cups with a sharp knife, and remove muffins to cooling racks. Serve warm or at room temperature. (Muffins may be stored at room temperature overnight, refrigerated up to 2 days, or frozen. Reheat at 375°F for 3 to 5 minutes, or until warm.)

Makes: 12 muffins

These muffins will probably be the closest thing to bread you'll sample during Passover. You'll be pleasantly surprised to find that muffins can rise so high and taste so good without flour or leavening.

Prep Time: 20 minutes

Bake Time: 25 minutes

Advance Prep: Muffins may be stored at room temperature overnight, refrigerated up to 2 days, or frozen.

Carrot Raisin Muffins

6 large eggs
¾ cup vegetable oil
1 cup packed light brown sugar
½ cup matzah meal
1 cup matzah cake meal
2 teaspoons vanilla extract (optional)
1 teaspoon ground cinnamon
¼ teaspoon salt
1 cup shredded carrots (about 2 medium)
¼ cup golden raisins

Place rack in center of oven and preheat to 350°F. Spray or grease 12 muffin cups.

To Make Muffins: In a large bowl, whisk eggs until blended. Whisk in oil, brown sugar, matzah meal, cake meal, vanilla, if using, cinnamon, and salt until incorporated. Stir in carrots and raisins. Spoon into muffin cups, filling almost to the top.

To Bake: Bake for 25 minutes, or until tops are firm and golden and a toothpick comes out clean. Cool 10 minutes, go around edges of muffin cups with a sharp knife, and remove muffins to cooling racks. Serve warm or at room temperature. (Muffins may be stored airtight at room temperature overnight, refrigerated up to 2 days, or frozen.)

Makes: 12 muffins

Banana Coffee Cake with Cinnamon Streusel

Streusel Topping
½ cup firmly packed light brown sugar
⅔ cup matzah meal
1 teaspoon ground cinnamon
½ stick (4 tablespoons) nondairy or regular margarine or butter, melted

Cake
6 large eggs, separated
½ cup plus ¼ cup granulated sugar
2 teaspoons vanilla extract (optional)
½ teaspoon salt
½ cup matzah meal
½ cup potato starch
4 large, very ripe bananas

Place rack in center of oven and preheat to 325°F. Grease or spray with nonstick spray a 9 × 13-inch glass baking dish.

To Make Streusel Topping: In a small bowl, combine brown sugar, matzah meal, and cinnamon. With a fork or your fingers, blend in margarine until mixture resembles coarse meal.

To Make Cake: In food processor with metal blade or mixing bowl with electric mixer, process or mix egg yolks with ½ cup granulated sugar until very thick and light colored, about 1 minute. Add vanilla, if using, salt, matzah meal, and potato starch. Chop 2 of the bananas and add to yolk mixture. Process or mix until bananas are pureed.

In separate mixing bowl, beat egg whites until soft peaks form. Slowly add remaining ¼ cup granulated sugar, beating until whites hold stiff but not dry peaks. Thinly slice remaining 2 bananas. Pour yolk mixture and bananas over whites. Fold together gently but thoroughly. Pour batter into prepared pan, smoothing top. Sprinkle streusel evenly over the top.

To Bake: Bake for 30 to 35 minutes, or until golden and tester inserted in center comes out clean. Remove from oven and cool in pan. It will fall as it cools. (Cake may be kept at room temperature, tightly covered, overnight, refrigerated for 3 days, or frozen.)

Makes: 12 servings

Here's a new slant on the traditional Passover sponge cake. To intensify the banana flavor, some of the fruit is pureed into the batter, and the remainder is sliced and folded into it. The top of the cake is enhanced with a crumbly brown sugar and matzah meal streusel.

Prep Time: 20 minutes

Bake Time: 30 to 35 minutes

Advance Prep: Cake may be stored at room temperature overnight, refrigerated for 3 days, or frozen.

Extra Points

THE INVITATIONS

Decorate a piece of white construction paper with 2 blue horizontal stripes at top and bottom and a Jewish star in the center to resemble the Israeli flag. Glue the flag to a popsicle stick and mail in a padded envelope.

THE PICNIC

Use blue and white paper plates and napkins. Purchase Israeli flag picks from a party supply shop and insert into the platters of food.

Israel Independence Day

✧

Since the State of Israel was established in May 1948, Jews around the world celebrate the miraculous return of the Jewish people to their homeland. In Israel, Independence Day, Yom ha-Atzma'ut, is as festive as the Fourth of July. The entire country celebrates with jubilant dancing in the street, parades, fireworks, festivals, and picnics. Although the holiday is relatively new, its popularity is gaining here in the United States. In many neighborhoods, friends gather together for Israeli folk dancing, song fests, poetry readings, picnics, and barbecues.

Kibbutznik Picnic Wrap-ups

Because vegetables are so plentiful in Israel, for this picnic I incorporate them into several fresh, easy-to-pack, sturdy dishes. For any size group, the recipes can be multiplied as desired. Eggplant, so prevalent in Israeli recipes, is chopped into Eggplant Salsa (see page 73) for a spirited dip or side dish. You might also offer Hummus dip (see page 74). Both the Hye Roller sandwiches are best made close to toting time as possible, but no more than 4 hours ahead or the bread will become soggy. Accompany the sandwiches with Israeli Chopped Salad with Bagel Chips or Tabbouleh (see page 101), variations of two of Israel's finest chilled chopped-vegetable dishes. Either Caesar Pasta Salad with Romaine Ribbons (see page 47) or Orzo Salad with Feta and Sun-Dried Tomatoes (see page 63) would make a good go-along.

For dessert, to the strains of "Hatikvah," proudly bring forth Israeli Flag Cake, a blueberry-carrot extravaganza slathered with white-chocolate icing and decorated with blue marzipan. Turn on some spirited Israeli folk music, join hands, and kick up your heels to the hora.

Menu

Eggplant Salsa
(see page 73)

◆

Tuna Hye Roller
(see page 100)

PB&J Hye Roller
(see page 100)

Israeli Chopped Salad
with Bagel Chips

◆

Israeli Flag Cake

GAME PLAN

As Far Ahead As Desired	Make unfrosted cake and freeze or refrigerate up to 2 days
	Make salsa and freeze or refrigerate up to 3 days
2 Days Ahead	Defrost cake, if frozen
	Make salad dressing
1 Day Ahead	Decorate cake
	Defrost salsa, if frozen, and assemble

DAY OF PARTY

6 Hours Before Serving	Prepare vegetables for salad
4 Hours Before Serving	Make Hye Rollers
Shortly Before Serving	Toss salad
	Slice Hye Rollers

Israeli Chopped Salad with Bagel Chips

Salad
1 large hothouse seedless cucumber, peeled and cut in small cubes
½ teaspoon salt
1 large green pepper, seeded and cut into small dice
6 tomatoes, seeded and cut into small dice
1½ cups thinly sliced green onions with tops (about 2 bunches)
10 inner leaves of romaine, sliced in thin shreds (about 5 cups)
½ cup finely chopped parsley
½ cup finely chopped fresh mint

Dressing
⅓ cup olive oil
⅓ cup orange juice
¼ cup plus 1½ tablespoons fresh lemon juice
2 cloves garlic, minced
Salt and freshly ground black pepper to taste

2 bags (6 ounces each) bagel chips, cut into quarters or crumbled

To Make Salad: In a large colander, sprinkle the cucumber with salt and let drain for 30 minutes. Meanwhile, prepare vegetables and make dressing. Rinse cucumber and pat very dry. In a large bowl, combine green pepper, tomatoes, cucumber, green onions, romaine, parsley, and mint. (Salad may be refrigerated, wrapped in paper towels, up to 6 hours.)

To Make Dressing: In a small bowl or jar, whisk together oil, orange juice, lemon juice, garlic, and salt and pepper. (Dressing may be refrigerated up to 2 days. Bring to room temperature and whisk well before using.)

Before Serving: Pour dressing over salad, add bagel chips, and toss well. Serve immediately.

Makes: 12 side-dish servings

Israel has such an abundance of outstanding vegetables that variations of this salad are served at most meals. The bagel chips are my addition —don't be surprised if you begin using them in place of croutons in all your salads. For toting, pack the salad, bagel chips, and dressing separately, and toss before serving.

Prep Time: 15 minutes

Standing Time: 30 minutes

Advance Prep: Dressing may be refrigerated up to 2 days. Salad may be refrigerated up to 6 hours. Toss with dressing before serving.

This cake, decorated like the Israeli flag, turns any Jewish holiday into a celebration. The star and stripes are cut out of rolled marzipan, painted with blue food coloring, and sprinkled with blue sugar crystals. Undecorated, this fragrant, cinnamon-scented cake, dotted with blueberries and rippled with carrots, makes a grand finale for any occasion, especially when serving a crowd.

Prep Time: Cake, 20 minutes; frosting, 10 minutes; decorations, 15 minutes

Bake Time: 60 to 70 minutes

Advance Prep: Unfrosted cake may be refrigerated up to 2 days or frozen. Frosted cake may be refrigerated overnight.

Israeli Flag Cake (Blueberry-Carrot Cake)

Cake
1 cup vegetable oil
2 cups granulated sugar
3 large eggs
2 teaspoons vanilla extract
3 cups all-purpose flour
2 teaspoons ground cinnamon
1 teaspoon baking powder
1½ teaspoons baking soda
1 teaspoon salt
2 cups grated carrots (about 2 medium)
1½ cups fresh or frozen blueberries, not defrosted

White Chocolate Frosting
3 ounces white chocolate (preferably Lindt or Baker's, chopped, or good-quality vanilla chips)
4 ounces regular or light cream cheese, at room temperature
2 cups powdered sugar, sifted if lumpy
3 tablespoons regular or low-fat sour cream

Flag Decorations
1 package (7 ounces) marzipan
Blue food coloring
Blue sugar crystals (optional) (found with cake-decorating items)

Preheat oven to 350°F. Spray a 9 × 13-inch baking pan with nonstick coating. Line bottom with parchment paper or wax paper and spray the paper.

To Make Cake: In a mixing bowl with electric mixer, beat oil and granulated sugar on medium speed until light and fluffy, about 2 minutes. Add eggs, one at a time, beating well after each addition. Beat in vanilla. Add flour, cinnamon, baking powder, baking soda, and salt. Mix on low speed until combined. Mix at medium speed for 2 minutes. Add carrots and mix on low to blend. Fold in blueberries. Batter will be stiff. Pour into prepared pan, smoothing the top.

To Bake: Bake for 60 to 70 minutes, or until top is golden and toothpick inserted in center comes out clean. Cool 10 minutes and invert onto rack. Pull off paper. Cool completely. (Cake may be refrigerated up to 2 days or frozen.)

To Make Frosting: Melt white chocolate in a microwave-safe bowl at 50% power for 60 to 90 seconds, or until smooth, stirring once. Or melt on stove in double boiler. Cool slightly. In a mixing bowl, beat cream cheese and powdered sugar until very smooth, about 2 minutes. Mix in chocolate. It will look grainy. Add sour cream and mix until smooth, about 1 minute. Spread a thin layer over the top and sides of cake. Spread remainder to cover as smoothly as possible. Refrigerate until set.

To Decorate: Roll marzipan between 2 sheets of wax paper to ⅛-inch thickness. Cut out a 4-inch Jewish star. Re-form pieces of marzipan into a 1-inch rectangle. Roll into a strip 13 inches long by 2 inches wide. Cut in half lengthwise, making 2 stripes. Wearing rubber gloves, pour blue food coloring into a paper cup. Using a paintbrush, paint star and stripes. Sprinkle with blue sugar, if using, and allow to dry completely. Place star in center of cake. Place 1 stripe about 1 inch from bottom of rectangle and the other 1 inch from top. (Cake may be refrigerated overnight.) Serve chilled or at room temperature.

Makes: 15 servings

Shavuot

◆

The word Shavuot means weeks, and this holiday was so named because it occurs seven weeks after Passover. It commemorates Moses' receiving the Ten Commandments on Mount Sinai. While theologians and scholars may debate what actually happened at Sinai, the giving of the Torah is central to Judaism. The Torah teaches us to be compassionate and responsible human beings, and to be concerned with the community and the world around us. Today, Shavuot is celebrated by a confirmation ceremony and by graduation from Hebrew and Sunday school, as well as by attending synagogue services.

Shavuot is also referred to as Hag ha-Bikurim, the feast of the first fruits. It celebrates the beginning of the agricultural season and the end of the grain harvest. Fresh fruits, especially those new to the season, are often served at meals and used in centerpieces. In honor of the holiday, decorate your home with lush flowers and foliage.

Shavuot is also known as the "Cheesecake Holiday," because of the predominance of dairy dishes that are enjoyed at this time. The exact reason for this is unknown. Some believe it's because the Hebrews abstained from eating meat the day before they received the Torah. Others suggest it's because the holiday occurs during the season when grazing animals give birth and find lush pastures, thereby producing an abundance of milk. Or perhaps it's because the whiteness of milk is symbolic of the purity of the Torah. Whatever the reason, isn't it wonderful to have an excuse to partake in so many of the foods we love on such a jubilant holiday?

Extra Points

THE INVITATION

To make a torah invitation, write the information on a sheet of stiff white paper, about 8½ × 5 inches. For each invitation, you will need two ⅜-inch dowels 8 inches long. Glue dowels onto the two long sides of the paper. Roll toward the center like a Torah scroll. Tie with gold twine or ribbon. Mail in a padded envelope.

THE RITUALS

Two candles are lit at sundown with the following blessing:

We praise You, Eternal God,
Sovereign of the universe:
You hallow us with Your Mitzvot,
and command us to kindle the
(Sabbath and) Festival lights.

Ba-ruch a-ta Adonai,
Eh-lo-hei-nu meh-lech ha-o-lam,
a-sher ki-d'sha-nu b'mitz-vo-tav
v'tzi-va-nu l'had-lik ner shel
(Shabbat v'shel) yom tov.

We thank You, O God, for the joy of Yom Tov, and for the opportunity to celebrate it in the company of those we love.

The leader lifts a glass of wine, and the following blessing is recited:

We praise You, Eternal God,
Sovereign of the universe,
Creator of the fruit of the vine.

Ba-ruch a-ta Adonai,
Eh-lo-hei-nu meh-lech ha-o-lam,
bo-rei p'ri ha-ga-fen.

It is followed by one of the most important Jewish blessings, the She-heh-cheh'yanu, which is recited on every new occasion or event in the cycle of the year, including the first night of holidays:

We praise You, Eternal God,
Sovereign of the universe, for
giving us life, for sustaining us, and
for enabling us to reach this season.

Ba-ruch a-ta Adonai,
Eh-lo-hei-nu meh-lech ha-o-lam,
sheh-heh-cheh-ya-nu, v'ki-y'manu,
v'higi-anu la-z'man ha-zeh.

One or two challot (plural for challah) are covered with a decorated cloth. Everyone breaks off a piece of bread and recites the following blessing:

We praise You, Eternal God,
Sovereign of the universe, for
You cause bread to come forth
from the earth.

Ba-ruch a-ta Adonai,
Eh-lo-hei-nu meh-lech ha-o-lam,
ha-mo-tzi leh-chem min ha-aretz.

THE TABLE

For a centerpiece, let the kids help make a fresh fruit pyramid (the pyramid symbolizes Mount Sinai). You will need a triangular piece of Styrofoam, as large as desired, but thick enough to stand on a platter or your table. Cover the Styrofoam with foil. Select 10 fruits, one for each of the Ten Commandments, such as grapes, pineapple, oranges, lemons, limes, or melons. Cut into slices, wedges, or chunks. Attach the fruit to the Styrofoam pyramid with toothpicks, covering it completely. Arrange lettuce leaves or other greens around the bottom. Guests have the option to eat it or not.

Wrap silverware in napkins to resemble a scrolled Torah. Fold the napkin in half and place on a flat surface. Place silverware with the handles toward the top of the napkin. Roll each side toward the center like a Torah scroll. Tie with cord, ribbon, or raffia.

Menu

Challah
(see page 4)

Tomatillo-Avocado
Salsa (see page 111)

◆

Chunky Vegetable
Lasagna

Mixed Greens with
Apples, Blue Cheese,
and Sweet 'n' Spicy
Walnuts

Herb Monkey Bread

◆

Cheesecake Pear Tart

A Torah Celebration Supper

When I was young, my mother's annual Shavuot dinner consisted of cheese with crackers, blintzes, and cheesecake. Perhaps she served a salad, too, but I don't remember. It is lost in the delirium of the dairy. I have attempted to design a menu that feels like Shavuot, but doesn't use up your cholesterol allotment for the entire month. Following is a well-balanced, light dairy menu, perfect for any size crowd. Although cheese is incorporated into most of the dishes, it is used judiciously.

The meal begins with Tomatillo-Avocado Salsa, a zippy puree of vegetables for dipping. A fitting accompaniment or substitution would be Cheese Pastry Torahs (see page 185). Chunky Vegetable Lasagna celebrates both aspects of Shavuot: the harvest, with its abundance of fresh vegetables, and the dairy, with its layering of ricotta and shredded cheeses. I suggest you use either regular or low-fat cheese, but don't use nonfat cheese because it doesn't taste or melt like the real thing. If you prefer serving a variation on blintzes, substitute Blintz French Toast Casserole (see page 195). Although challah traditionally begins the meal, I like to accompany the lasagna with Herb Monkey Bread, an impressive ring of crispy little rolls linked together with butter, garlic, and herbs. Mixed Greens with Apples, Blue Cheese, and Sweet 'n' Spicy Walnuts offers a refreshing counterpoint to the hearty lasagna. Another choice would be Spinach Salad with Mandarin Orange Dressing (see page 55).

Cheesecake Pear Tart is a delectable dessert with a thin cheesecake baked in a crunchy walnut crust and crowned with a garland of juicy pears. Lofty Coconut Chiffon Cheesecake (see page 147) would make a stellar alternative.

GAME PLAN

As Far Ahead As Desired

Make challah and freeze
Make nuts for salad and freeze or store at
    room temperature up to 2 days

1 Week Ahead

Make vinaigrette

2 Days Ahead

Make lasagna
Make salsa

1 Day Ahead

Prepare greens for salad
Make tart
Defrost nuts, if frozen

DAY OF PARTY

3 Hours Before Serving

Bring challah to room temperature
Bring lasagna to room temperature

2 Hours Before Serving

Make monkey bread

Shortly Before Serving

Toss salad

20 Minutes Before Serving

Reheat challah
Reheat lasagna

Uncooked lasagna noodles, sliced potato, frozen vegetables, canned black beans, and a picante tomato sauce make this casserole a winner in your busy schedule as well as on your table.

Prep Time: 15 minutes

Bake Time: About 65 minutes

Cool Time: 20 minutes

Advance Prep: Lasagna may be refrigerated up to 2 days.

Chunky Vegetable Lasagna

Tomato Sauce
2 cloves garlic, peeled
½ medium onion, peeled and cut into quarters
1 can (28 ounces) whole tomatoes with juice
½ cup jarred salsa picante or chunky salsa, medium or mild, to taste
1 package (1¼ ounces) taco seasoning mix
½ cup water

Ricotta Cheese Layer
1 large egg
1 cup regular or low-fat ricotta
2 tablespoons whole or low-fat milk

Noodles and Vegetables
1 box (8 ounces) uncooked dried lasagna noodles (10 noodles)
1 package (16 ounces) frozen mixed vegetables, such as Japanese style
  with broccoli, not defrosted
1 cup frozen corn
1 can (16 ounces) black beans, rinsed and drained
1 large baking potato (about 8 ounces), peeled and thinly sliced
1½ to 2 cups shredded regular or low-fat sharp Cheddar, Jack,
  or mozzarella cheese, or a combination (about 6 to 8 ounces)

Preheat oven to 425°F. Grease or spray with nonstick spray a 9 × 13-inch casserole.

To Make Sauce: In a food processor with the metal blade, mince garlic. Add onion and pulse to chop. Add tomatoes, reserving the juice, salsa, and taco seasoning. Pulse until tomatoes are in small pieces; do not puree. Transfer to a bowl and stir in juice from tomatoes and ½ cup water.

To Make Ricotta Layer: In a small bowl, with a fork mix egg slightly. Stir in ricotta and milk.

To Assemble: Spread 1 cup sauce over the bottom of prepared casserole. Top with 5 noodles, overlapping slightly, half the frozen vegetables, half the corn, and half the beans. Arrange all the potato slices in a single layer over the vegetables. Spread 2 cups sauce over potatoes. Spoon ricotta cheese mixture over and spread lightly. Sprinkle with half the shredded cheese. Top with remaining noodles, vegetables, corn, beans, and sauce.

To Bake: Place casserole on rimmed baking sheet (to catch drippings), cover with foil, and bake for 1 hour, or until noodles and vegetables are tender when pierced with a skewer or knife. Remove foil, sprinkle with remaining shredded cheese, and bake for 5 minutes. Cool at least 20 minutes before serving. The casserole will stay warm for up to an hour and can be reheated, if desired. (Lasagna may be refrigerated up to 2 days. Bring to room temperature and reheat, covered, at 375°F for 15 to 20 minutes or in a microwave until heated through.)

Makes: 10 to 12 servings

Mixed Greens with Apples, Blue Cheese, and Sweet 'n' Spicy Walnuts

Apple-Walnut Vinaigrette
¼ cup plus 2 tablespoons walnut oil
3 tablespoons olive oil
4 tablespoons plus 2 teaspoons raspberry vinegar
1 tablespoon Dijon mustard
3 tablespoons apple juice
Salt and freshly ground black pepper to taste

Salad
8 ounces stemmed and trimmed spinach leaves, cut into ½-inch strips
  (about 8 cups, loosely packed)
8 cups Boston or butter lettuce, washed and torn into 1-inch pieces
1 can (14 ounces) hearts of palm, drained and sliced
2 medium tart green apples, such as Granny Smith, peeled, cored, and
  chopped into ¾-inch pieces
¼ cup crumbled blue cheese
¾ cup Sweet 'n' Spicy Walnuts (recipe follows)

To Make Vinaigrette: In a small bowl or jar, whisk together oils, vinegar, mustard, and apple juice until blended. Season with salt and pepper. (Vinaigrette may be refrigerated up to 1 week. Whisk well before using.)

To Make Salad: In a large bowl, toss greens, hearts of palm, apples, and blue cheese with dressing. Divide among plates and sprinkle each serving with walnuts.

Makes: 8 servings

Faster: Substitute 12 ounces baby or field greens (mesclun) for the spinach and Boston lettuce.

This is an irresistible salad with contrasting tastes and textures: sweet, juicy apples; pungent, creamy cheese; and crunchy candied nuts.

Prep Time: 15 minutes

Advance Prep: Nuts may be stored airtight at room temperature up to 2 days. Vinaigrette may be refrigerated up to 1 week. Salad greens may be prepared a day ahead and tossed before serving.

Besides being sprinkled over salad, these deliciously spiced and crunchy nuts are great in stir-fries and as hors d'oeuvres. But be forewarned: They are addictive.

Besides being sprinkled over salad, these deliciously spiced and crunchy nuts are great in stir-fries and as hors d'oeuvres. But be forewarned: They are addictive.

Prep Time: *5 minutes*

Bake Time: *25 to 30 minutes*

Advance Prep: *Nuts may be stored airtight up to 2 days.*

Sweet 'n' Spicy Walnuts

¼ **cup sugar**
¼ **cup plain regular, low-fat, or nonfat yogurt**
¾ **teaspoon salt**
¾ **teaspoon cayenne**
1½ **cups walnut halves or large pieces**

Preheat oven to 300°F. Line a baking sheet with heavy foil. Grease or spray the foil with nonstick spray.

To Make Coating: In a 2-quart (8-cup) microwave-safe bowl, stir together sugar, yogurt, salt, and cayenne. Microwave on high (100%), uncovered, for 2 to 3 minutes, or until sugar melts. Stir in nuts.

To Bake: Transfer nuts to prepared baking sheet. Spread in an even layer. Bake for 25 to 30 minutes, or until golden. Stir after 15 or 20 minutes, if they are browning unevenly. Watch nuts carefully the last 10 minutes; they burn quickly. They will be slightly soft, but will firm up as they cool. Remove from oven and immediately loosen with spatula. Cool 5 minutes and remove to a plate or airtight container. Cool completely. (Nuts may be stored airtight at room temperature up to 2 days. If the coating becomes sticky, bake at 300° for 10 minutes, or until crisp.)

Makes: 1½ cups

Change of Pace: To make Sweet 'n' Spicy Pecans, substitute pecan halves for the walnuts.

Herb Monkey Bread

2 loaves (1 pound each) frozen white bread dough, thawed according to
  package directions (usually sold in a 3-pound package)
2 tablespoons butter or margarine
2 cloves garlic, minced
2 tablespoons chopped fresh parsley or 1 tablespoon dried parsley
1 teaspoon dried basil
½ teaspoon dried oregano
½ teaspoon dried thyme
2 tablespoons grated Parmesan cheese, divided
1 tablespoon sesame seeds, divided

Grease or spray with nonstick spray a 10-inch tube pan with a removable
bottom.

To Assemble Bread: Place thawed bread on lightly floured board. Divide
each loaf into quarters and cut each into quarters again, making 16 pieces
per loaf. Shape into balls and place 16 of them in bottom of prepared pan.
Melt butter with garlic and brush half of it over rolls. In a small bowl, combine parsley, basil, oregano, and thyme. Sprinkle a heaping tablespoon
over rolls. Sprinkle with 1 tablespoon Parmesan cheese and ½ tablespoon
sesame seeds. Arrange remaining rolls over. (There will be space between
them.) Stir remaining herbs into butter and brush over rolls. Top with
remaining Parmesan and sesame seeds. Cover with damp cloth, place in a
warm, draft-free place, and let rise 45 minutes, or until double in bulk,
almost to top of pan.

To Bake: Place rack in bottom third of oven. Preheat oven to 375°F. Place
bread pan on baking sheet to catch any drippings and bake for 30 to 40
minutes, or until golden. Cool on rack 10 minutes, remove sides of pan, and
lift bread out. Serve warm.

Makes: 8 to 10 servings

I love to watch guests devour this loaf. Even though it looks and tastes homemade, it's assembled with packaged frozen bread dough. They rave so much that I am almost embarrassed to tell them.

Prep Time: 10 minutes

Rise Time: 45 minutes

Bake Time: 30 to 40 minutes

Advance Prep: Bread is best made as close to serving as possible.

Prep Time: *10 minutes*

Bake Time: *30 minutes*

Advance Prep: *Tart may be refrigerated overnight.*

Cheesecake Pear Tart

Walnut Crust
½ cup sugar
¼ pound (1 stick) butter or margarine, cut into 8 pieces
¾ cup all-purpose flour
⅔ cup walnuts

Filling and Topping
8 ounces cream cheese
1 large egg
¼ cup sugar
1 teaspoon vanilla extract
1 can (29 ounces) pear halves, well drained
½ teaspoon ground cinnamon

Place oven rack in lower third of oven. Preheat oven to 425°F. Spray bottom and sides of a 9-inch tart pan with removable bottom with nonstick spray.

To Make Crust: In food processor with metal blade, pulse sugar and butter until combined. Add flour and pulse until crumbly. Add walnuts and process until mixture is the consistency of wet sand. Reserve ½ cup and set aside. Press remainder into bottom and sides of prepared tart pan.

To Make Filling: In same food processor bowl (no need to wash it), process cream cheese, egg, sugar, and vanilla until smooth. Pour into crust. Arrange pear halves in a circle around the top, with one half in center. Stir cinnamon into remaining crust mixture and sprinkle over top.

To Bake: Bake at 425°F for 10 minutes. Reduce oven temperature to 350°F and bake for 20 minutes more, or until edges are golden. Remove to rack and cool 20 minutes. Go around edges of crust with tip of sharp knife and remove sides of pan. Cool. (Tart may be refrigerated overnight.) Serve warm, chilled, or at room temperature.

Makes: 8 servings

Bar or Bat Mitzvah

✧

A Bar or Bat Mitzvah is not a holiday, it is a once-in-a-lifetime event, one of the most eagerly anticipated and widely celebrated of all Jewish occasions. B'nai Mitzvah (plural for Bar or Bat Mitzvah) literally means Children of the Commandment, and marks the time when our children accept the responsibility of abiding by the laws of the Jewish religion. It celebrates a child's entry into adulthood, when he or she begins to separate from parental bonds. Traditionally held when a child turns thirteen (although it may be twelve for a girl), a Bar or Bat Mitzvah is one of the most important rituals of Jewish life. B'nai Mitzvah are given the honor of reading from the Torah, known as the Five Books of Moses, and reciting specific blessings in the presence of the synagogue community, family, and friends who come to partake in the tribute. The child studies long and hard, sometimes for many years, to share this day with the Jewish community. It is an important time for families to reflect upon the significance of traditions in the Jewish religion and the beauty of passing down these traditions from one generation to the next.

THE RITUALS

Because the celebration dinner for family members and friends who may have come from afar falls on Friday evening, the same blessings apply as for Shabbat (see page 2).

Menu

*Polenta Stars with
Sun-Dried Tomato
Salsa*

*Spinach-Mushroom
Quiche Squares*

*Cheese Pastry Torahs
with Fresh Fruit or
Vegetable Platter*

◆

Challah (see page 4)

*Tournedos of Salmon
with Dill Piccata Sauce*

*White and Wild Rice
Timbales*

*Stir-fry Carrots,
Zucchini, and
Mushrooms*

◆

*Chocolate Mitzvah
Cake*

Out-of-Towners' Celebration Dinner

This very elegant menu was originally designed to be served at the reception after the synagogue service. But, the more it developed, the more I worried that it would be overlooked, because so many people have this special event catered. It seemed a shame to offer these outstanding recipes, which are equally as good for a party of six as for sixty. So, I suggest you prepare this menu for Shabbat dinner before the service, for the many relatives and friends who come from out of town. However, should you choose to cater your own Bar/Bat Mitzvah reception, each of these dishes can be multiplied easily. This is such a hectic time, you may want to enlist your friends' help by giving each of them a dish to prepare.

APPETIZERS

Although you certainly don't need to serve three hors d'oeuvres, each offers distinct advantages. Polenta Stars with Sun-Dried Tomato Salsa is made with a polenta base cut into Jewish stars (or any other shape), and it can be refrigerated or frozen. Before baking they are topped with a dollop of tangy salsa. They are attractive and unique, and taste great served warm or at room temperature. Spinach-Mushroom Quiche Squares are easy to make because they are baked in one pan, can be cut ahead, and reheated before serving. Flaky Cheese Pasty Torahs can either be arranged on a platter with fresh fruit or served on their own. For eight people or less, one appetizer is enough. For a gathering of ten to fourteen, choose two appetizers, and for a larger group, consider serving all three. If you're entertaining fourteen people or more, offer a platter of fresh vegetables and/or fruit as well.

ENTRÉE AND SIDE DISHES

It is seldom I find an entrée that boasts the flexibility of Tournedos of Salmon. They adapt easily to any size group—just be sure to leave ample space between them on the baking sheet so they don't steam. You can even bake them ahead and serve them at room temperature. The boned salmon steaks are rolled up like a jelly roll and wrapped in strips of tortillas. They are served coated with a silken hot Dill Piccata Sauce, but if you wish, you may substitute chilled mayonnaise-based Emerald Sauce (see page 46). White and Wild Rice Timbales are cooked and molded ahead, so all you need to do is microwave them before serving. Or if you have oven space and don't mind assembling a last-minute dish, consider Crisp Potato Kugel (see page 132). Stir-fry Carrots, Zucchini, and Mushrooms, with their sparkling color and sprinkling of Parmesan cheese, artistically complete the plate. Peas with Leeks (page 12) go well with this entrée, too.

DESSERT

My friend and collaborator Joanne Neuman created the show-stopping Chocolate Mitzvah Cake for a friend's son's Bar Mitzvah reception. It is so extraordinary that I include it here in the hopes you will try it. It is much easier to make than it looks. Should you choose to make it for your pre-Bar/Bat Mitzvah dinner, be prepared for it to outshine the professional cake at the reception. The *tallit* decoration is a bonus, as the cake is delicious without it. Coconut Cheesecake (see page 147), Upside-Down Apple-Walnut Pie (see page 209), and/or Mocha Fudge Torte (see page 145) would also make great finales for this dinner, depending on the number of people you're entertaining.

These recipes are all designed to be multiplied or divided to serve any number.

THE TABLE

For a centerpiece, fill a round glass bowl like a fish bowl with water. Tint the water blue and float flowers in it. Add silver and blue Mylar balloons held down with tiny weights. Purchase blue Jewish-star garlands from a party-supply shop and wind them with ivy and silver ribbon around the centerpiece and down the center of the table.

PLACE CARDS

Make cards that resemble a tallit by punching holes in both sides of a white card. Pull pieces of blue yarn through each hole, loop them around to secure, and then cut yarn to resemble fringes. With a blue felt marker, make one thin and one thick stripe down each side next to the holes.

Or purchase blue or white cards and decorate them with stickers, for example, Jewish star or a torah. Write names in contrasting color.

GAME PLAN

As Far Ahead As Desired

Make challah and freeze

Make polenta stars and salsa and freeze
or refrigerate 1 to 2 days

Make quiche squares and freeze or
refrigerate up to 2 days

Make pastry torahs and freeze or
refrigerate up to 3 days

Make rice timbales and freeze up to 2
weeks or refrigerate up to 2 days

Make unfrosted cake and freeze

1 Day Ahead

Defrost polenta stars and salsa, if frozen

Defrost quiche squares, if frozen

Defrost rice timbales, if frozen

Frost and decorate cake (do not defrost
first)

Prepare salmon and sauce

DAY OF PARTY

In Morning

Defrost pastry torahs, if frozen

6 Hours Ahead

Cut vegetables for stir-fry

4 Hours Ahead

Bring challah to room temperature

1 to 2 Hours Before Serving

Assemble and bake polenta stars

Bring rice timbales to room temperature

**15 Minutes or More Before
Serving**

Bake salmon

Reheat challah

Shortly Before Serving

Reheat quiche squares

Reheat pastry torahs

Unmold and reheat rice

Stir-fry vegetables

Reheat sauce for salmon

Polenta Stars with Sun-Dried Tomato Salsa

Polenta
1½ cups water
1½ cups whole or low-fat milk
¾ teaspoon salt
1 teaspoon Dijon mustard
1 cup yellow cornmeal or polenta
1 tablespoon butter or margarine
⅓ cup grated Parmesan cheese plus ⅔ cup for sprinkling on top

Sun-Dried Tomato Salsa
¼ cup sun-dried tomatoes (about 6 halves), rehydrated in boiling water
1 large clove garlic, peeled
2 medium plum tomatoes, cored, seeded, and quartered
⅓ cup lightly packed fresh basil leaves, chopped
Dash of sugar
Salt to taste
¾ teaspoon balsamic vinegar

To Cook Polenta: Cover a flat baking sheet with heavy foil; grease or spray the foil. Pour water and milk in a 3- to 4-quart (12- to 16-cup) microwave-safe bowl. Stir in salt, mustard, and cornmeal. Microwave, covered, on high (100%) for 9 to 14 minutes, stirring every 4 minutes, until mixture is very thick but still spreadable. Stir in butter and ⅓ cup cheese. Spoon onto baking sheet. Cover with plastic wrap and spread with hands or rolling pin into an 11 × 12-inch rectangle, ⅜ inch thick. Refrigerate until firm and cold, 2 hours or overnight.

To Make Stars: Using a 2-inch cutter, cut out Jewish stars. (Stars may be refrigerated overnight or frozen.)

To Make Salsa: Squeeze sun-dried tomatoes dry. In a food processor with the metal blade, process garlic until minced. Add fresh and dried tomatoes, basil, sugar, and salt, and pulse until very finely chopped, almost pureed. Remove to a bowl and stir in vinegar. (Salsa may be refrigerated up to 2 days or frozen.)

To Bake: Preheat oven to 425°F. Place stars on greased baking sheet. Drain excess juices from salsa and spoon ½ teaspoon in center of each star. Sprinkle with Parmesan cheese. Bake for 10 to 15 minutes, or until tops and bottoms are golden. (Stars may be held at room temperature up to 2 hours. Reheat at 425°F until hot.)

Makes: about 36 stars

Faster: Cut polenta into 2-inch squares instead of star shapes.

The difference between cornmeal and polenta is confusing. Polenta is the Italian name for cornmeal, but it also refers to a cooked dish that resembles cornmeal mush. The product sold under the label polenta is more coarsely ground than regular cornmeal (and is more expensive). For this recipe, use either regular or finely ground cornmeal, or polenta, which will give you a coarser end result. Spread the cooked polenta onto a baking sheet, cut it out with a Jewish-star cookie cutter, and top with spicy salsa and a sprinkling of Parmesan cheese.

Prep Time: Polenta, 5 minutes; salsa, 10 minutes

Microwave Time: 9 to 14 minutes

Chill Time: At least 2 hours

Advance Prep: Stars and salsa may be refrigerated 1 to 2 days or frozen. Assemble up to 2 hours before serving.

Spinach-Mushroom Quiche Squares

1 tablespoon vegetable oil or margarine
1½ pounds mushrooms, cleaned and sliced
6 ounces cleaned and stemmed baby spinach (8 cups, loosely packed)
8 large eggs
1 pint regular or low-fat sour cream
1 pint regular or low-fat cottage cheese
⅔ cup all-purpose flour
2 teaspoons ground rainbow peppercorns or seasoned black pepper
1 cup grated Romano or Parmesan cheese
4 cups shredded jalapeño Jack cheese or 4 cups shredded Jack cheese and
   1 jalapeño, seeded and minced
1 cup sliced green onions, including tops (about 1 bunch)

Preheat oven to 350°F. Grease or spray a 15½ × 10½ × 1-inch rimmed baking sheet (jelly-roll pan).

To Make Quiche: Heat oil in a large skillet. Cook mushrooms over high heat, stirring frequently, until dry, about 10 minutes. Add spinach and toss just until wilted, about 2 minutes. Cool.

In a food processor with the metal blade, process eggs until blended. Remove to a large bowl. Process sour cream, cottage cheese, flour, and pepper until pureed. Add to eggs. Stir in cheeses, mushrooms, spinach, and green onions. Pour into prepared pan, smoothing the top.

To Bake: Bake for 50 to 60 minutes, or until golden. Remove from oven and cut into 1½-inch squares. (Cooled quiche may be refrigerated up to 2 days or frozen. Bring to room temperature and reheat at 350°F for 8 to 10 minutes, or until hot.)

Makes: 70 quiche squares

Faster: Purchase mushrooms cleaned and sliced.

Cheese Pastry Torahs

10 tablespoons (1¼ sticks) unsalted butter or margarine,
  at room temperature
1⅔ cups shredded Gruyère or Swiss cheese
2 cups all-purpose flour
1 heaping teaspoon salt
1 teaspoon paprika
½ teaspoon baking powder
½ cup whipping cream
1 egg yolk mixed with 2 teaspoons water, for glaze
Sesame, poppy, or caraway seeds

To Make Dough: In a large bowl with electric mixer or food processor with metal blade, mix or process butter and cheese until blended. Add flour, salt, paprika, and baking powder, and mix or pulse until incorporated. Add cream and mix or pulse until combined. Divide dough in half and shape into 2 flat balls; wrap in plastic. Refrigerate until cold enough to roll. (Pastry may be refrigerated overnight or frozen. Bring to room temperature until soft enough to roll but still very cold.)

To Make Torahs: Preheat oven to 375°F. Grease or spray with nonstick spray or line baking sheets with parchment paper. On a lightly floured surface, roll out 1 ball of dough ¼ inch thick. Using a 4-inch cutter, cut out torah shapes and place on baking sheet. Reroll and cut scraps. Repeat with remaining dough. Brush tops lightly with egg yolk mixture. Sprinkle with seeds.

To Bake: Bake for 10 to 12 minutes, or until lightly browned. If baking 2 sheets in one oven, rotate them halfway through the baking time. Serve warm. (Torahs may be refrigerated up to 3 days or frozen. Before serving, bring to room temperature and reheat at 375°F for about 3 minutes.)

Makes: 30 torahs

This rich cheese pastry can be cut into any shape desired. However, a Torah is appropriate for a Bar/Bat Mitzvah. Look for Torah cutters in Jewish gift shops and some party-supply stores. When the pastry bakes, it separates into dozens of flaky layers. Serve these appetizers on their own, as part of a fruit or vegetable platter, or in place of bread.

Prep Time: 20 minutes

Bake Time: 10 to 12 minutes

Advance Prep: Torahs may be refrigerated for 3 days or frozen.

Tournedos of Salmon

Photograph, page 16

**12 salmon steaks (6 to 7 ounces each), cut ¾ inch thick, boned, and
  skinned**
4 tablespoons chopped green onions with tops
4 tablespoons chopped fresh dill
6 burrito-style flour tortillas (about 10-inch diameter)
Salt and pepper
Dill Piccata Sauce (recipe follows)
Fresh dill and lemon wedges, for garnish

To Prepare Fish: Place each salmon steak on a work surface in a long
strip skin side down. (Some of the steaks will break into 2 pieces when
boned; place them in 1 long strip.) Sprinkle each with 1 teaspoon green
onions and 1 teaspoon dill. Roll up jelly-roll fashion, as illustrated. Place
flat side down. Cut tortillas into 24 strips, each 1 inch wide; discard the
ends. Wrap 2 strips around each salmon roll. Secure ends with toothpicks.
Transfer salmon rolls to greased or sprayed baking sheets (not cushioned
ones), placing them at least 1½ inches apart. (Tournedos may be refrigerated, covered, overnight.)

To Bake: Preheat oven to 400°F. Sprinkle salmon rolls with salt and pepper. Bake, uncovered, for 15 minutes, or until cooked through. The more
fish you bake in one oven and the colder they are, the longer the baking
time. If baking 2 sheets in one oven, rotate their positions after 8 minutes.
Transfer salmon rolls to plates, spooning sauce over top and sides. Garnish
with sprigs of fresh dill and lemon wedges.

Makes: 12 servings

---

*T*his sensational
salmon recipe is
adapted from one
served at Château Lake
Louise, in Canada. It
is terrific for any
gathering, for lunch or
dinner, or any special
occasion when you
want to make an
impression. Because
the tournedos are
prepared in individual
portions, it's easy to
divide or multiply the
recipe. For even greater
ease, have the salmon
skinned and boned at
the fish market. If
you're serving a large
crowd and are short of
oven space, bake the
tournedos up to 2 hours
ahead. Then serve them
at room temperature,
topped with a warm
and lemony Dill
Piccata Sauce.

*Prep Time: Salmon, 20
minutes; sauce, 10
minutes*

*Bake Time: 15 to 20
minutes*

*Advance Prep:
Tournedos may be
refrigerated overnight
before baking. Sauce
may be refrigerated
overnight.*

Dill Piccata Sauce

1 cup dry white wine or imported dry vermouth
1 cup vegetable or chicken broth
3 tablespoons fresh lemon juice
3 tablespoons whipping cream
1 tablespoon plus 2 teaspoons cornstarch, dissolved in 2 tablespoons water
3 tablespoons capers, rinsed
3 tablespoons chopped fresh dill
Salt and freshly ground black pepper to taste

In a medium saucepan over moderately low heat, simmer wine, broth, lemon juice, and cream for 5 minutes. Remove from heat and whisk in cornstarch. Return to heat and bring to a boil, stirring constantly. Stir in capers, dill, and salt and pepper (Sauce may be refrigerated overnight. Reheat before serving.)

Makes: about 1⅔ cups; serves 12

This recipe is as easy as preparing a packaged mix, only it takes longer to cook. Once you taste the timbales, I know you'll agree the extra cooking time is worth it. Besides, you can't mold white and wild rice made from a mix; the grains are too dry and they won't hold together. The cooked rice is packed into small paper cups or small soufflé dishes or molds and inverted into neat little domes. The recipe may be multiplied or divided for any number.

Prep Time: 10 minutes

Cook Time: 65 minutes

Advance Prep: Timbales may be refrigerated for 2 days or frozen for 2 weeks.

White and Wild Rice Timbales
Photograph, page 16

Rice
⅔ cup wild rice (about 4 ounces)
4 cups chicken or vegetable broth
2 tablespoons butter or margarine
1⅓ cups uncooked long-grain white rice
4 teaspoons soy sauce
½ cup chopped parsley

Garnish
⅓ cup chopped parsley
12 (5-ounce) paper cups or ½-cup soufflé dishes or molds
1 jar (7 ounces) roasted red peppers, drained

To Make Rice: Rinse and drain wild rice, and place in a large saucepan. Add broth and butter, and bring to a boil. Cover, reduce heat to medium, and boil slowly for 45 minutes, or until almost soft. Stir in white rice and soy sauce. Cover and continue cooking over medium heat until all the liquid is absorbed, about 20 minutes. Remove from heat and let sit, covered, for 5 minutes. Stir in chopped parsley.

To Assemble: Spoon 1 teaspoon parsley into the bottom of each paper cup or soufflé dish. Using a ½-inch Jewish star or desired shape cutter, cut out small designs from red peppers. Place in bottom of cups. Add ½ cup rice and press down tightly. (Timbales may be refrigerated up to 2 days or frozen for 2 weeks. Defrost in refrigerator. Bring to room temperature at least 1 hour before serving.)

To Serve: Invert cups and unmold. To reheat, unmold around outer edge of 1 or 2 microwave-safe platters. Microwave, uncovered, on high (100%) until hot, 3 to 4 minutes, rotating once.

Makes: 12 servings

Stir-fry Carrots, Zucchini, and Mushrooms

Photograph, page 16

1½ pounds carrots, peeled
1½ pounds zucchini, trimmed
12 ounces mushrooms, sliced
1 tablespoon olive oil
4 cloves garlic, minced
2 teaspoons dried tarragon
Salt and freshly ground black pepper to taste
¼ cup shredded Parmesan cheese

To Prepare Vegetables: Cut the carrots and zucchini into 2½-inch-long pieces. Then cut into matchstick strips, about ¼ inch wide. (Carrots, zucchini, and mushrooms may be prepared 6 hours ahead. Wrap zucchini in paper towels and refrigerate vegetables separately.)

To Cook: In a 12-inch skillet or wok over high heat, heat olive oil until hot. Add carrots and sauté until crisp-tender, 3 to 5 minutes. Add zucchini, mushrooms, garlic, tarragon, and salt and pepper. The pan will be very full, but the vegetables will shrink down as they cook. Stir-fry until tender to the bite, 3 to 5 minutes. Sprinkle with Parmesan cheese, toss, and serve immediately with a slotted spoon.

Makes: 12 servings

The compelling combination of garlic, tarragon, and Parmesan cheese is so easy to prepare, especially if you use a mandolin to cut the vegetables into matchstick strips. Mandolins are hand-operated gadgets with adjustable blades for slicing and julienning that can be found in most cookware shops. They do the job much more precisely and uniformly than a food processor. If you wish to double the recipe, you will need to cook it in 2 pans.

Prep Time: 20 minutes

Cook Time: 6 to 10 minutes

Advance Prep: Vegetables may be prepared up to 6 hours ahead. Cook before serving.

Prep Time: Cake, 20 minutes; icing, 5 minutes; marzipan tallit, 40 minutes

Bake Time: 35 to 40 minutes for each layer

Advance Prep: Unfrosted cake may be refrigerated up to 2 days or frozen. Frosted cake may be held at room temperature overnight.

Chocolate Mitzvah Cake

Chocolate Cake

(For 9 × 13-inch cake)
1¾ cups all-purpose flour
2 cups sugar
¾ cup unsweetened cocoa powder
1½ teaspoons baking powder
1½ teaspoons baking soda
1 teaspoon salt
2 large eggs
1 cup whole milk
½ cup vegetable oil
2 teaspoons vanilla extract
1 cup boiling water

(For ½ sheet cake)
3½ cups all-purpose flour
4 cups sugar
1½ cups cocoa
3 teaspoons baking powder
3 teaspoons baking soda
2 teaspoons salt
4 large eggs
2 cups milk
1 cup oil
1 tablespoon plus 1 teaspoon vanilla extract
2 cups boiling water

Chocolate Icing
36 ounces semisweet chocolate (squares or chips)
3 cups regular or light sour cream
¾ teaspoon salt

Items Needed
1 cardboard or other cake tray, 15 × 22 inches
Floral foil to cover cardboard (available at floral-supply stores and craft shops)

Marzipan Tallit Decoration
2 packages (7 ounces each) marzipan
Red, yellow, green, and blue food coloring
1 paintbrush

Preheat oven to 350°F. Spray pan(s) with nonstick cooking spray.

To Make Cake: For 9 × 13-inch layer, mix flour, sugar, cocoa, baking powder, baking soda, salt, eggs, milk, oil, and vanilla in large mixing bowl on medium speed for 2 minutes, or until well blended. Add boiling water and mix until incorporated. The batter will be thin. Pour into prepared pan. While it bakes, make batter for ½ sheet cake in same manner.

To Bake: Bake 9 × 13-inch cake for 30 minutes, ½ sheet cake for 35 to 40 minutes, or until cake tester inserted into center comes out clean. Remove from oven and cool 10 minutes. Invert onto cooling rack. (Cakes may be wrapped in heavy foil and stored at room temperature up to 2 days or frozen. It is easiest to frost cakes frozen.)

To Make Icing: Place chocolate in a large microwave-safe bowl. Microwave on high (100%) for 2 to 4 minutes, or according to package directions, until melted, stirring frequently. Stir in sour cream and salt until smooth. Use while warm.

To Frost: If possible, work with frozen cakes. Cover cardboard cake tray with floral foil. Place ½ sheet cake in center. Tuck wax paper underneath edges of cake to catch frosting drips. Using about half the frosting, spread over top and sides. Cut off two corners of 9 × 13-inch cake, as shown in illustration. Place on top, about 3 inches from front of cake. (Back edges will not be even.) Spread top and sides with icing, reserving about 1½ cups for piping. Spoon some of reserved icing in a piping bag fitted with a star tip. Beginning with the front, because the frosting is the right temperature and easiest to work with, pipe along the bottom of the cake. Refill bag as needed. If icing begins to harden, reheat in microwave for 10 to 20 seconds. Stir until smooth and cool until firm enough to pipe.

To Make Tallit Decoration: Roll 1 package of marzipan between 2 sheets of wax paper into a 14 × 5-inch rectangle, flipping it occasionally to loosen the bottom. Repeat with second package. Trim edges even. (A pizza cutter works well.) Working on the wax paper, press the 2 rectangles together into a 28-inch strip. Pour each food coloring into a paper cup. Wearing plastic gloves, paint four ½-inch-wide stripes on each end, beginning about 4 inches from end. Cut fringe with pizza cutter or sharp knife. Drape over cake. It is easiest to do this with 2 people. (Completed cake may be held at room temperature, uncovered, overnight.)

Makes: 50 servings

Brit Milah or Baby Naming

✧

Brit Milah means covenant of circumcision. Circumcision has been given to us as a sign of our covenant with God, as it is written: "God said to Abraham, you shall keep my covenant, you and your children after you. He who is eight days old shall be circumcized, every male throughout your generations."

The ceremony itself is usually held on the eighth day after birth at home in the morning. It is both a religious ritual and a medical procedure, performed by a *mohel* (circumciser) who is well trained in both aspects of the ceremony. Family and friends gather together to welcome the new life into the Jewish community. A Hebrew name is given to the child at this time as well.

Historically, the birth of a girl has gone relatively unmarked in Judaism. Traditionally, the father went up to the pulpit during a Shabbat morning service and said a prayer for his newborn daughter. However, in this century Jews have become more concerned with equality for women and have begun a new ritual of baby naming for a girl. It is similar to a Brit Milah in that family and friends gather together for the *simcha* (joyful occasion), the baby is given a Hebrew name, and enters into a covenant with God to live a Jewish life. This ceremony is usually performed at home within the first few months of the baby's birth.

Mazel Tov Buffet Brunch

With all the excitement and tension that goes along with welcoming a new baby, it's more important than ever to keep the food simple. The celebration of a precious new life is so heartwarming, the food becomes merely an extra.

Blintz French Toast Casserole is the impressive star of the buffet. It should be assembled a day ahead and refrigerated overnight, so when things get hectic, all you need to do is put it in the oven. If you are having a large group, you might offer several fruity sauces to complement the casserole. Any one of the three suggested here works well.

What would a festive Jewish breakfast or brunch be without a lox and bagel platter from the deli? Supplement it with a creamy fish spread, Confetti Tuna Mousse, molded and decorated to look like a baby block. A beautiful platter of fresh fruit with berries, grapes, melons, apples, and pears rounds out the menu. You can purchase many of the fruits already cut up from the supermarket.

Each of the three desserts is very distinctive. Apricot Crumble Cake is a melt-in-your-mouth white cake with ribbons of apricot preserves swirled throughout. Its moist and luscious texture is attributed to the cream cheese in the batter. It's best to eat it within two days, as the texture is not quite the same after freezing. If you are the plan-ahead type who prefers to fill the freezer in advance, consider making Lemon Yogurt Cake (see page 27), Banana–Chocolate Chip Coffee Cake (see page 65), Double Apricot Strudel (see page 102), Shikker Cake (see page 119), or Israeli Flag Cake (see page 168). Both Lemon Logs and Peanut Butter Cup Cookies are very special pastries that can be prepared at your leisure and are truly worthy of this momentous occasion.

FESTIVE NOTE

Plant a new tree in the yard for the baby to enjoy as he or she grows up. In keeping with ancient tradition, a cypress tree is planted when a baby girl is born; for a boy, a cedar. When they marry, branches are cut from their trees and used to support the chuppah *(canopy) they stand under at their wedding.*

Menu

Blintz French Toast Casserole

Blueberry Sauce, Ruby-Red Raspberry Sauce (see page 196), and/or Strawberry Sauce (see page 159)

Confetti Tuna Mousse

Bagel, Lox, and Cream Cheese Deli Platter

Fresh Seasonal Fruits

◆

Apricot Crumble Cake

Peanut Butter Cup Cookies

Lemon Logs

Extra Points

THE INVITATIONS

For a baby naming it's not traditional to send out invitations; it's considered a mitzvah just to be invited. But if you want, you can write a note and tie it around a rattle or insert it into a toy plastic baby bottle. Mail in a padded envelope.

THE TABLE

Tie weights onto balloons and place them inside a pastel-colored shopping bag. Fill with colored tissue paper. Fill baby bottles with flowers and balloons and place around the table.

To make napkin rings, shape mini bagels out of frozen bread dough, bake, and varnish them. Be sure to make the holes large enough to insert napkins and silverware, if you plan to use them on a buffet table.

GAME PLAN

As Far Ahead As Desired	Make peanut butter cookies and freeze or refrigerate
	Make Lemon Logs and freeze, refrigerate for 1 week or store airtight at room temperature for 2 days
2 Weeks Ahead	Make Blueberry Sauce, if serving
1 Week Ahead	Make raspberry sauce, if serving
2 Days Ahead	Make tuna mousse Make apricot cake Make Strawberry Sauce, if serving
1 Day Ahead	Make blintz casserole Defrost cookies, if frozen

DAY OF PARTY

4 Hours Ahead	Unmold and garnish mousse Cut up fresh fruits, if serving
1 Hour Before Serving	Bake blintz casserole Cut apricot cake

Blintz French Toast Casserole

Bread and Batter
12 slices white bread, crusts removed
4 large eggs
3 egg whites
1 cup regular or low-fat milk
¼ cup maple syrup
¾ cup orange juice

Filling
8 ounces regular or low-fat cream cheese, at room temperature
1 cup regular or low-fat ricotta cheese
1 cup regular or low-fat small-curd cottage cheese
2 large eggs
⅓ cup sugar
1 tablespoon vanilla extract

1 recipe Blueberry Sauce (see page 196), Ruby-Red Raspberry Sauce
  (see page 196), or Strawberry Sauce (see page 159), for serving

To Prepare Bread and Batter: Place bread in a rimmed baking sheet or jelly-roll pan. In a large bowl, whisk eggs, whites, milk, syrup, and orange juice until blended. Pour over bread, turning to coat both sides.

To Make Filling: In food processor with metal blade or bowl with electric mixer, process or mix cream cheese, ricotta, and cottage cheese until blended. Mix in eggs, sugar, and vanilla. Grease or spray a 9 × 13-inch glass baking dish. Arrange 6 slices of bread on bottom. Spoon filling over and spread evenly. With a spatula, place remaining bread over filling. Cover and refrigerate overnight.

To Bake: Preheat oven to 350°F. Bake for 50 to 60 minutes, or until top is golden and casserole is puffed. Serve with desired sauce.

Makes: 6 to 8 servings

For those who love blintzes but don't have time to make them, here are all the delectable flavors layered in a new casserole. Batter-soaked bread is sandwiched between a mixture of three creamy cheeses and refrigerated overnight. After baking, the casserole is as lush as a velvet custard with a topping as crisp as golden French toast. It makes a good choice for a buffet because it stays warm for a long time.

Prep Time: 20 minutes

Chill Time: At least 12 hours

Bake Time: 50 to 60 minutes

Advance Prep: Casserole should be refrigerated overnight and baked before serving.

I don't know whether my love for blueberry topping on blintzes comes from my childhood or whether it's strictly an adult passion, but for me blueberry sauce is the perfect partner for Blintz French Toast Casserole.

Prep Time: 5 minutes

Cook Time: 8 to 10 minutes

Advance Prep: Sauce may be refrigerated up to 2 weeks.

Blueberry Sauce

1 pint fresh or frozen blueberries (2 cups)
½ cup sugar
1 teaspoon grated lemon peel
½ teaspoon ground cinnamon
¼ teaspoon ground nutmeg
¼ cup water

In a medium-size saucepan, stir all ingredients together. Bring to a boil over moderate heat and cook, stirring often, for 8 to 10 minutes, or until sauce thickens slightly and sugar is dissolved. The sauce will continue to thicken as it cools. (Sauce may be refrigerated, covered, up to 2 weeks.)

Makes: 2½ cups sauce

*T*his simple topping is so versatile—it's delicious on ice cream and blintzes, plain cakes and pancakes. The Chambord heightens the raspberry flavor.

Prep Time: 10 minutes

Advance Prep: Sauce may be refrigerated up to 2 weeks.

Ruby-Red Raspberry Sauce

3 packages (10 ounces each) frozen raspberries in syrup, defrosted
½ cup sugar
⅓ cup Chambord (black raspberry liqueur)
½ pint fresh raspberries (optional)

In food processor with metal blade, process raspberries and sugar until pureed. Place a medium-mesh strainer over a bowl. Push raspberries through the strainer to extract as much juice and pulp as possible, scraping the bottom often. Discard seeds. Stir in Chambord. Refrigerate until ready to serve. (Sauce may be refrigerated up to 2 weeks.)

If desired, stir in fresh raspberries before serving.

Makes: 2¼ cups sauce

Confetti Tuna Mousse

Tuna Spread
2 cans (12 ounces each) water-packed tuna, drained
2 packages (8 ounces each) regular or light cream cheese, cut into cubes
½ cup regular, low-fat, or nonfat mayonnaise
1 can (5 ounces) water chestnuts, drained and chopped
2 medium stalks celery, chopped (about 1 cup)
⅓ cup chopped red onion
Mini bagels or crackers, for serving

Garnish (optional)
Sliced black olives
Carrots, sliced into rounds
Carrot or celery, cut into thin strips

To Make Mousse: In food processor with metal blade, process half the tuna, half the cream cheese, and half the mayonnaise until smooth. Remove to a bowl. Repeat with remaining tuna, cream cheese, and mayonnaise. Stir in water chestnuts, celery, and red onion.

To Form Baby Block: Line a 4- to 5-cup square container with plastic wrap. Fill with spread and refrigerate for at least 4 hours. (Spread may be refrigerated up to 2 days.)

To Decorate: Several hours before serving, invert spread onto a platter, remove container, and pull off plastic wrap. Decorate edges of block with olives and carrot rounds, (see illustration). Form an **A** or the baby's initial on the top with carrot or celery strips. Refrigerate until serving. Serve with bagels or crackers.

Makes: about 5½ cups; serves 24

For a Brit Milah, mold this spread into a baby block by packing it into a square-shape container or box lined with plastic wrap. For other occasions, you can shape it into a fish, either by hand or in a mold. For a smaller gathering, the recipe may be cut in half, but leftovers make terrific sandwiches.

Prep Time: 20 minutes

Chill Time: At least 4 hours

Advance Prep: Spread may be refrigerated up to 2 days.

Apricot Crumble Cake

If you believe that you can't tell a book by its cover, then you'll not judge this cake by its appearance. It looks like any ordinary coffee cake, but wait until you taste it. The texture is rich, the crumb tender, and the flavor, with its marbling of apricot preserves and broiled coconut topping, is divine. My gratitude to Mary Markovitz for sharing this recipe.

Prep Time: Cake, 10 minutes; topping, 5 minutes

Bake Time: 35 to 40 minutes

Advance Prep: Cake may be stored at room temperature up to 2 days.

Cake
1½ cups granulated sugar
1 package (8 ounces) regular or low-fat cream cheese, at room temperature
¼ pound (1 stick) butter or margarine, at room temperature
2 large eggs
1 teaspoon vanilla extract
2 cups cake flour
1 teaspoon baking powder
½ teaspoon baking soda
¼ teaspoon salt
¼ cup whole or low-fat milk
1 jar (10 ounces) apricot preserves, heated in microwave until warm

Topping
2 cups flaked coconut
⅔ cup firmly packed brown sugar
¼ pound (1 stick) butter or margarine, melted
1 teaspoon ground cinnamon
½ cup chopped pecans or walnuts

Preheat oven to 350°F. Grease or spray a 9 × 13-inch baking pan with non-stick spray.

To Make Cake: In a large mixing bowl with electric mixer, beat sugar, cream cheese, and butter on high speed until smooth. Add eggs and vanilla, and mix until well blended, about 2 minutes. In a medium bowl, stir together flour, baking powder, baking soda, and salt. Add to creamed mixture alternately with milk, mixing continuously on low speed. Mix on medium speed for 1 minute. Pour half the batter into prepared pan. Dot with preserves. Cover with remaining batter.

To Bake: Bake for 35 to 40 minutes, or until toothpick inserted near center comes out clean.

While cake bakes, **Prepare Topping:** In a medium bowl, stir coconut, brown sugar, butter, cinnamon, and nuts together. Remove cake from oven and spread over top. Place under broiler until golden and bubbling, 1 to 2 minutes. Watch carefully so it doesn't burn. Cool completely. (Cake may be stored, covered, at room temperature up to 2 days. Although it can be frozen, the texture becomes drier.)

To Serve: Cut into squares.

Makes: 15 servings

Peanut Butter Cup Cookies

¼ **pound (1 stick) butter or margarine**
½ **cup granulated sugar**
½ **cup firmly packed light brown sugar**
½ **cup creamy or chunky peanut butter (not the natural variety)**
1 **large egg**
½ **teaspoon vanilla extract**
1¼ **cups all-purpose flour**
¾ **teaspoon baking soda**
¼ **teaspoon salt**
1 **package (14 ounces) Reese's Miniature Peanut Butter Cups**

Preheat oven to 350°F.

To Make Dough: In a large mixing bowl with electric mixer on high speed, beat butter, sugars, and peanut butter until smooth and creamy. Mix in egg and vanilla until blended. Add flour, baking soda, and salt, and mix on low speed until incorporated. Mix on medium speed for 1 minute.

To Form: Spoon a scant tablespoon of dough into ungreased 1½-inch muffin cups that measure ¾ inch deep.

To Bake: Bake for 8 to 10 minutes, or until lightly browned. Remove from oven and immediately press a peanut butter cup into center of dough until only the top shows. Cool 10 minutes and remove from tins by inserting the tip of a sharp knife into one edge. (Cookies may be stored in an airtight container at room temperature up to 1 week, refrigerated for 2 weeks, or frozen.)

Makes: 48 cookies

Peanut butter cookie dough is spooned into miniature muffin tins (make sure they are ¾ inch deep) and baked until barely set. When they are removed from the oven, a miniature peanut butter cup is pressed into the center. The cookies look like little tarts and taste heavenly. You won't want to wait for a baby to make them.

Prep Time: 10 minutes

Bake Time: 8 to 10 minutes

Advance Prep: Cookies may be stored airtight at room temperature for 1 week, refrigerated for 2 weeks, or frozen.

One recipe of buttery, almond pastry makes 4 logs, which are filled, baked, and sliced. You can fill them all with lemon curd, or prepare each with a different filling, so they look like four types of cookie. Here, I offer lemon and lime curd and apricot preserves topped with sliced almonds. Experiment with various types of jams, alternating the colors on the platter.

Prep Time: Lemon curd, 5 minutes; cookies, 20 minutes

Bake Time: 18 to 23 minutes

Advance Prep: Cookies may be stored airtight at room temperature for 2 days, refrigerated for 1 week, or frozen.

Lemon Logs

Lemon Curd Filling
1 tablespoon cornstarch, packed
⅔ cup granulated sugar
⅓ cup fresh lemon juice
1 egg

Pastry
1 cup sliced or slivered almonds (about 4 ounces)
2 cups all-purpose flour
¾ cup granulated sugar
¾ cup (1½ sticks) butter, at room temperature
1 large egg
2 teaspoons vanilla extract
Powdered sugar, for sprinkling on top

Place oven racks in upper and lower third of oven and preheat to 350°F. Grease or spray 2 flat cookie sheets without sides.

To Make Filling: In a medium saucepan, stir together cornstarch and sugar. Whisk in lemon juice and egg until well blended. Cook over moderate heat, whisking constantly, until mixture comes to a boil and thickens. Remove from heat and refrigerate or put into a bowl of ice water, stirring often, until cold. (Filling may be refrigerated for 1 week.)

To Make Pastry: In food processor with metal blade, process almonds with flour and sugar until ground. Add butter, egg, and vanilla, and process until dough holds together. Shape into a ball.

To Form Cookies: Divide pastry in quarters. On prepared baking sheets, shape each into a log about 14 inches long and 1 inch wide, at least 3 inches apart. (They will spread when baking.) Using the handle of a wooden spoon or your finger, make a depression down the center of each log about ½ inch wide, pressing only about halfway down into dough. If you press too far, the cookies will break. Spoon filling into depression.

To Bake: Bake for 18 to 23 minutes, or until tops are pale brown and bottoms are golden. If baking sheets in one oven, rotate their positions after 10 minutes. Cool 2 minutes and loosen bottoms with a spatula. Sprinkle with powdered sugar. Cool 10 minutes, remove to a cutting board, and slice into ¾-inch diagonal slices. (Cookies may be stored airtight at room temperature for 2 days, refrigerated for 1 week, or frozen.)

Before Serving: Sprinkle with powdered sugar.

Makes: 52 cookies

Variations: For lime curd filling, substitute fresh lime juice for the lemon and add 1 to 2 drops green coloring.

To make Apricot Almond Jam Logs, substitute ½ cup apricot jam or preserves for the lemon curd. Fill logs with jam. Sprinkle with ¾ cup sliced almonds and powdered sugar. Bake as for Lemon Logs.

Faster: Purchase lemon or lime curd from the supermarket or specialty food store. You will need ¾ cup curd to fill 4 logs.

Havdalah

✧

After sundown on Saturday evening, when the first three stars are sighted, Shabbat officially ends with a ceremony called Havdalah. In Hebrew *havdalah* means distinction, and the ceremony is intended to distinguish between the sacred and the ordinary, between Shabbat and the rest of the week. A Havdalah service also marks the conclusion of Passover, Sukkot, Shavuot, and Yom Kippur. During the service, sweet-smelling spices are passed around in a special box for everyone to sniff. They are meant to cheer the soul, to help one get over the disappointment that the Sabbath has ended. Traditionally, the spices are cinnamon and cloves, but they can be any with a fragrance; even a flower. A beautiful multicolored twisted candle is lit. The flame represents the beauty and light of the Sabbath; the shadows on the wall, the ordinary days of the week. This is such a lovely service that it is becoming more and more popular to celebrate it at home with friends and family.

THE RITUALS

The leader lifts a cup or glass of wine, and the following blessing is recited:

We praise You, Eternal God,
Sovereign of the universe,
Creator of the fruit of the vine.

Ba-ruch a-ta Adonai,
Eh-lo-hei-nu meh-lech ha-o-lam,
bo-rei p'ri ha-ga-fen.

The leader holds up the spice box and says:

We praise You, Eternal God,
Sovereign of the universe,
Creator of the world's spices.

Ba-ruch a-ta Adonai,
Eh-lo-hei-nu meh-lech ha-o-lam,
bo-rei mi-nei v'sa-mim.

The spice box is circulated, and all present inhale its fragrance.

A twisted candle is lit, the leader holds it up and says:

We praise You, Eternal God,
Sovereign of the universe,
Creator of fire.

Ba-ruch a-ta Adonai,
Eh-lo-hei-nu meh-lech ha-o-lam,
bo-rei m'o-rei ha-eish.

We praise You, Eternal God, Sovereign of the universe: You make distinctions, teaching us to distinguish the commonplace from the holy; You create light and darkness, Israel and the nations, the seventh day of rest and the six days of labor.

All present sip from the cup of wine. The candle is extinguished by immersing it in the cup.

Extra Points

THE INVITATIONS

Place spices such as cloves, allspice, broken cinnamon sticks, and potpourri in the center of a small square of cellophane. Pull up the edges like a money bag and tie with ribbon. Attach a note and mail in a padded envelope.

THE TABLE

Insert cloves into oranges. Arrange oranges in a basket and intersperse with fresh leaves, vines, and/or fresh flowers.

PLACE CARDS

Glue pieces of cinnamon stick and cloves onto white or colored cards.

FOR THE KIDS

Make mini spice bottles. Save or purchase small, clear jars or bottles. Fill them with cloves, cinnamon sticks, allspice, snippets of garland, glitter, and potpourri. Decorate the outside with ribbons, beads, and puffy paints.

Menu

*Streamlined
Chopped Liver*

◆

*Butter Lettuce Salad
with Balsamic
Vinaigrette*

*Stuffed Cabbage
Casserole*

Bow-tie Noodles

Crisp Rolls or Bread

◆

*Upside-Down
Apple-Walnut Pie*

A Dinner with Distinction

Havdalah, falling on Saturday night, is the ideal time for a party, so I've chosen food that can be multiplied for any size group. If you want to serve a selection of hors d'oeuvres, offer Streamlined Chopped Liver with Eggplant Salsa (see page 73), Warm Baby Potatoes Stuffed with Egg Salad (see page 136), and/or Hummus (see page 74).

Stuffed Cabbage Casserole has all the convenience of a lasagna. It is an entire meal in a casserole, can be refrigerated overnight or frozen, and is baked and served from the same dish. Since it contains meat, vegetables, and rice, you won't need to serve many side dishes. I like to accompany it with bow-tie noodles, crusty rolls or bread, and a straightforward Butter Lettuce Salad with Balsamic Vinaigrette that does not compete with its complexity of flavors.

Warm and wonderful Upside-Down Apple-Walnut Pie completes this homespun meal, but for a crowd, you may wish to substitute or add Strawberry, Raspberry, and Rhubarb Crisp (see page 146) or Warm Brownie Pudding (see page 13).

GAME PLAN

As Far Ahead As Desired   Make casserole and freeze or refrigerate
                                   up to 2 days

2 Days Ahead   Make chopped liver
                                   Make vinaigrette

1 Day Ahead   Prepare lettuce for salad
                                   Defrost casserole
                                   Make pie

DAY OF DINNER

30 Minutes Before Serving   Bring water to a boil for noodles,
                                   if serving
                                   Reheat casserole

Shortly Before Serving   Assemble and toss salad
                                   Cook noodles, if serving
                                   Reheat pie

If it looks like chopped liver and tastes like chopped liver, than it must be chopped liver, right? Not exactly. This version fools most people, but it never would have gotten past my bubbe. She lived to the age of ninety eating the schmaltz (chicken fat) variety, having never heard the word cholesterol.

Prep Time: *10 minutes*

Cook Time: *15 to 20 minutes*

Advance Prep: *Liver may be refrigerated up to 2 days.*

Streamlined Chopped Liver

½ medium eggplant, peeled (about 6 ounces)
1 to 2 tablespoons vegetable oil
1 medium onion, chopped
1½ cups sliced mushrooms (about 4 ounces)
8 ounces chicken livers
1 hard-boiled egg, cut in eighths
¾ teaspoon salt or to taste

For Serving
Lettuce leaves
Chopped egg whites and yolks
Finely chopped onions
Crackers, bread rounds, and/or fresh vegetables

To Cook Vegetables: Cut eggplant into ½-inch slices and then into ½-inch cubes. You should have about 2 cups. In a large skillet (preferably non-stick), heat 1 tablespoon oil over medium-high heat. Sauté eggplant for 1 minute. Add onion and sauté for 1 minute. Reduce heat to medium low, cover, and cook, stirring frequently, until lightly browned and soft, about 10 minutes. Add mushrooms, cover, and cook for 3 to 4 more minutes, or until cooked through. Uncover and sauté over moderately high heat, stirring, until liquid evaporates.

To Cook Livers: Rinse livers and pat dry. Cut in half and add to skillet. Add remaining oil, if needed. Sauté over medium-high heat, turning, until livers are cooked through but not dry. Remove from heat and cool at least 10 minutes.

To Process: Transfer mixture to a food processor with the metal blade. Add egg and salt, and pulse until finely chopped but not pureed. Line a 2-cup mold or bowl with plastic wrap. Add liver mixture and refrigerate. (Chopped liver may be refrigerated, covered, up to 2 days.)

To Serve: Line platter with lettuce leaves. Unmold liver and remove plastic wrap. Garnish top with rings of chopped eggs and onions. Serve chilled with crackers, bread rounds, and/or vegetables.

Makes: 1¾ cups; about 10 servings

Butter Lettuce Salad
with Balsamic Vinaigrette

Balsamic Vinaigrette
2 small cloves garlic, minced
1 tablespoon plus 2 teaspoons balsamic vinegar
2 teaspoons red wine vinegar
6 tablespoons olive oil
1 teaspoon Dijon mustard
1 teaspoon honey
Salt and freshly ground black pepper to taste

Salad
2 heads butter or Boston lettuce (about 12 ounces)
2 ripe avocados, peeled, pitted, and sliced
1 cup shredded carrot
2 tablespoons roasted sunflower seeds (optional)

To Make Vinaigrette: In a small bowl or food processor with metal blade, mix all ingredients until blended. (Vinaigrette may be refrigerated up to 2 days. Bring to room temperature and whisk well before using.) Makes about 1 cup.

To Make Salad: Wash and dry lettuce. Tear into bite-size pieces and wrap in paper towels. Refrigerate until ready to use. (Lettuce may be refrigerated overnight.)

To Assemble: Divide lettuce among salad plates. Garnish with 3 or 4 avocado slices and spoon shredded carrots into the center. Drizzle with as much vinaigrette as desired. Sprinkle with sunflower seeds, if using.

Makes: 6 to 8 servings

Faster: Purchase shredded carrots from the supermarket.

This is a simple salad to pair with a complex entrée. Leaves of tender lettuce, buttery slices of avocado, and golden shreds of carrot make a pretty presentation, drizzled with a mild yet flavorful vinaigrette.

Prep Time: 10 minutes

Advance Prep: Vinaigrette may be refrigerated up to 2 days. Assemble salad before serving.

There is nothing stuffed about this recipe. It uses all the ingredients of my mother's famous stuffed cabbage, but it is layered in a casserole— shredded cabbage, sauerkraut, tomatoes, and rice sandwiching a ground-beef filling. This dish tastes very similar to Mom's, but it takes a lot less time to prepare.

Prep Time: 20 minutes

Bake Time: 1½ hours

Rest Time: At least 20 minutes

Advance Prep: Casserole may be refrigerated up to 2 days or frozen.

Stuffed Cabbage Casserole

Cabbage Layer
1 can (1 pound 12 ounces) whole tomatoes in juice, chopped
1 can (14½ ounces) sauerkraut, drained
1 can (10¾ ounces) tomato soup
Scant ⅔ cup packed brown sugar
¼ cup lemon juice
4 cups thinly sliced green cabbage (about ½ small cabbage)
⅓ cup uncooked white rice

Meat Layer
2 large eggs
1½ pounds lean ground beef
½ teaspoon salt
½ teaspoon freshly ground black pepper
½ cup water

16 ounces cooked bow-tie noodles, for serving (optional)

Preheat oven to 375°F.

To Make Cabbage Layer: In a large bowl, stir together tomatoes with their juice, sauerkraut, soup, brown sugar, and lemon juice. Stir in 3½ cups cabbage and mix well. Spread half the mixture in an ungreased 9 × 13-inch casserole. Sprinkle with rice and stir to combine.

To Make Meat Layer: In a medium bowl, mix eggs until blended. Add beef, salt, pepper, and water, and mix thoroughly. Drop by spoonfuls over cabbage and spread into an even layer. Top with remaining cabbage, spreading evenly.

To Bake: Place casserole on a baking sheet and bake, covered, for 1 hour. Remove cover and bake for 30 more minutes. Let rest, uncovered, at least 20 minutes before cutting into squares. There will be some sauce on the bottom to spoon over casserole when serving. (Casserole may be refrigerated up to 2 days or frozen. Bring to room temperature and reheat, covered, at 375°F for 20 to 30 minutes or reheat in microwave.)

If desired, serve with bow-tie noodles.

Makes: 8 servings

Upside-Down Apple-Walnut Pie

Apple Filling
5 large or 5 medium Granny Smith apples (about 2½ pounds)
¾ cup granulated sugar
3 tablespoons all-purpose flour
2 teaspoons ground cinnamon

Praline
4 tablespoons (½ stick) butter or nondairy or regular margarine
¾ cup packed light brown sugar
¾ cup chopped walnuts

Pie Crust
3 cups all-purpose flour
½ teaspoon salt
1 cup shortening
7 to 8 tablespoons cold water

Vanilla ice cream, for serving (optional)

Place rack in center of oven and preheat to 400°F. Spray a 9 × 1¼-inch metal pie pan. Line pan with a 14 × 14-inch piece of wax paper. Spray the paper with nonstick spray.

To Make Filling: Peel, quarter, and core apples. Cut into ¾-inch slices. Place in a large bowl. Add granulated sugar, flour, and cinnamon, and toss well to coat. Set aside.

To Make Praline: In a small saucepan over moderate heat, melt butter. Add brown sugar and cook, stirring, until melted, about 3 minutes. Stir in nuts. Remove from heat.

To Make Pastry: In a food processor with the metal blade or a large bowl, mix flour and salt. Add shortening and pulse or cut in with a pastry blender or 2 knives until the size of peas. Add 7 tablespoons water and pulse or mix with a fork until mixture holds together and is thoroughly moistened. If needed, add the extra water, 1 teaspoon at a time. Remove to a floured board, pat into a ball, and divide in half. Place 1 piece between 2 sheets of wax paper, flatten with hands, and roll into a 12-inch circle. Repeat with second piece of dough.

To Assemble: Spread praline over bottom of wax paper in pie pan. Top with a crust. Pour the apple filling with its juices into the crust, mounding in the center. Press down firmly. Place top crust over apples. Trim edges, leaving a ¾-inch border. Fold top and bottom crusts together and flute. Cut a 1-inch circle from center of pastry.

This is the king of all apple pies. It comes from the Buttercup Grill in Walnut Creek, California, and it is the best ever. A brown sugar and walnut praline is spread on the bottom of a metal pie pan (it must be metal for the praline to bake properly), topped with a crust, mounded with a thick layer of cinnamon-spiced apples, and then topped with another crust. After baking, the pie is inverted and the praline becomes a scrumptious, crunchy caramel topping. Do not substitute store-bought refrigerated pie crusts for homemade; they are not substantial enough for this recipe.

Prep Time: 35 minutes

Bake Time: 1¼ hours

Chill Time: 12 hours

Advance Prep: Pie should be made 1 day ahead.

To Bake: Place on a baking sheet (not a cushioned one) and bake for 15 minutes. Reduce oven temperature to 325°F and bake for 1 more hour. Top will be pale, but edges will be lightly golden. Remove from oven and cool completely. Refrigerate overnight, covered with foil.

To Invert: Heat a large skillet or griddle over moderately high heat for 2 minutes. Place pie in skillet or on griddle and heat for 1 to 2 minutes, or until the bottom is hot. Invert onto an ovenproof serving platter and peel off wax paper. (Pie can be held for several hours at room temperature or refrigerated.) To serve warm, bake at 350°F for 5 to 10 minutes. Serve with ice cream, if desired.

Makes: 8 servings

Faster: To peel, core, and slice apples quickly, use an apple peeler-corer-slicer gadget, available at cookware shops.

Bibliography

Cunningham, Marion, ed. *Fannie Farmer Cookbook*. New York: Alfred Knopf, 1990.

Fellener, Judith B. *In the Jewish Tradition*. Smithmark Publishers, 1995.

Feuerstadt, Ivy, and Melinda Strauss. *New Kosher Cuisine for All Seasons*. Berkeley, CA: Ten Speed Press, 1993.

Fiszer, Louise, and Jeannette Ferrary. *Jewish Holiday Feasts*. San Francisco: Chronicle Books, 1995.

Goldin, Barbara Diamond. *The Passover Journey*. New York: Viking, 1994.

Greene, Gloria Kaufer. *The Jewish Holiday Cookbook*. New York: Random House, 1985.

Hertzberg, Arthur. *Judaism*. New York: George Braziller, 1961.

Levy, Faye. *Faye Levy's International Jewish Cookbook*. New York: Warner Books, 1991.

London, Anne, and Betrah Kahn Bishov. *The Complete American-Jewish Cookbook*. New York: Harper & Row, 1971.

Marks, Copeland. *Sephardic Cooking*. New York: Donald I. Fine, Primus, 1992.

Nathan, Joan. *The Jewish Holiday Kitchen*. New York: Schocken Books, 1979.

Oberman, Phyllis, and Bessie Carr. *The Gourmet's Guide to Jewish Cooking*. Octopus Books Limited, 1973.

Plotch, Batia, and Patricia Cobe. *The International Kosher Cookbook*. The 92nd Street Y Kosher Cooking School. New York: Fawcett, Columbine, 1992.

Prager, Dennis, and Joseph Telushkin. *The Nine Questions People Ask About Judaism*. New York: Simon & Schuster, A Touchstone Book, 1986.

Sirkis, Ruth. *A Taste of Tradition*. Los Angeles: Ward Ritchie Press, 1972.

Strassfeld, Michael. *The Jewish Holidays*. New York: Harper-Collins, 1993.

Trepp, Leo. *The Complete Book of Jewish Observances*. New York: Behrman House, 1980.

Waskow, Arthur. *Seasons of Our Joy*. Boston: Beacon Press, 1982.

Zeidler, Judy. *The Gourmet Jewish Cook*. New York: William Morrow, 1988.

Index

AUG   1997

DATE DUE